Radical Religious Movements
in
Early Modern Europe

EARLY MODERN EUROPE TODAY

Editor: Professor J. H. Shennan

Radical Religious Movements
in
Early Modern Europe

MICHAEL A. MULLETT
Lecturer in History, University of Lancaster

London
GEORGE ALLEN & UNWIN
Boston   Sydney

First published in 1980

GEORGE ALLEN & UNWIN LTD
40 Museum Street, London WC1A 1LU

© Michael A. Mullett, 1980

British Library Cataloguing in Publication Data

Mullett, Michael A
    Radical religious movements in early modern
    Europe. – (Early modern European history series).
    1. Heresies and heretics – Modern period, 1500–
    2. Church history – Modern period, 1500–
    I. Title   II. Series
    274   BT1476   80-40545

ISBN 0-04-901028-X

Set in 10 on 11 point Times by Inforum Ltd, Portsmouth
and printed in Great Britain
by Biddles Ltd, Guildford, Surrey

Contents

Early Modern Europe Today

In introducing a new historical series it is difficult not to begin by offering some justification for its appearance. Yet if we accept that history is ultimately unknowable in the sense that our perception of the past as distinct from the past itself is forever changing, then no apologia is required. That is certainly the premise on which this series is based. In the last several decades the changes have been particularly rapid, reflecting fundamental shifts in social and political attitudes, and informed by the growth of new related disciplines and by new approaches to the subject itself. The volumes contained within this series will seek to provide the present generation of students and readers with up-to-date history; with judgements and interpretations which will no doubt in turn form part of the synthesis of future scholarly revisions. Some of the books will concentrate on previously neglected or unconsidered material to reach conclusions likely to challenge conventional orthodoxies in more established areas of study; others will re-examine some of these conventional orthodoxies to discover whether, in the light of contemporary scholarly opinion, they retain their validity or require more or less drastic reassessment. Each in its own way, therefore, will seek to define and illumine some of the contours of early modern Europe, a coherent period at once remote from our own world yet crucial to an understanding of it. Each will combine considerable chronological range with thematic precision and each, finally, will be completed by a significant bibliographical chapter. It is hoped that this last, prominent feature, which will make the series especially distinctive, will be of value not only to readers curious to explore the particular topic further but also to those seeking information on a wide range of themes associated with it.

Introduction

This study of radical religious movements is intended to help students understand some features of the 'middle period' of British and European history. The chronological scope of the book is extensive, and it is assumed that the reader will already have some knowledge of key developments in the religious, political, social and economic history of early modern Europe. At the end of the book suggestions for further reading and bibliographical chapter will offer advice on books which provide a context for this study.

The reader will look in vain for any concise definition of radical Christianity in this volume: in fact the whole study is intended to contribute to such a definition. In many cases radicalism means fundamentalism – strict fidelity to the texts of the Christian Scriptures. However, those texts are themselves variegated and sometimes offer the most perplexing guidance to the seeker after truth. Therefore, Christian groups and individuals have often applied principles of selectivity to the Scriptures, and they have done so either in group analysis or in isolated individual contemplation. Selectivity is the result of the application to the Scriptures of the social and intellectual needs of a group or of an individual. It is a common approach of Christian movements, and it has always characterised the major churches, which have interpreted, highlighted and even disregarded passages of the Bible in accordance with their own requirements and aspirations. Thus those 'radical' Christians who move away from total fidelity to Scripture share with the major churches the view of Scripture as a tool. We may adumbrate three types of approach to the Bible: conservative relativism, which has characterised established churches of the type of the mediaeval Catholic Church; radical fundamentalism, which has characterised such movements as the Evangelical Anabaptists, and which involves an attempt to apply the New Testament literally; and radical relativism, which has characterised such groups as the early Quakers and involves a detached attitude to the Bible. It ought to be said that relativism is, paradoxically, a more 'fundamentalist' attitude for Christians, for the New Testament itself seems to have been composed in the light of the religious, and perhaps the social, needs of the first Christians.

Two chapters of this book have to do directly with political history, and with the relations of religious radicals and states. New-Testamentarian Christians are not concerned with the state, either positively or negatively. However, when we come to look at early modern religious radicals we often find in them highly developed political awareness and, usually, antipathy to the states under which they lived. This hostility arose because those states purported to be religious: they supported official churches and persecuted religious dissenters. This book offers three models of the state. The first model is of the mediaeval state. This institution was adorned, but also inhibited, by its religious legitimation. The states of the West borrowed heavily from Christian propaganda, but their liberty of action was marginally circumscribed by Church teaching on such subjects as just warfare, and by their membership of the supra-national society of Christendom and the Catholic Church. In the sixteenth century our second model of the state came into existence with the widespread nationalisation of churches in the Reformation and Counter-Reformation. Viewed from the mediaeval point of view, the intermediate, early modern state was rational, functional and impressively effective. Whether officially Protestant or Catholic, the new state subordinated the church to its needs and made churchmen national subjects. However, this type of state was only *comparatively* modern. In incorporating the church, the Renaissance state entered into a compact with it. Clerics advertised the national state, and marshalled mass religious opinion in its support. But the support of national churches for national states was conditional. In making the church a part of itself, the nation-state built up its authority nationally and developed its sovereignty by cutting its links with the community of Christendom. But internally the conduct of states was determined by their social contracts with mass lay and clerical ecclesiastical opinion. Clerics, in particular, supported their states. Bishop Bossuet's image of kings – *Vous êtes des dieux* – seems to represent the high point of state-worship, but in fact Bossuet and the French church were aware of the heavy – and inhibiting – religious commitment of the Bourbon House, a commitment which hampered the full operation of the state as we would understand the term. In particular, the state, allied in near-equal partnership to the church, was *required* to repress religious dissent, so that the support of ecclesiastical opinion was won at the cost of alienating dissident religious opinion – a cost that could only be calculated when the state was, as happened in France and England in the sixteenth and seventeenth centuries, brought to its knees in religio-civil wars.

Our third model of the state is of the state proper – the modern state, the outcome of the organic and inexorable growth of the institution itself. Such a state is, quite properly, unconcerned with religious questions. It requires no legitimation beyond its own existence. It is in theory and practice omnicompetent and is in no way checked – or validated – by religious sanctions. According to its dominant secularist principles, churches are at best voluntary associations and only their rights as denominations – if those – can be guaranteed by the state. Since the American, French and Russian revolutions such pluralistic states have come to preponderate within the traditional confines of Christendom, except perhaps in such societies as Ireland, Poland, Spain and Italy, where mass membership of the Roman Catholic Church conditions the relationship of religion and regime. Elsewhere in the modern world the dominance of the rational state has emancipated both religious dissidence and the state itself.

Mediaeval and early modern states were awesome mechanisms, at least in appearance. The state's formidable aspect was the consequence of its possession of 'the sword' – the means of justice and punishment. Indeed, in the sixteenth century Western states assumed greater control of the machinery of structured violence in their societies. The prime function of the early modern state was to deter and punish malefactors – rather than to direct society towards salvation as in the mediaeval ideal, or to distribute material welfare as in modern cases. The image of the state as the wielder of the sword – and the image of statesmen as 'magistrates' – were endorsed by religious thinkers. This was because the anthropological premises of theologians were pessimistic: fallen, sinful man needed curbing at every turn. But such discouraging abstract premises were borne out in observation: no one who had witnessed the behaviour of the *Landsknechte* in Rome in 1527 or of the mutinous 'Catholic' troops at Antwerp in 1576 could persist for long in seeing man as anything but vicious and corrupt. Such vivid but occasional glimpses were reinforced by daily observation of the lustful, violent, avaricious and cruel behaviour of Europeans in peace and war. Dejection about man seems to have reached a crescendo in the age of Callot and Hobbes – that 'iron age' of war and economic crisis in the mid-seventeenth century, a time of war of every man against every man. Hobbes's grim depiction of 'the nature of man' was in fact an accurate anthropology for the times and it fully justified the repressive equipment of the state that Hobbes had in mind as a corrective against anarchy. It is clear, though, that the incessant turbulence that Hobbes saw around him is much less a feature of modern than of early modern Western societies. The social behaviour of modern Europeans is markedly less aggressive, less disorderly, than was the daily behaviour of their pre-modern ancestors, so that it is possible now to be less uncertain about the distinction between formal peace and war than Hobbes was. For modern states the relative docility of masses of citizens has interesting consequences: it diminishes the punitive and judicial functions of the state and allows the modern state to combine an appearance of liberalism with a reality of absolutism – in contrast to the early modern state which combined an appearance of absolutism with a reality of ineffectiveness. How is it that the mass behaviour of modern Europeans is more controlled than that of those pre-industrial Europeans who, like N. Z. Davis's sixteenth-century Frenchmen, made violence an everyday part of their lives? The answer falls into two parts. First, modern European society is normally pacific because of its high levels of affluence. It is possible that the Reformation and the radical reformation made some contribution to the economic developments that resulted in this general prosperity – a point that will be considered in Chapter 2. A second possibility is that Europeans have been gradually subjected to the restraining influences of the Reformation. Seen as a psychological revolution, the Reformation can be viewed as a long-term indoctrination of Europeans in the values of personal inhibition, thrift, non-violence – all in all, the creation of the 'bourgeois' type familiar from Max Weber and Michael Walzer. If it is the case that the Reformation has tamed Hobbes's frighteningly self-assertive Europeans, it may also be the case that the *radical* reformation has played a part in this didactic transformation.

As well as incorporating primary research, this book sets out to synthesise some of the work that has appeared in recent years on dissenting Christianity and on millenarianism. The extent to which I am indebted to the scholarship and ideas of Professor Trevor-Roper (Lord Dacre) and Dr Christopher Hill will be immediately obvious. Professor J. H. Shennan has given me constant encouragement, and has been endlessly helpful and patient in suggesting ways of improving and clarifying this work. I have profited from a number of discussions with Sir Charles Carter, Mr R. M. Bliss and Mr Harro Höpfl, who has also helped with some translation. Professor H. J. Perkin has given me every assistance in the preparation of this book, and I must also thank Dr John Andrews and the staff of the Lancaster University Library, as well as the staff of the John Rylands Library, Manchester. I am deeply indebted to Mr Ralph Randles, the archivist at Friends' Meeting House, Lancaster, and to Mrs Parker, who took such pains over my difficult manuscript. My wife has helped at every stage, and to her go my deepest thanks.

MICHAEL MULLETT

List of Abbreviations

DNB	*The Dictionary of National Biography . . . from the earliest times to 1900* 22 vols (London: Oxford University Press, 1921–2)
LFMH	Friends' Meeting House, Lancaster
LW	*Luther's Works* ed. J. Pelikan and H. T. Lehmann, 55 vols (St Louis, Missouri: Concordia, in progress)
TRHS	*Transactions of the Royal Historical Society*

Glossary

In this glossary of specialised and technical terms I have made a point of explaining certain words according to the sense in which I have used them. Asterisks have been employed to indicate where terms used in one place in the glossary will be explained elsewhere in it.

Albigensians:
semi-Christian heretics in southern France in the twelfth and thirteenth centuries; the Albigensians (or 'Cathars') posited a sharp distinction between 'evil' matter and 'good' spirit.

Anabaptism:
a *radical religious movement, arising in the sixteenth century, which rejected all the main churches, was indifferent or hostile to the state and insisted on the adult baptism of its converts as a mark of their 'rebirth'.

ancien régime (French – 'the old order'):
the social and governmental systems prevailing in France, and in Europe generally, between the sixteenth century and the French Revolution.

Antichrist:
the chief enemy of Christ, mentioned in several places in the New Testament; this figure has a special place in Christian *eschatology: according to eschatological tradition, Antichrist will be particularly strident before the return of Christ to earth, will claim to *be* Christ, but will be vanquished by Him.

antinomianism:
the belief that the true Christian, internally prompted, will do what is right, regardless of external law (cf. *libertarianism).

avaritia:
Latin – a greedy desire for wealth.

(the) ban:
ecclesiastical and social ostracising of a member of a church as a result of a disciplinary process.

Beghards:
lay men in the Middle Ages living piously and communally.

Beguines:
the female equivalent of Beghards; both Beguines and Beghards were especially to be found in the Netherlands.

biblicism:
pronounced belief in the value and authority of the

Bible; biblical scholarship and familiarity with the Bible (cf. *literalism, *Verbum Dei, *fundamentalism).

Burgundian: of the (originally French) House of Burgundy which ruled the Low Countries in the late Middle Ages.

Camisards (French – 'shirted ones'): radical Calvinist rebels in the Cévennes mountains of southern France in the late seventeenth and early eighteenth centuries.

casuistry: the application of moral principles to individual cases.

catholicity: the universality of the church.

christocephalism: the belief that Jesus Christ is the sole head of the church.

'church-type': a term used (notably by Ernst Troeltsch) to describe a sort of Christian church (e.g. traditionally, the Church of England) which sets out to uphold a social order and makes its membership coincide with that of a whole civil society (cf. *comprehensive (church), *sect, *denomination).

Ciompi (Italian – wool carders in Florence): plebeian insurgents who set up a popular government in Florence in 1378.

classical (Reformation): the relatively conservative Reformation associated with Luther, Calvin, Cranmer et al. (cf. *magisterial).

clericalism: belief in the leadership of the church and of Christian society by the clergy (cf. *laicism, *sacerdotalism).

comprehensive (church): used to describe a non-*separatist church; a church which includes all members of a political society (cf. *'church-type', *sect, *denomination).

consubstantiation: the belief that in the Eucharist the substance of bread and wine coexists with that of the body and blood of Christ (cf. *transubstantiation).

contado (Italian – countryside around a city): the country area ruled by a city state.

covetousness: eager and sinful desire for wealth.

cupiditas: Latin – a sinful lust for wealth.

denomination: a large-scale religious association which is not in overt conflict with its social environment; the denomination is held to be characteristic of Protestantism and of modern *pluralistic societies (cf. *sect, *'church-type', *comprehensive (church)).

discipline: the correction by the church of the moral faults of its members.

Dissenter: in England Protestants not members of the Anglican Church; the word is sometimes used to suggest a more uncompromising rejection of the Church of England than that of the *Nonconformists.

Donation of Constantine: a forged document, dating from the eighth or ninth century, which purported to be a grant from the Roman Empire to the papacy of an imperfectly defined but

extensive rule by the popes over the church and western
Europe.

ecclesiola (Latin – a   a small informal religious society.
small church):

ecclesiology: theories of the church and its government.

election: the act of divine will choosing some men for salvation
                       (cf. *predestination, *free will).

enthusiasm: a high degree of emotionalism in religion, a sense of
                       divine inspiration.

erastianism: the belief that the church ought to be subordinate to the
                       state.

eschatology: the doctrine of the last things; expectation and study of
                       the end of the world (cf. *millenialism).

Establishment: the Church of England, 'by law established' and sup-
                       ported by the state.

evangelical: according to the Gospels and the teachings of Jesus
                       found in them.

Evangelical: pertaining to the churches of the Lutheran Reformation.

Free Spirit: a mediaeval religious movement characterised by a
                       belief in the ability of its devotees to perfect themselves
                       through mystical contemplation and thus to rise into the
                       freedom of the spirit.

free will: freedom of choice between good and evil and the conse-
                       quent ability to choose eternal damnation or salvation
                       (cf. *election, *predestination).

Friends: since the early 1650s the Quakers' term for themselves;
                       in the first place 'Friends in the truth' or simply 'Friends'
                       was used to betoken Christian affection and shared
                       belief; in the eighteenth century 'Religious Society of
                       Friends' became the official label for the Quakers as a
                       denomination.

fundamentalism: insistence on the example of the early church and on the
                       binding authority of the Bible as the word of God and as
                       a rule for Christians (cf. *biblicism, *literalism).

Gallican: used of the Catholic Church in France, and especially its
                       administrative independence of Rome; also Gallico-
                       Catholic, i.e. Catholic in doctrine, French in government.

governo popolare   a republican form of government in an Italian city-state,
(Italian – popular   especially Florence.
government):

grace: supernatural divine aid to make possible the attainment
                       of sanctification.

gubernatorial: referring to a governor; specifically, the role of the Eng-
                       lish monarch as 'supreme governor' of the Church of
                       England.

hat-honour: the disparaging term which early Quakers used to refer
                       to the custom of doffing the hat to a social superior, a
                       habit which they rejected on grounds of Christian equal-
                       ity (cf. *'thou').

humanism: in the Renaissance, commitment to the employment of classical Greek and Latin literature and grammar so as to realise educational, literary, philosophical, civic and religious ideals.

Hussites: inclusive name for the Czech reformist movement which separated from the Catholic Church after the execution in 1415 of their titular martyr, John Hus.

Hutterites: the branch of the *Anabaptists named after Jacob Hutter (d. 1536); settled in Moravia, the Hutterites were characterised by strong communalism.

Independency: in England a variant of Calvinism which upheld the independence of each local congregation of the church (hence also, and later, 'Congregationalism'); Independency's heyday was in the mid-seventeenth century; its radicalism, with regard to church–state relations and even to religious toleration, was relative rather than absolute.

irenic: avoiding controversy, seeking agreement over religious questions.

Jansenism: stemming from the writings of Bishop Cornelius Jansen (d.1638), a revival in seventeenth-century French Catholicism of the determinist theology of St Augustine, involving a heavy emphasis on the importance of divine *grace and a repudiation of the freedom of the human will; like Calvinism, with which it had some theological features in common, Jansenism was strongly marked by *puritan asceticism.

Joachimism: the thought of Joachim of Fiore (c.1132–1202) and the prophetic system and ideology arising therefrom; Joachim, who was preoccupied with the theology of the Trinity, divided human history into three stages – the first age, that of God the Father, the second, that of the Son, and the future age of the Holy Spirit – an era (or 'state') of supreme spiritual illumination. Joachim's scheme, especially when stripped of its more ethereal qualities, endowed a number of dissident religious movements with confidence in a future vindication.

joyeuse entrée   in the province of Brabant in the mediaeval and early
(French – joyful   modern Netherlands the ceremonies (and charter of
entry):   liberties) which accompanied the entry of a ruling duke into his inheritance.

jure divino (Latin – the religious theory of monarchy according to which a
by divine right):   legitimately descended king is ordained to rule by God, consequently has a moral claim to be obeyed by his subjects and cannot be displaced or actively resisted by them.

laicism: belief in the importance of the laity, as distinct from the clergy, in social and religious life (cf. *clericalism, *sacerdotalism).

(Christian) liber- tarianism:	the belief that the true Christian is freed from imposed obedience to elaborate laws (cf. *antinomianism).
literalism:	a belief in the truth and authority of the literal words of the Bible (cf. *biblicism, *fundamentalism, *Verbum Dei).
Lollards:	pre-Reformation English heretics and critics of the Catholic Church who took their ideas from John Wyclif and from the translation of the Bible which he sponsored (cf. *Wyclifites).
magisterial (Reformation):	the mainstream, non-*radical Reformation of the sixteenth century which emphasised the need to work along with civil powers ('magistrates') so as to sanctify or discipline entire societies (cf. *classical (Reformation)).
martyrology:	the study and cult of Christian martyrs; emphasis on martyrdom as a characteristic of the church.
Mennonites:	a branch of the *Anabaptists taking their name from the Netherlands religious leader Menno Simmons (1496–1561); the Mennonites were (and are) pacifistic, indifferent to the state, congregationalist and democratic in their *ecclesiology.
millenialism, mil- lenarianism:	the Christian doctrine of a future thousand-year age of felicity; the doctrine of the millennium, which has Old Testament roots, was developed in the New Testament Book of Revelations (Apocalypse), and though the doctrine has often been interpreted in a metaphorical sense, insistence on its literal meaning and on the imminence of its predictions has been a recurrent theme in Christian history, especially amongst *radical movements.
Muggletonians:	an idiosyncratic *millenarian sect founded in England in the early 1650s by Ludowicke Muggleton and John Reeve.
Nonconformists:	English Protestants who have been (and are) unconvinced of the unqualified Protestantism of the Church of England; the term is often used interchangeably with *Dissenters.
numinous:	of the deity; inspiring great reverence; not fully explicable in rational terms.
papalism:	belief in the authority of the pope over the Catholic Church as its visible head on earth.
perfectionism:	the pursuit of elevated and evangelical moral and devotional standards, above the level of average Christian norms; belief in the possibility of the temporal attainment of saintly standards.
Piagnoni (Italian – weepers, mourners, moaners):	the followers and party of Girolamo Savonarola, so called because they lamented sins and seemed (especially to their opponents) to have a joyless outlook.
pluralism:	ecclesiastical historians use this word for the abuse of a cleric's holding more than one benefice; it is also used to

describe the condition of ideological and religious variety in a given society.

polis (Greek – a city): a city or city-state as a political community.

politique (French – [*homme*] *politique* – a person occupied with political issues): in the French Wars of Religion a religious moderate, a believer in religious toleration and the strengthening of the crown as a means to bring about peace; by extension, one who put reasons of state before doctrinal tenets.

popolo minuto (Italian – the lesser people): the mass of ordinary citizens of the city of Florence.

predestination: God's 'eternal decree' according to which men are fore-ordained to salvation or damnation (cf. *election, *free will).

prophecy: the disclosure by the individual prophet, through inspiration, of divine teaching.

Purgatory: in Catholic doctrine the phase of painful purification for the imperfect after death and before admission into Heaven.

puritanism: in general, fundamentalist Christian morality, with an emphasis on self-denial; specifically, an English religious movement, especially in the sixteenth and seventeenth centuries, to complete the Protestant Reformation.

radical [reformation; religion; Christianity]: used to describe a concern with religious criticism and reform based on the roots of Christianity, especially the New Testament roots; also visionary and individualistic religion.

Reformed: used of the churches of the Calvinist Reformation.

Regenten (Dutch – governors): in the early modern Dutch Republic the bourgeois republican oligarchy whose wealth was originally in trade and whose religion inclined towards moderate Calvinism.

Reich (German – realm): 'the Holy Roman Empire of the German Nation' in the mediaeval and early modern periods; Germany as a political community.

Reichstadt (plural: *Reichsstädte*; German – imperial city): a free city of the Reich.

Reichstag (German – imperial Diet): the representative assembly of the German Reich.

sacerdotalism: belief in the supremacy in the church of an ordained priesthood (cf. *clericalism, *laicism).

sacral: concerning the divine.

Scholasticism: the methods, employed in the mediaeval Schools, of using reason and philosophy, to understand the articles of revealed faith (cf. *Thomism).

sect: a religious *separatist protest movement aiming at *perfectionist standards, with membership on the basis of high individual religious attainment (cf. *denomination, *'church-type', *separatists).

separatists: in general, those who reject membership of *comprehensive churches to found purist religious groups; in particular, the sectarians of Elizabethan and Stuart England.

statism: belief in the necessity of a high degree of state authority.

supernal: divine and above the things of this world.

Test and Corporation Acts: the 1661 Corporation Act reserved municipal office in England to Anglicans; the 1673 Test Act excluded non-Anglicans from all offices under the crown.

thaumaturgic: pertaining to the performance of miracles, especially miracles of healing.

Thomism: the thought-system, within *Scholasticism, of Thomas Aquinas (c.1225–74), according to which revealed truths were seen as not contrary to reason.

'thou': the Quaker insistence on the archaic single-person form of address, indicating a refusal to acknowledge social gradations through speech (cf. *hat-honour).

tithe: the payment to a parson, or other proprietor of parochial income, of a tenth part of the produce of land in a parish.

Tory: a political party, originating in England in the later seventeenth century, committed to the defence of the Church of England, monarchy and landownership (cf. *Whig).

transubstantiation: the belief that in the Eucharist the real substance of bread and wine (though not their surface appearance) is converted into the very substance of Christ, God and man (cf. *consubstantiation).

trinitarian: belief in the Christian deity as three persons in one God.

universalism: belief in the unity of man and of the church.

Verbum Dei (Latin – the word of God): the Scriptures viewed as God's word (cf. *literalism, *biblicism, *fundamentalism).

Waldensians: members of the *evangelical movement originating in the twelfth-century preaching of Peter Waldo of Lyons; the Waldensians survived, especially in Piedmont, down to the Reformation and beyond.

Whig: an English political party of later seventeeth-century origin, dedicated to the ideals of constitutional monarchy, liberty, Protestantism, property, trade and religious moderation (cf. *Tory).

Wyclifites: those who followed the dissenting Oxford theologian John Wyclif (c.1330–84) in demanding a simple, biblical Christianity (cf. *Lollards).

For Lorna, Lena and Margaret

CHAPTER 1

Religious Radicalism, the Nation and the State

A survey of the period of religious reformation between the late fourteenth century and the mid-seventeenth century makes it obvious that a force akin to nationalism played a crucial role in religious change. Historians are, rightly, cautious in applying an essentially modern concept like nationalism to the early modern period. Yet there is evidence of strong feelings of nationality in Europe in those centuries. This proto-nationalism had several sources. In the first place, the localisation of universalist forces – primarily the Roman Church and the Holy Roman Empire – encouraged the growth of national awareness in the various kingdoms. Secondly, the Middle Ages closed on a note of warfare in Europe, most notably the Anglo-French Hundred Years' War in the West and the Czech–German Hussite wars in central Europe. Such conflicts, involving invasions and the violation of native soils and peoples, fostered hostile feelings between aggressors and their victims, helping in turn to strengthen the sense of national identity of both aggressor and victim.[1]

In the Anglo-French wars the war effort focused on the national dynasties of the combatants. Though the English developed their national consciousness and extended their national myth through their involvement in France, the presence of the English in France in the first place was justified in terms of their obligation to uphold the inherited personal rights of their kings. On the French side, too, resistance to the English became possible through reawakening loyalty to the charismatic symbol of the national monarchy. The third factor, then, in creating an increased national awareness was the rise of the national monarchies. In their monarchs Europeans, especially in the sixteenth century, could actualise inchoate feelings of national identity, and monarchy provided the essential feature of early modern nationality, so that we ought to speak of national-monarchism.

If monarchy was the indispensable force in the growth of nationalism, language was a highly important factor. The emergence and differentiation of the national vernaculars – Tuscan, Castilian, French, English, Dutch and German – made it possible to identify the people of a land as a community and to set up feelings of hostility towards, and separateness from, unintelligible peoples. A further cultural factor in the development of nationality entered with the classical Renaissance – the support given by the new scholarship to the national ideal. An example of this lies in the revival by humanists and antiquarians of the imperial Roman names for the subdivisions of Europe. In progressive educated circles the magniloquent geographical expressions coined by the Romans – Hispania, Gallia, Germania, Italia, Britannia – were much in vogue; these classical labels conveyed a sense of national unity and lent literary and historical support to national consolidation and aggrandisement.

We must, however, beware of exaggerating the extent of this process. In the Renaissance the Romance-speaking peoples of western Europe – Spaniards, Italians, Portuguese, French – took pride in the fact that their national tongues descended directly from Latin. The Germans for their part derived inspiration from the fact that Tacitus, rediscovered in the fifteenth century, had praised them for their enduring racial qualities of strength, simplicity and valour. But these Renaissance insights, encouraging as they were to incipient national feelings, tended to be the preserve of courtly and academic élites. The provincial divisions of Europe had been in existence for centuries and had attracted their own form of loyalty – the sense of *pays*, of region. The myriad regional divisions of the continent were traditional and natural foci for local allegiance – Catalonia and Galicia, Brittany and Languedoc, Swabia and Saxony, Flanders and Friesland, Lombardy and Calabria, or, for that matter, the North of England. In political organisms like France and the Netherlands the development by the dynasty of supra-provincial institutions and representative bodies often encountered determined opposition from the regions; and even in England, usually thought of as the model of advanced national development in the sixteenth century, entrenched sectionalism was manifested in Cornwall in 1496 and 1549 and in the North in 1536–7. Strongly differentiated regional dialects and even alternative languages; aristocratic leadership and patronage networks within local areas, flourishing regional political and ecclesiastical institutions; opposition to administrative centralism and fear of economic subordination; sheer familiarity with the local scene; these things made many early modern Europeans cling on to the manageable concept of the province, as against the remote notion of the nation. Yet, difficult as it was for nationalism to develop, pressing as the traditional force of regionalism was, religious change in the early modern period both encouraged the growth of nationalism and drew strength from national feelings already apparent. The protest of John Wyclif against Catholic corruption, priestly power and papalism took root in an England which already had formal parliamentary statutes restricting foreign papal intervention in the realm's affairs. In sponsoring the translation of the Scriptures into the national language Wyclif further contributed to the alliance of nationality and religious reform. At the other end of Europe, in Bohemia, a similar alliance between nationhood and reformation is evident. Though the opening moves in the Czech Reformation were made by German evangelisers in the late fourteenth century, the national reformer Jan Hus was thoroughly Czech in his language and approach; his academic career exemplified the struggle of the Czech intelligentsia to de-Germanise the University of Prague. In general terms the Czech Reformation can be seen as an assertion before the whole of Christendom of Czech national consciousness – a movement which took off from an outraged attempt to undo the insult done to the Czech people by the pronouncement of heresy against Hus by the Council of Constance; and in particular terms the Czech Reformation may be viewed as a national struggle of Czechs against Germans – as a campaign first to wrest control of academic, ecclesiastical and urban life in Bohemia from German hands and then later as an aggressive Czech crusade deep into the German lands.[2]

The Protestant Reformation of the sixteenth century exhibits similar strongly marked national features. Martin Luther – the 'German Hercules'[3] – was acclaimed as the epitome of the national character. His protest, initially a negative one against foreign Roman financial and spiritual corruption, seemed in the early 1520s, in alliance with the nationalist knight Ulrich von Hutten, to turn into a fully fledged positive national and religious movement of renewal, ideally under the leadership of Germany's national monarch, the Holy Roman Emperor. In Switzerland the humanist-influenced Protestant reformer Ulrich Zwingli vociferated the emergent nationalism of the Confederation in his passionate denunciations of the iniquitous traffic in Swiss blood, in the form of mercenary troops sold to foreign powers. In Geneva the apparently cosmopolitan reformer John Calvin found his strongest supporters amongst fellow-French residents and had dedicated his *Institutes of the Christian Religion* to the King of France; Calvin's obvious standing as a citizen both of the republic of letters and of the international Reformed church cannot conceal the fact that the goal of his life was not so much the reformation of his adoptive city, Geneva, as the religious and moral transformation of his mother-country, France. In fact, outside Geneva Calvinism took its deepest hold in alliance with the force of intense nationalism: in Scotland, where Calvinism was in the late 1550s and early 1560s, as again in the late 1630s and early 1640s, the expression of a national struggle against a foreign government; and in the North Netherlands, where Calvinism provided the ideological motor for successful national resistance to Spanish overlordship.

Examples can be multiplied. The Scandinavian Reformations were carried through by national monarchies and, pre-eminently in the case of Sweden, the Lutheran Reformation was the religious concomitant of a simultaneous assertion of national autonomy. Tudor England provides an exceptionally clear instance of a nationalist Reformation. In the first, Henrician phase of the religious revolution – in the 1530s – the negative repudiation of the pope's authority led on to a positive assertion, defended by recourse to history, of the traditional integrity and sovereignty of the realm: 'this realm of England is an empire'. In the Elizabethan phase of the Tudor Reformation the doctrine of the historic Englishness of the English Church, articulated by Elizabeth's first Archbishop of Canterbury, became the approved rationale for the compromise nature of a national ecclesiastical institution subordinate neither to Geneva nor to Rome.[4] This nationalism, bolstered by historical scholarship and implied in the concept of a protestant nation with a unique religious destiny – a new Israel, a godly people, God's Englishmen – received its fullest expression in the second English Reformation, that is, in the 1640s and 1650s.[5]

It is clear, then, that the pre-Reformation and the Protestant Reformation were intimately linked with the rise of nationalism in Europe. For our purposes, though, we must distinguish between the 'classical' or 'magisterial' Reformation and the 'radical' reformation running alongside it. An examination of radical Christianity in the late mediaeval and early modern centuries will show that it was either indifferent or antithetical to contemporaneous manifestations of monarchical nationalism. Those developments which, as we saw, were important in fostering national awareness – the decline of universalism and the sense of a community of the realm, the intensification of international warfare, national monarchy and Renaissance culture – were of little significance to dissident Christians. For sectarian Christians the concept of the community of the realm gave way to that of the fellowship of the church; the radical distinction between elect and unregenerate took primacy over that between native and foreigner. At the same time, the decline of universalism was halted, in the case of religious radicals, by their revival, or retention, of Christian universalism. Missionary activities on the part of religious radicals traversed all national and political frontiers. The Anabaptist mission of the sixteenth century was conducted throughout all the lands of high and low German speech and even down into Italy.[6] Anabaptist missionaries like Melchior Hoffmann and Menno Simmons operated, like their model Paul of Tarsus, in an unrestricted geographical framework, impelled onwards by the constant push of persecution and by their sense of spiritual pilgrimage, of actual alienation from the world around them: they were the true exiles of the period. In their exile in the Netherlands Elizabethan and Jacobean English Separatists found themselves in a world of luxuriant religious cosmopolitanism; [7] in the seventeenth century English religious radicals extended the concept of the elect nation into a militant religious outreach to Europe or, like the Quakers, took in a world preaching mission from North America to Constantinople.[8] Now it is true that religious internationalism characterised almost all the mainstream forms of the Reformation. There was a Lutheran international movement, as there most certainly was a Calvinist international movement. Yet it is clear that Lutheranism, depending for much of its intellectual and emotional force on the German language, took hold primarily in the German lands or amongst German communities outside the Reich itself. It is significant, further, that the doctrinal divisions in the early Protestant Reformation – especially that between the Swiss and German Reformations – also tended to coincide with national divisions; then, in the Calvinist phase of the classical Reformation the emergent Reformed church quickly crystallised into a number of *national* churches, each with an individual confession of faith: the Gallic and Belgic Confessions of 1559 and 1561, the English 39 Articles of 1563, the Scottish National Covenant of 1580 and the Dutch Canons of the Synod of Dort (1619).

The conscious creation by Evangelical and Reformed Protestants of comprehensive, social, national churches, working actually or ideally in close co-operation with national political authorities so as to achieve the moral renewal of whole societies, this was an essential goal of the magisterial Reformation. Essential to this task was a view of the church as a confederation of visible national churches and this conflicted with the universalist and élitist conceptions of the church which characterised religious radicals. At the same time, the task which the classical Reformation set itself could be achieved only with a degree of overlapping of functions between state and church; to this was opposed the radicals' purist and New Testamentarian view of the absolute distinctness of state and church and, in fact, the primacy of church over state. The national church was a concept totally foreign to radical religious elements: for the Quakers, indeed, the term 'national worship' was one of intense opprobrium.

The nebulous force of early modern nationalism vitally required for its actualisation the tangible figure of the sovereign prince. The classical Reformation gave this figure a deeper dimension in the character of the *godly* prince, the initiator of reformation. In German territories like Electoral and Ducal Saxony, Brunswick-Wolfenbüttel or Prussia the implementation of reform was the work of the ruler.[9] Martin

Luther himself, for all his reservations about the confusion of spiritual and secular functions, gave considerable impetus, in widely disseminated works like *To the Christian Nobility of the German Nation*,[10] to the notion of the religious responsibilities of the ruler; the ideal type of the quasi-episcopal ruler was fully brought out by Evangelical theoreticians like Brenz – the prince had 'the power of judging and deciding the doctrine of religion' – and Capito: 'The prince is the pastor, he is the father, he is the visible head of the church on earth.' In addition, in *Reichsstädte* like Nuremburg or Swiss cities like Zürich major responsibilities in initiating, protecting and regulating religious reform were conceded by the pastors to the political authorities. Again, just as England seems to represent the flowering of national consciousness in sixteenth-century Europe, so its religious Reformation was to a very high degree influenced by the prevalent royalism, though in 1559 German views on the prince as bishop were renounced in favour of a purely gubernatorial conception of the prince's office *vis-à-vis* the church. But it can hardly be denied that Reformation in sixteenth-century England depended entirely on the policies of the monarch and that the prince and the royal council directed the changing currents of religious life. In the reign of Elizabeth the development of the English concept of the reforming prince reached a climax in the martyrologist John Foxe's characterisation of the queen as a new Constantine, a monarch who introduced true religion.

Yet there were uncertainties attached to this relationship between state and religion and these uncertainties were perceived most clearly by religious radicals. In delineating the episcopal role of the prince, spokesmen of the German Reformation inherited from their Catholic antecedents the demand for a temporal and visible residuum of authority over the church. Religious radicals, on the other hand, discarded this form of authority in favour of the sole headship of the transcendent figure of Christ as only 'prophet, priest and king'. This christocephalism clearly left no room for the *cura religionis* of the prince, whether as chief bishop or as supreme governor. A further area of tension opened up over the conflicting priorities of state and church. The state's needs, especially its financial needs, often conflicted with the well-established models of religious reformation which were common to all the churches, Catholic, magisterial and radical. Even before the sixteenth century it had become obvious that to reform the church so as to equip it to perform its most elementary tasks of preaching and instruction a complete overhaul of ecclesiastical finances was necessary – a redeployment of resources, especially in the direction of the education and maintenance of the lower clergy. The state, however, whether in Catholic France, Anglican England or Lutheran Germany, clearly had a vested interest in the retention of those existing structures of ecclesiastical finance which, though they hampered the carrying out of the church's basic tasks, yet allowed the state to supplement its incomes and reward its servants and dependants.[11]

In numerous instances during the period of the proto-Reformation and the Reformation the needs of the state, whether financial or political, impeded the implementation of blueprints of religious reform. Where religious radicalism already existed it was left isolated by the state's inevitable retreat from total change; where religious reformism was present frustration at the reassertion of statist priorities frequently converted it into religious radicalism. The most pressing of the state's political needs with regard to religious settlements was for national consensus, for conservative respectability and the middle ground. The early history of the Wyclifite movement provides an example: in the 1370s eminent members of the English political establishment patronised John Wyclif; however, as Wyclif's critique of familiar abuses was extended into a politically dangerous attack on the Mass, so his high-placed backers withdrew their support. Across the continent, in Bohemia, the full working-out of anti-sacerdotalism, lay religion, moral puritanism and eschatology was checked by the need to hold together a military, political and intellectual coalition embracing the baronage and the University of Prague. In Elizabethan England the essentially political need to placate Catholic opinion at home and abroad imposed on the Anglican Church an unreformed church order and liturgy; Separatism was the most articulate form of protest against the compromise.

The constant attenuation of radical religious developments by political exigencies – especially those of 'consensus' – frequently left religious radicals hostile or indifferent to the state, and remote from the mood of nationalist statism which characterised the magisterial Reformers.

A further reason for the diffidence of religious radicals towards the national-monarchical state lay in the history of persecution. The sixteenth-century Anabaptists, as the heirs of the late mediaeval dissenting tradition, inherited a prudent suspicion of those political authorities who had in the past collaborated with inquisitorial and episcopal tribunals in repressing religious nonconformity. Though the prince might now call himself 'Evangelical', the name-change did not change the prince's insistence on religious uniformity, and an attitude of ancestral mistrust towards the state was vindicated by the way in which Reformation princes, fully supported by the pastors, prepared to suppress the religious radicals: G. H. Williams reminds us that the Reichstag at Speyer, which launched the word Protestant, also witnessed a total agreement between Catholic and Evangelical estates to put down Anabaptism.

Persecution lay at the centre of radical Christian thought in the Reformation period. Martyrdom was a mark of the authenticity of the church and a link with the apostolic model. Because of the spiritual value given to persecution, the records of suffering were jealously conserved. These records, read or recalled, led to the inescapable conclusion that the perennial oppressor of the true church – from Nero to Charles II of England and Louis XIV of France – was the secular prince. The voluminous Collections of Sufferings made by seventeenth- and eighteenth-century English Quakers brought home to the reader first an impression of the fortitude of the sufferers and martyrs and then a conviction of the antichristian iniquity of the initiator and agent of persecution, the royal state.

Such a conclusion was a dangerous one to hold and escape routes were sought, such as the belief that bishops were the real instigators of the persecution of the saints. These were beliefs, however, that could not for long stand up in face of the facts – the fact, for instance, that bishops were, in England as elsewhere, royal appointees. Historical martyrology, a science much cultivated in the Protestant Reformation, put the blame for centuries of persecution on the shoulders of the princely state. Foxe's *Acts and Monuments* (the 'Book of Martyrs') was a classic of Reformation martyrology. The intention of the work was to celebrate the Protestantism of the Tudor monarchy, epitomised in Elizabeth; in the process, however, Foxe's work recounted a history of persecution in the later Middle Ages and in the sixteenth century, all of it at the hands of the princely state. The martyrs among the 'secret multitude of true believers', the Lollards, died under the provisions of that concordat between the church and the Lancastrian monarchy, the statute *De Haeretico Comburendo*; the anti-transubstantiationists burned under Henry and Mary Tudor were victims of royal doctrinal orthodoxy. Now conclusions like these were not those that John Foxe intended to be drawn. None the less, soon after its publication in English in 1563, the *Book of Martyrs* quickly became a source-book for radicals in their resistance to the Elizabethan state's demand for conformity. 'It may be showed', said the Separatist Robert Hawkins in answer to his episcopal interrogators in 1567, 'in the book of the monuments of the church, that many which were burned in Queen Mary's time died for standing against popery, as we now do.' Not surprisingly, the answers given by the dissidents in this examination show scant respect for monarchy and its rule over the church: 'It had been better we had never been born than to suffer God to be dishonoured, and his word defaced for prince's pleasure . . . the servants of God are persecuted under her.'[12] The decade in which the *Book of Martyrs* appeared was a good time to look back on the vicissitudes of godliness in Tudor England and to see how ill it had fared, on the whole, at the hands of the dynasty. Tudor nonconformists had already drawn the conclusion that the best guarantee of the church's integrity was its separation from the state. This conclusion, fully based on historical study and reflection, was drawn up by the eighteenth-century Congregationalist historian Daniel Neal in his summing up of the reign of Mary: 'It will appear in the course of this reign, that an absolute supremacy over the consciences of men, lodged with a single person, may as well be prejudicial as serviceable to true religion: for if king Henry VIII. and his son king Edward VI. reformed some abuses by their supremacy, . . . we shall find queen Mary making use of the same power to turn things back into their old channel, till she had restored the grossest and most idolatrous part of Popery . . . It is sad when the religion of a nation is under such a direction.'[13]

Such a conclusion – that political authorities have political priorities or conservative personal preferences which are hostile to the interests of 'true religion' – was also brought home to religious radicals in the sixteenth and seventeenth centuries. It resulted in the further distancing of religious dissidents from the nationalist consciousness forming around the figure of the sovereign prince.

Hereditary monarchism conflicted with the social egalitarianism characteristic of religious nonconformists like the Quakers. George Fox's manner of address to the King of England – 'Friend', along with the familiar single-person form – showed a total lack of regard for the pretensions of monarchy. The elective principle of church government found in groups like the English Sectaries was also inconsistent with the very nature of monarchy. The eschatology of groups like the Anabaptists pronounced all human institutions transitory and denied validity to the exalted claims of divine-right monarchy. Thus innate characteristics of fundamentalist Christianity left its proponents critical of national monarchism. As monarchism developed, primitive features, such as military leadership, continued to adhere to it and to harmonise monarchy with national mythologies. Kings took seriously their responsibilities as commanders-in-chief of their armies: Charles V and Francis I at Pavia, Louis XIV pretending to direct the fall of Strasburg, and, as late as the mid-eighteenth century, George II pluckily leading his troops to battle on the field of Dettingen. Warfare, which was crucial to the advancement of national awareness, was also inextricably involved with monarchy. Now it is clear that many Christian radicals in the early modern centuries adopted a markedly militarist ethic influenced by eschatology and by the Old Testament. The Bohemian Taborites in the fifteenth century, the Münster Anabaptists in the sixteenth, the New Model Army in the seventeenth, all took up arms on behalf of the gospel. It ought to e said, though, that in none of these cases was *national* struggle the sole justification for warfare. In addition, it is clear that Christian radicals, from the Waldensians for most of their history through the mainstream Anabaptists to the Quakers, have generally conformed to Christian pacifism.[14] The Anabaptist Michael Sattler's refusal to countenance warfare even went beyond the normally pacifist Erasmus's acceptance of anti-Turkish war. Nationalism intensified warfare and warfare intensified nationalism, but those groups who renounced war put themselves outside the complex of ideas associated with patriotism, militarism and monarchism. A particularly vivid example is to hand during the Seven Years' War (1756–63) between France and Britain. Under the influence of the Earl of Chatham this struggle for trade and colonies took on the character in Britain of a war for national glory and survival, and the national jingoism reached fever pitch in the 'Year of Victories', 1759, with the conquests of Clive of India and Wolfe in Canada. The mood sweeping the country was certainly encouraged by the establishment, which sponsored 'Rejoicing Nights' to give thanks for the string of victories. For Quakers, of course, such celebrations were pagan rituals, but all the more objectionable in that they glorified war. In refusing to participate in the rejoicings, however – for instance by illuminating their shops and homes – Quakers cut themselves off completely from the prevailing militaristic nationalism. Twenty-four years later, American Quakers put themselves in the same position, and left their 'patriotism' dangerously open to question by their refusal to celebrate the achievement of American independence and the military victories that had made it possible. In both cases the nationalist commitment of the Quakers really was less intense than that prevailing in the community around them. The reasons for this were threefold: first, that the Quakers looked inwards to their church communities rather than to the community of the nation; second, that Quakers were aware of their place in a supra-national transatlantic community, with frequent contacts; and third, the Quakers as typical Christian pacifists could never fully share a national consciousness which received its most solemn, hysterical and religious expression in times of war.[15]

We saw how support was given to the development of national consciousness by Renaissance culture, and especially by Renaissance works of history. History, especially if it discounted the history of the church in favour of the history of the nation, if it recounted the achievements of kings and the victories of the past, provided essential emotional and intellectual stimulus for national feelings. 'The strongest cause for the feeling of nationality', wrote J. S. Mill, 'is identity of political antecedents; the possession of a national history, and consequent community of recollections; collective pride and humiliation, pleasure and regret, connected with the same incidents in the past.'[16] The historical recollections that were to feed such national feelings were, in the Renaissance period, dynastic, national and militaristic rather than hagiographic, ecclesiastical and miraculous; and, especially in the approach characteristic of Machiavelli, the historiographical outlook was decidedly classical and pre-Christian. A new historical method, albeit derived from Roman historians, characterised the national histories, though it is important to recall that Renaissance historical research, and the arts of rhetoric and philology which helped support it, were the carefully cultivated preserves of scholars. Such scholars were favoured by royal courts, as was the imported Italian historian Polydore Vergil, who dedicated to Henry VIII his *Anglica Historia*, a humanist work of non-legendary history, exalting the English nation and its kings.[17] The 'new learning' deeply affected the writing of history and helped produce historical literature that was decidedly secular and dedicated to a realism, accuracy and stylistic perfection quite foreign to the diverse traditions of ecclesiastical history and of the bourgeois vernacular city chronicle. The latinity and secularity of humanist historical literature tended to restrict it to humanist circles and to withhold it from popular currency, at least until popular drama and poetry were able to popularise the fruits of national-oriented historical research.

Early modern nationalism, though sometimes acting in alliance with the Protestant religion, was also often characterised by a rational, empirical, realistic and non-transcendent view of life, history and politics. Those attracted to fundamentalist and dissenting forms of Christianity, on the other hand, were in their reading and overall culture estranged from the relatively rationalist perceptions which were inseparable from nationalist and statist culture. We too easily forget how restricted was the circulation of such works as Marsiglio's *Defensor Pacis* or Machiavelli's *Il Principe* or Hobbes's *Leviathan*. Those whose staple culture and reading derived from the Christian Scriptures had no access to the Renaissance outlook which accompanied the rise of early modern nationalism. We must try to imagine – something difficult to do in an age of the mass dissemination of ideas – a situation in which members of dissenting groups can be effectively insulated from dominant or approved cultures. In Philip Gosse's *Father and Son* we have a picture of a group of Victorian fundamentalist Christians who were totally unaware of essential features of Victorian secular culture – for example, the novel and the drama – and whose own culture was effectively that of seventeenth-century Puritanism. Similarly, Quakers, for the greater part of their history, have deliberately cut themselves off from the currents of English and American culture – from non-religious literature, music, sports, amusements and art. In the early modern period, the existence of cultural diversity in European societies and of cultural dissent from 'Renaissance' culture was made all the more likely by the typical recondite Latin form of expression of the new civilisation of the Renaissance. The 'civilisation of the Renaissance' did not confront prevailing barbarism, but rather encountered the existence of other, older, more popular, more vernacular and more religious cultural forms. What we think of as Renaissance culture was hardly communicable on any mass level. In fact, our thinking about the cultural history of the early modern period has been too much influenced by the concept of the Renaissance. Perhaps our awareness of the significance of the invention of printing has blinded us into believing that the fifteenth, sixteenth and seventeenth centuries made up an age like our own – an age of the mass distribution of new ideas, especially of nationalist and statist propaganda. In fact, the intellectual culture of the Renaissance, however much its values may in the long run have triumphed, however much its insights were necessary to the ultimate exaltation of the nation-state, was in the first place the culture of exclusive coteries; this fact was frequently underlined by forms of communication which confirmed the impression of exclusiveness – leisured Platonic dialogues, private Latin epistles. The Renaissance preference for a pure Latin and the vogue for Greek confirmed this effect of removing the neo-classical Renaissance civilisation from popular currency. We must not make the old mistake of equating the terms 'Renaissance' and 'pagan'. And yet, a career like that of Cardinal Bembo[18] is just typical enough to remind us that the Renaissance stood for a fastidious, aristocratic and relatively worldly culture totally foreign to that of the petit-bourgeois and artisan elements who gravitated in large numbers towards radical religious movements. However, this civilisation of the Renaissance rode in harness with monarchist and nationalist impulses and lent its full support to the ideal of the nation and of the nation-state. It was Renaissance art that provided nationalist and royalist iconography; it was Renaissance pragmatism and realism – the thought of writers from Marsiglio to Hobbes – that created the *raison d'être* of the early modern nation-state, existing by right of history and by virtue of its own purposes.

This pragmatism and realism can be examined by looking at the most obvious element in the national-statist complex of ideas, the idea of kingship. Renaissance writers saw this institution realistically, in terms of the professional success or failure of individual kings in attaining the limited and human goals of monarchy. Thus, for Machiavelli, Ferdinand the Catholic, through his cunning, assiduity and force of character, achieved the ends that kings should have before them. The natural goals of kingship were to remain on the throne, to enforce the laws evenly, to conserve, and perhaps add to, the territory of the state. To perform these functions, Renaissance profiles of the ideal monarch showed how the king received before his accession a practical, all-round education (especially in history), how he appointed the best advisers, and how, like Philip II and Louis XIV, he worked hard at the daily tasks of kingship. The picture of a king that was built up was of a dynamic and human agent. Admittedly, artists and courtiers, more or less convincingly, magnified the king's attributes – his grace, culture, vitality, religion, martial prowess, sagacity – but they did so in such a way as to present the king's individual human qualities, and in such a way, too, as to show him to be superbly well qualified to carry out the professional work of kingship; if the king was flattered, he was also humanised and individualised, and in works like Holbein's Henry VIII, or Titian's Charles V series, or Van Dyck's studies of Charles I, we have portraits which are regal, complimentary – and thoroughly personal and non-typological. This view of kingship – as a human and practical function – differed markedly from older and more popular views of kingship. These older views fall into two categories – of the king who *is* and of the king who *becomes*. Both these attitudes to kingship are de-personalised, non-practical and non-human, or super-natural rather than super-human. In the first category resides the conventional mediaeval image of the king. According to this image the king *is* certain things – residuum of ancient law, fount of justice, righter of the wrongs of the commons. In line with this essentially traditional view, the king is a symbolic and inert force: 'amicis adjutorium, inimicis obstaculum, humilibus solatium, elevatis correptio, divitibus doctrina, pauperibus pietas, peregrinis pacificatio, propriis in patria pax et securitas'.[19] Action is largely irrelevant in this idea of kingship, and the English concept of the petition of right reveals a traditional expectation that the king – not as a working administrative officer but as custodian of ancient justice – can make right be done by his word. The king is not individualised, either pictorially or literarily – and certain kings are picked out – Charlemagne, Louis IX – only for their conformity or contribution to the model. Accounts of such kings are not fables but rather further opportunities for developing the stereotype of the just and pious king.[20]

This view of kingship was prevalent and popular in Europe in the Middle Ages, though not always well articulated. It obviously had its social value, for it sustained beliefs that grievances could be attended to and that justice did have an abode in human society. The strong survival on various lower-class levels of the traditional ideal of kingship is brought home to us by the number of European peasant uprisings designed to restore weakened kingly authority and to bring to the king's notice his subjects' grievances so that, as source of justice, he would correct them. Such a view of the king as conservator of the good old laws is also revealed in fifteenth-century documents like the *Reformation of the Emperor Sigismund*.[21] A development of this conventional notion of kingship lies in the idea of the king, not as one who *does* or *is*, but as one who *becomes*. This messianic vision of kingship is somewhat analogous to the common myth of the once-and-future king – Arthur, Frederick Barbarossa, Sebastian of Portugal – the sleeping and returning king. But the messianic king is a thoroughly Christianised figure. In the prophecies of the Second Charlemagne the apotheosised king has an eschatological function totally at variance with the rational aims of Renaissance monarchy.[22]

Nonetheless, in the fifteenth and sixteenth centuries the conduct of kings at least occasionally approached the stereotype of the paternal king. The Christian piety of Henry VI of England, the chivalry of Emperor Charles V, the care for justice of Philip II, these were at least aspects of the ancestral image of monarchy. Yet in all cases these traditional and valuable features were lost sight of behind a new structure of Realpolitik. In fifteenth-century England the bewildering changes in the succession to the throne produced a theory of rightful tenure in which actual possession counted for nine points of the law. As for Charles V, though some of his ideologues were beguiled by a Dantean vision of world monarchy, and though shreds of Charlemagne *redivivus* clung to the emperor, yet Charles's actual conduct often showed a clear preference for personal and dynastic advantage over the realisation of Christian goals.[23] In Philip of Spain's case, the king's ruthlessness in Spain and the Netherlands concealed the traditionalist Christian and Castilian king behind the persona of an unscrupulous implement of the Counter-Reformation.

Political reality left unsatisfied the popular quest for either a traditional or messianic king. Philip II privately working at the tasks of kingship was not a substitute for Louis IX *being* a king – publicly dispensing his justice under an oak in the woods of Vincennes (though in the fifteenth century Edward IV of England showed a shrewd awareness of the force of popular fantasy by briefly resuming his royal place on the King's Bench). As for prophetic monarchy, Charles VIII of France in the 1490s was the last European king to respond to the messianic summons to transfiguration on Calvary. Prophetic expectations of monarchy formed part of a Christian culture which was being increasingly left behind by the realism of the Renaissance – though it should be said that some men of the Renaissance, for example, Egidio da Viterbo and Christopher Columbus, were strongly influenced by prophecy. Renaissance realism, when applied to the state, left out of account the unanalysable, mythological and numinous aspects of kingship, part of a popular and Christian culture that was being superseded, but for which rational nationalism and pragmatic statism provided inadequate substitutes.

In the early modern period those whose culture was overwhelmingly religious and traditional and who inclined towards a fundamentalist, dissenting variant of Christianity were also immune to the intellectual and cultural currents lending support to nationalism and nationalist monarchism. In so far as proto-nationalist and national-monarchist ideas rested on the progressive and realist assumptions, and especially on the historical writings, of Renaissance thinkers, the new nationalism remained outside the range of ideas of all those for whom Renaissance ideas remained a closed book. The magisterial Reformation seemed to offer the possibility of reviving transcendent monarchy, but in fact the general result of the state Reformations was either to subordinate religion to the priorities of the state or to project the prince as merely the protagonist of his state's religious denomination.

Religious radicals in early modern Europe remained cut off from nationalist tendencies and formed a 'counter-culture' opposed to the developing state-oriented nationalism. Seeing the state as transient and the nation as unregenerate, Christian radicals and sectarians inclined, as we have seen, to a variant of mediaeval Christian universalism.

In the fifteenth, sixteenth and seventeenth centuries national monarchy in Europe assumed more rational functions than it had possessed in the Middle Ages. In the past historians overstated the idea of a 'new monarchy' in the sixteenth century: in particular they overestimated the 'absolute' and 'middle class' aspects of the new royalism in France, Spain and England. Yet we ought to be aware that, though there were important continuities between mediaeval and early modern monarchy, and that early modern monarchy was more religious and less effective than the modern state, a different, functional image of monarchy developed in the Renaissance period, partly under the influence of Renaissance ideas. Though the Renaissance prince might become 'supreme head', 'supreme governor' or even 'chief bishop' of a local branch of the Christian church, in doing so he added to his administrative responsibilities. The tendency away from charismatic, numinous, thaumaturgic monarchy was only partly halted by royal assumptions of control over the church. Early modern monarchy was in process of becoming a thoroughly practical and natural institution, fully subject to historico-philosophical analysis in terms of its origins and developments and subject to scientific political analysis in terms of its stated functions – to maintain itself in power, to govern for the material good of the realm. In the transition there was lost the sacramental or magical element of monarchy, the essential popular element. This element was brought out in the public semi-sacrament of coronation and was confirmed in the magical royal act of touching to cure the scrofula. Both these facets of monarchy were particularly to the fore in the mediaeval French monarchy. They also had a surprising persistence in the English monarchy: James I, his grandson James II and his great-grand-daughter Queen Anne touched for the 'King's Evil'.[24] However, the scepticism of James I with regard to touching against the scrofula reveals a king dangerously failing to share a popular belief in his own supernatural powers – as it also discloses a widespread surviving acceptance of this belief. The lessening of emphasis under Renaissance and Reformation influences on the 'superstitious' popular dimensions of monarchy was paralleled by a geographical distancing of the sovereign from his subjects. The tendency of Renaissance and Baroque monarchy, justified by the new insistence of the administrative functions of the king, was to remove the sovereign from contact with his subjects. Court ceremonial, designed to amuse potentially dissident aristrocrats, provided no substitute for visual awareness of the king on the part of the mass of his lesser subjects. The sixteenth and seventeenth centuries witnessed the effective end of mobile monarchy. The courts of the Louvre and Versailles, of Whitehall, the Escorial, the Vatican, Dresden, Vienna and Berlin localised the prince. With their expensive and rigid rituals, such courts, as Professor Trevor-Roper says, imposed demands on national resources which, along with the strain of war, set off a rash of popular and tax-payers' revolts in mid-seventeenth-century Europe. But we might also ask how much the removal of the king from his subjects' gaze also had a hand in causing the anti-state manifestations of popular feelings in the 1640s and 1650s. Philip II once criticised his father Charles V for wasting his time, health and substance on travelling between his territories; as an administrator-king, Philip chained himself to a desk in a 'rational' attempt to discharge his bureaucratic duties. But Philip failed to share his father's instinctive appreciation of the elusive secret of traditional monarchy, popular contact. This charismatic and popular aspect of monarchy gave way to a relatively utilitarian and institutional view of kingship. Early modern monarchy certainly lacked the power and impersonality of the modern state; it has to be seen as a transitional form of government, lying between religious and feudal monarchy and the rational and bureaucratic state institutions of the modern world. Many highly traditional features clung to early modern monarchy, above all its religious character. However, early modern European monarchical states had wider scope than their predecessors and had a number of express rational functions to perform: the pacification of the nobility, the encouragement of commerce and the acquisition of territory. Yet in pursuing these rational goals monarchy lost some of the paternal and mythical dimensions which had created a public political religion among the European peasantries and provided a contrary force of attraction to the quasi-democratic and republican tendencies evident in some of the major cities of mediaeval Europe.

In the early modern period the vacuum created by the decline of popular monarchy was filled, sometimes by the emergence of aristo-cratic leaders of resistance and revolt, for example the Duke of Guise in Paris in the 1580s or the Prince of Orange in the Revolt of the Netherlands; or by popular religious pseudo-kings and messiahs like Jan of Leyden at Münster in 1535 or Sabbatai Zevi in the Jewish communities in 1666; or by a non-human transcendent monarchism like that of 'King Jesus' amongst the English Fifth Monarchists.

Proto-nationalism was supported by a realist and progressive out-look, characteristic, for example, of Thomas Cromwell in sixteenth-century England, and was associated with the new monarchism which adopted that pragmatic viewpoint. In methods of government like those proposed by Sully and Colbert for France, or by Pepys and Petty for England, the emphasis lay on applied science, statistics, 'political arithmetic', and the balances of power and trade. Religion was still indispensable to the support of these 'intermediate' states, though the religion in question may itself have been modernistic, as with the Newtonian-influenced religion that was in vogue amongst moderate progressives in England after the Glorious Revolution. Rational, prac-tical and statist ideas proved attractive, especially in England, to the more highly placed members, or former members, of the Protestant Dissenting community. But there was a difference – one of education, culture, class orientation and religious zeal – between a Sully and a Camisard, as there was between a Locke and a Bunyan; the difference lay in the fact that radical religionists from the lower social strata possessed an overwhelmingly or entirely religious culture which pre-cluded the rational and scientific values which accompanied the exalta-tion of the nation and the state. The social composition of radical religious movements is a complicated matter. In even the most subver-sive groups there were found disaffected clerics and university gradu-ates, along with restive members of the landed gentries, especially disgruntled younger sons – and members of the military and political classes in general. But it is clear that the typical rank-and-file member-ship of radical Christian groups, such as the Waldensians, the Ana-baptists, the Lollards or the Quakers, was made up of lower and lower-middle class elements – schoolmasters, clerks and printing workers, skilled craftsmen, weavers and workers in all the metallurgi-cal, catering and textile trades, urban and rural industrial and mining workers in general, plus some peasants and small farmers. Such groups and individuals were often literate or semi-literate in their own ver-naculars but were shut off from the sophisticated Renaissance classics of secular literature, political theory, ethics, jurisprudence, speculative theology, national history or science: works necessarily written in either Latin, Italian or recondite versions of the vernaculars. In place of the Renaissance classics, the literature of the lower orders consisted of readily intelligible, mass-produced works like the cheap, ephemeral pamphlets and cartoons of the German Reformation, or the broad-sheets and tracts of the English civil war; on a less ephemeral, but still accessible, level than these lay religious works like the *Theologia Deutsch*, the French Calvinist-inspired *Calendrier historial*, the Italian crypto-Lutheran *Beneficio di Christo Crocifisso*, or *Pilgrim's Progress*; but looming much larger in importance than any of these was the Bible, generally obtainable in good vernacular translation by the middle of the sixteenth century and made available for large-scale, relatively inexpensive distribution by printing. However, any account of the literary culture of the lower classes leaves out of account the popular culture's aural dimension. Through the sermon, the most common form of structured communication and entertainment in early modern Europe,[25] the non- or semi-literate were involved in scriptural and Christian culture. The sermon in fact bridged the gap between the aural and scriptural media for it, along with the Scripture readings delivered in annual cycles during divine worship, constantly recited the word of Scripture. The English Protestant expression 'preaching the word' has a peculiar force, for a sermon, based on a scriptural text and constantly citing passages of Scriptures, made audiences familiar with *the* authoritative text without their necessarily reading it. In this sense the sermon was the religious equivalent of the mediaeval academic lecture – the oral presentation of the contents of a book or books. Sermons like those delivered by Jan Hus at the Bethlehem Chapel were largely the concatenations of Scripture passages, and, through the repeated delivery of such edited excerpts of the Bible, congregations were thoroughly schooled in the contents of the crucial Christian text. Given the normally high level of aural concentration and aural memory in non-literate societies,[26] we can expect an equally high level of retention of the preached word of Scripture – forming a Bible-based culture of the apparently uneducated, and equipping them with a set of biblical and especially New-Testamentarian norms from which to evaluate contemporary political and ecclesiastical institutions. This audio-biblical culture was especially to be found in the towns of Europe, where special provisions were made for preaching. Endowed preaching provisions, such as the puritan lectureships set up by godly borough corporations to supply adequate preaching in the English county towns and market towns, ensured a plentiful urban supply of preaching.[27] In fact, English religious radicals sometimes displayed such a sermon-hunger that they would go to listen to those ministers of the established church who had the words of life.[28] The skilled preacher was a valued member of society – a demotic rhetorician, a popular poet, a populariser of religious ideas, a trained artist and master of the formal art of preaching, which was the sacred counterpart of the secular art of rhetoric. The extent of such an individual's influence as the spokesman and creator of popular urban culture and consciousness may be realised through a study of Savonarola's career in Florence. But we must remember that Savonarola was not a unique figure, either in Florence or in any of the major towns and cities of early modern Europe. Like any popular artist the preacher articulated as well as shaped the minds of his audience. The culture he expressed was, obviously, essentially religious and, indeed, grounded in the source of his evidence and information, the Bible. In so far as 'social questions' were broached, they were explored in the traditional biblical and Christian terms of economic justice and charity, personal frugality, the perils of wealth and the virtues of poverty. In so far as political questions were discussed, they were considered in the terms familiar to urban audiences, those of urban politics.

The political culture of urban popular elements in Renaissance Europe consisted of nostalgia for quasi-democratic institutions. This is not to say that the great towns and cities had held out completely against the royalist ideal in its popular mediaeval form, and where sovereigns like Elizabeth I and Charles V retained the aura of traditional monarchy they were normally assured of cordial receptions in their cities. Nor do I intend to say that mediaeval European cities were possessed of urban democratic forms as we would understand that term. None the less, in two areas of Europe particularly – central and northern Italy and the Low Countries – urban autonomy and tendencies in a democratic direction has emerged together in the course of the Middle Ages, though socioeconomic change and the rise of the Burgundian and Medician proto-monarchies in Flanders and Tuscany brought to an end the existence of relatively popular institutions in communes like Ghent and Florence. In even pro-Burgundian Antwerp, and with even a comparatively old-fashioned dynast like Charles V, there were signs of tension between monarchical and allied aristocratic forces on the one hand and urban popular elements on the other; take this minor incident: 'The Emperor having been ill-used last summer by some of the base sort in Antwerp, and reminded of this by late misorders, has thought fit to show himself their sovereign by no longer overslipping in silence their lewd demeanour. Wherefore by sending thither the Prince of Orange . . . and other nobles . . . he has finally sent in one body seven ensigns of Germans who made the Emperor full master of the city.'[29] Whether or not this imperial conduct displays a Spanish influence, it certainly does show Charles in one of his new-monarchist moments, extending the modernising state's authority at the expense of mediaeval municipal franchises. In Ghent autonomist traditions were much stronger than in Antwerp and in that city resistance to the fiscal encroachments of the centralising Burgundian-Habsburg state led in 1540 to the abrogation by the emperor of the mediaeval constitution, though nearly forty years later, under the auspices of radical Calvinist preachers, Ghent briefly restored the mediaeval constitution before superseding it with a demagogic theocracy. In Florence in 1494 Savonarola gave a religious sanction to the deposition of the near-monarchical but non-legitimate Medici house and lent his prophetic support to the restoration of the mediaeval republican *governo popolare*. Examples like these could be multiplied to show that the popular religious and political culture, articulated by radical preachers, proved antithetical to the new monarchism and responsive to calls for a renewal of municipal democracy. But in restoring civic republican government the communes of Florence and Ghent were also reasserting urban autonomy and local patriotism. In Florence a combination of lower-class Savonarolan religious radicalism and traditional Florentine patriotism formed the ideology of the city's *popolo minuto* in the mid-1490s and for years afterwards. In the case of the revolution at Münster in the 1530s intense religious radicalism provided the necessity and the moral justification for the defence of urban autonomy in an actual siege situation. In John Bunyan's elaborate religious and political allegory, *Mansoul*, a left-wing puritan compares the human soul to a city attempting to preserve its autonomy and integrity against the blandishments of the centralising Stuart monarchy.[30]

In these cases radical Christianity, oblivious to the appeals of nationality and monarchism, stood for local urban patriotism, allied to representative or theocratic institutional forms. The culture of the urban elements involved in these struggles was left largely untouched by the intellectual and emotional force of the new monarchical nationalism which was proving so attractive to progressive forces and educated élites – university graduates, humanist scholars, merchants and financiers operating in a national and international framework, state servants drawn from the higher clergy and from the lower nobility and bourgeoisie.

The idea of the city possessed irresistible fascination for religious radicals in late mediaeval and early modern Europe. The biblical metaphor of Jerusalem and the Augustinian metaphor of the *Civitas Dei* were translated into reality in a number of actual urban situations. The Hussite Reformation, beginning in the city of Prague, progressed through the setting-up of five 'cities of the sun' in Bohemia and climaxed in the establishment of the radicals' city fortress of Tabor. It was in a Reformation city – Zürich – that Anabaptism arose in the sixteenth century and the career of Thomas Müntzer, played out in a series of urban environments, reached its climax in the defence of the city of Mühlhausen. The city of Amsterdam became in the seventeenth century a synonym for religious and political radicalism;[31] and London played a vital role in fostering the religious and political radicalism of mid-seventeenth-century England.[32]

In sponsoring religious dissent the city in early modern Europe was repeating a role that the city had occupied in the early Christian centuries, when the new ideas of Christianity circulated in the urban centres of the Mediterranean littoral. But in the early modern period the religious and political ideas which found favour with demotic city populations throve in an existing framework of urban politics and culture which were being systematically eroded. Both the independence and the quasi-democracy of mediaeval cities were being undermined by centralised states. First, the economic importance of independent, or largely independent, cities and confederations of cities – Bruges, Ghent, Venice, Florence, Nuremberg, Augsburg, the Hanse League – was diminishing in favour of the centrally organised national mercantile economies. Secondly, the city as a national entrepôt – London, Bristol, Bordeaux, Marseilles, Lisbon, Seville, or as a princely administrative capital – Paris, Rome, London – was overtaking the concept of the city as an independent political and regional economic entity. Thirdly, governments were methodically subjecting their internal cities to increasing supervision, regulation and de-democratisation. Examples of this process are widely familiar from the cases of Spain and France, but England too provides an instance in the later Stuart borough policy, which included the cancellation of London's charter in 1683, the effective abrogation of the city's mediaeval constitution and its replacement by royal letters patent ensuring immediate crown supervision of the city.

The aims of the *polis* and those of the new princely state were in natural conflict. The expression of the city's independence very often took the form of radical religious dissent – the religious radicalism characteristic of the *Ciompi* in Florence in the late 1370s[33] and of the Savonarolan *Piagnoni* in the 1490s, of the radical Praguers under Želivský in 1419,[34] of revolutionary Ghent in 1578, even of the demotic-extremist Catholicism of Paris in the 1580s, and of the radical puritanism of London in the 1640s.

This political antipathy between the emerging leviathan of the early modern national princely state and the urban commune was underlined by a cultural differentiation. The sovereign prince sought clerks, jurists, poets, bureaucrats, latinists, historians and propagandists to staff his state and shed glory on his reputation. He founded or patronised universities, either under the princely eye in state capitals – Wittenberg, Prague – or in politically safe backwater towns – Cambridge, Louvain. Surprisingly few of the city-states and great cities of mediaeval and early modern Europe possessed universities – neither London, nor Milan, nor Nuremberg nor Strasburg nor Ghent nor Bruges. The culture of the university supported the aspirations of the state. The prince's servants were recruited from the universities – the Thomas Wolseys, Stephen Gardiners and William Lauds of England, the *letrados* of the Spanish crown – and the endowed colleges of the European universities were built increasingly upon foundations of royal generosity. At the same time, the European universities stood towards the mediaeval Church in a relationship of reciprocal support. To a considerable extent the unwieldy system of parish tithes and dues operated as a grant-paying arrangement for needy scholars. The income of John Wyclif at Oxford, a virulent critic of such clerical abuses as non-residence, was derived from the parishes of which he was nominal and non-resident incumbent: the abuse financing its own condemnation. Through this set-up the Church recruited its leading personnel and ensured a constant succession of senior clerics trained in the rigorous intellectual disciplines of canon law and scholastic theology. In return for his education the scholar repaid the Church with his loyalty and service and put the skills he had acquired at the disposal of the institution which had made these skills available. Even the renegade ecclesiastical intellectuals – Marsiglio, Hus, Wyclif, Luther – were only carrying to the uttermost limits the Church's permission to its scholars constantly to re-examine Christian truth so as constantly to reassert it.

The mutually supportive relationship of official church and university was strengthened by the Reformation. The emphasis on the word of God as the only guide for Christians, especially in so far as it led to anarchic individual interpretations, sent the Evangelical churches off in hot pursuit of textual accuracy: *Verbum Dei* forced the churches to rely on the professional philological scholar, while the post-Reformation theological disagreements in both the Evangelical and Reformed churches over grace, free will, election and so on resulted in the emergence of a new, Protestant, scholasticism.

As we have seen, however, the university, which played so important a role in upholding the ethos of the princely state and of established churches, was not a necessary feature of the life of those early modern cities where independent urban cultural and political life flourished most vigorously. The very absence of this force helped to permit urban life in major cities to continue to flow in its accustomed cultural and intellectual channels. It was, as we shall see, a feature of Christian radicalism to disparage academic learning. This was a natural reaction in those city environments where an alternative lay culture developed outside the state-and-church-supporting curricula of the universities. The cast of mind of the mediaeval and early modern academic, a product of deference to unchallenged authorities, was intellectually authoritarian, and it is no accident that when dissident dons, like Wyclif and Luther, questioned the claims of the papal church they turned irresistibly to the magnification of the pretensions of the secular state. The lower and more popular level of education within the urban culture, the absence of intellectual specialisation and the existence of a degree of intellectual egalitarianism produced an urban mental life which was remote from the intellectual standards and methods with which the universities supported royal estates and official churches.

Many mediaeval and early modern European cities were episcopal centres. Like his late Roman administrative predecessor, the mediaeval diocesan operated from an urban capital and exercised political rights over his city base. As urban life gained ground in the eleventh century, bishops, like that of Liège, willingly or unwillingly took measures to emancipate their cities by granting them chartered rights of self-government. But whether, as at Cologne, the ruling bishop was an independent prince, or, as at London, a royal nominee, the political struggle between him and his townsmen was often bitter and long-drawn-out, sometimes coming to a climax in the Protestant Reformation. At London the *cause célèbre* of Richard Hunne in the second decade of the sixteenth century has usually been looked at from the point of view of demonstrating the intense anti-clericalism of the English capital. But 'anti-clericalism' in the Hunne case meant opposition to the authority of a resident diocesan who possessed formidable police powers in the city but who was also, like the rest of the English episcopate, a royal protégé. Behind the authority of London's Bishop Fitzjames stood that of his royal master.[35] No matter that as an upshot of the Hunne case King Henry began playing to the anti-clerical gallery with ominous murmurings about his prerogative royal: throughout the Tudor and early Stuart periods – with Queen Mary and Bishop Bonner, with Elizabeth and Aylmer, with Charles I and Laud – the royal-appointed Bishop of London was the crown's resident agent for the suppression of the city's religious nonconformity. In the Netherlands at the end of the 1560s opposition groups detected in Philip of Spain's plans for the reorganisation of the episcopate not only a manoeuvre to advance a monolithic and repressive Castilian Catholicism but also a major extension of royal authority at the expense of traditional municipal and sectional liberties. In Reformation Geneva the city's attempt to throw off the overlordship of Bishop de la Baume turned necessarily into a struggle against his ally, the Duke of Savoy.

The episcopal palace often acted as a fifth column for the invasion of a city's independence by the prince. Bureaucrat-clerics, like Philip II's Granvelle or Louis XIII's Richelieu, were impatient with the ancestral franchises that stood in the way of the streamlining processes of the early modern monarchical state. The episcopal administration, the university, the royal court, each of these allied forces possessed a distinct mode of expression, a cultural form: in the case of the bishop's palace the form was the canon law, set down in Latin and derived from the rational Roman jurisprudence; in the case of the university it was the written and printed text and the formal Latin disputation and lecture; in the case of the royal court it was esoteric literature and visual pageantry. These forms of expression ran counter to the dominant mode of urban expression, vernacular speech.

Codified law, such as that employed in episcopal administration, differed markedly, especially in Germanic parts of Europe, from familiar ways of ordering society. Though cities usually derived their original liberties from Latin charters, they often built impressive structures of self-government upon these charters, structures which depended for their validity on prescriptive custom and remembrance. Even in the sophisticated city of Nuremberg, in the very period of the reception of Roman law into Germany, remembered law was of great force, and the quaint Germanic custom was still observed of taking children to legal hearings, so that they would recollect and pass on to the future what they had heard: the aural culture was in evidence in the sphere of law.[36]

Cities of the Renaissance and Reformation became the major centres of the printing industry – Basle, Venice, Antwerp, Amsterdam. But this should not conceal the fact that in the city environment verbal forms of expression were at least as important as the written and printed forms in use at the universities. Even when the university expressed its ideas in verbal form it did so in a formalistic, highly technical and, above all, Latin medium which contrasted with the vernacular immediacy of urban speech.

Courtly pageantry played an important part in mediaeval urban life and sometimes allowed a city populace to express its views. The increasingly recherché quality of Renaissance court pageantry, however, de-popularised the medium. Roy Strong has shown how mediaeval, popular and readily intelligible pageantic themes retained a hold in sixteenth-century England, France and the Netherlands.[37] On the other hand a tendency arose to make official pageantry depend on intellectualised classical themes, satisfying to the *cognoscenti*, remote from the mass. Learned allegorical spectacle, replete with rhetoric and mythological references, like the pageant designed by Rubens for the entry of Archduke Ferdinand into Antwerp in 1635,[38] was much less popularly comprehensible than the homespun *joyeuses entrées* of the high Burgundian period. In fact a development took place in the direction of removing the pageant out of the streets altogether and, as part of the process of the localisation of the royal court, converting it into a private showing. The court masque, abounding with recondite allusions grasped by the immediate witnesses and performers, or by some of them, was consciously influenced by a platonic philosophical distrust of the distorting medium of speech – that essential medium of popular urban expression. Little wonder that a cultural bridge-builder like Ben Jonson turned to bitterness and depression, or that a spokes- man for London's word-revering puritanism like William Prynne turned to savage moralistic denunciation.[39] None the less, as court political pageantry was withdrawn from popular circulation, demotic religio-political displays, expressed in pre-classical form, continued as a vivid expression of popular culture. The London pope-burnings of the Exclusion period, coarse, cruel, bibulous, comical, traditional and totally intelligible, fully expressed London's extremist Protestantism and radical politics in an entirely vernacular and urban form.[40] A comparison between these shows and the Rubens Antwerp pageants affords the most effective contrast between the controlled, Catholic, official and neo-classical values of the court and the spontaneous, republican, oppositionist, ultra-Protestant and non-classical values of the city.

Indigenous urban culture was inconsistent with the Roman law outlook of the ecclesiastical hierarchies, the technical argumentation and latinate text book learning of the universities, and the increasingly remote allegorical forms of expression sought after by self-conscious princely courts. In place of these the city put the spoken word. Euro- pean speech as we know it grew up largely in city environments – the Tuscan of Dante's Florence, the East-Midland English of Chaucer's London. In the competitive commercial atmosphere of the city, citi- zens, constantly using speech, acted as fluent advocates of their stock- in-trade: the craftsman advertised his wares, the merchant his goods, the doctor recommended his remedies, the lawyer argued his case, the friar preached his faith. Though the countryman respected silence – in Quakerism the English north-country peasant farmer found a religious validation for his taciturnity – the townsman had to make himself heard above a hub-bub of conflicting voices. Speech mattered cru- cially. In the Netherlands the towns prided themselves on their *rederij- kerskamers* – 'chambers of rhetoric' – the major form of popular urban culture in the Burgundian period.[41] In Florence articulacy was a civic virtue. All had access to the Tuscan vernacular, though there was considerable popular snobbery about speaking it well, and gales of mockery for foreigners who spoke it with an accent, as Savonarola found to his cost before dropping his harsh Ferrarese Italian in favour of the polished Florentine. The verbal city culture revolved around the non-classical popular drama – carnival plays especially – whose roots lay in the miracle plays and which often expressed popular grievances; it received more formal and political expression in occasional fora like the *parlamento* – the 'speaking', a significant name for an urban institution – which was revived in Florence upon the fall of the Medici; it received religious expression above all in the sermon, and also in the public theological disputations arranged by city councils like those of Zürich and Nuremberg as a prelude to introducing religious reform in the early sixteenth century. Because the aural culture was in the nature of things ephemeral, the historian must make an imaginative effort to understand its force. Sufficient glimpses of it survive – cycles of morality and miracle drama, sermons taken down by auditors – to appreciate its existence. What is missing to us is the vehemence with which the popular aural culture was communicated. We cannot feel the impact of Savonarola's austere and tortured personality, and in reading his reiterated, incantatory prophecies and denunciations we read only cold words and sense none of the terror and hope they inspired. We cannot imagine the magnetic power of the Capuchin Berardino Ochino, drawing crowds to Italian churches with his evocation of the passion and death of Jesus. We cannot conceive how the biblical discussions of Cambridge graduates in English market towns could seem such a threat to order that these 'prophesyings' were supressed by order of Queen Elizabeth. We cannot be present among the huge crowds at the 'hedge preachings' outside Antwerp in the 1560s, occasions of such dramatic power that Breughel depicted them as the repentance preachings of John the Baptist.[42] History based on documents alone excludes by its nature a proper understanding of the popular culture grounded in speech. But it is clear that because the sermoniser, like any communicator, had to have the support of his audience, he was forced to articulate their ideals and aspirations. Because the preacher used the vernacular, because he had to convey the fruits of his reading and study to audiences who were more intelligent than they were educated, his medium was demotic – the common speech. For the same reasons the preacher's style had to be popular – broad humour, like that of the Roman people's priest Philip Neri, dramatic self-presentation, vivid cautionary tales. The mendicant orders were partly called into existence to carry out a preaching mission to the Italian towns of the thirteenth century – the Dominicans were properly called the 'Order of Preachers' – and these orders had perfected this urban art form whose purpose was the evocation of the drama of Christian history and whose result was to familiarise auditors with Christian doctrines. Through the emotional experience of the sermon the Christian religion, and a surprisingly sensitive, often radical, awareness of it, was made an essential component of the popular culture. Plentiful as sermons often were, serious-minded early modern men and women could not get enough of them, for they found in them the essential human theatrical elements of tragedy and release, but also, through the spoken word, access to the Word.

Not that the preacher was ever a one-way manipulator. As with the modern press, a two-way communication existed between audience and communicator. Savonarola frequently praised the 'intelligence' of the Florentines, but by this he can hardly have meant that they were, on the lower social levels, highly educated in the conventional sense, but rather that they were, typically, articulate, independent-minded, a difficult audience. We have seen how Fra Girolamo modified his dialect to meet Florentine standards. Donald Weinstein has also shown how he picked up and articulated the Florentines' ancestral republicanism and intense, prophetic city patriotism. Because the typical city preacher was sometimes imperfectly licensed by the authorities, or because he came from an order, like the Franciscans, with a radical tradition, or simply because he was in a reciprocal relationship with his audience, he played back to his hearers and developed for them their political and social views: proletarian moral puritanism as with the Prague Bethlehem Chapel preachers and the priests of Tabor, denunciations of the irreligious upper classes and their lower-class dependants as with the Florentine sermonisers of the thirteenth century,[43] and always condemnations of luxury, usury, exploitation and the defects of the official churches. These were also the essential themes of radical religious protest and they had their origin in the vocal city civilisation whose central expression was the vernacular sermon. Through this medium the preacher would communicate and popularise the contents of his reading, whether it was Joachimist prophecy, current political polemic or technical theology. But one text was absolutely indispensable – the Bible. The stylised art of the sermon has certain conventions, one of which is that the preacher should base his matter on a passage of Scripture, and another of which is that he should refer to other and related passages, forming, as we saw earlier, an edition of excerpts from the Bible, linked by the preachers' commentary. Through this exercise the texts of Scripture were time and time again repeated. The discrepancy between low early modern literacy statistics and the high familiarity of lower-class religious radicals with Scripture passages may be resolved if we bear in mind the acute aural memory of pre-industrial man. Non-literate people could both *listen* for long periods – four-hour sermons, for instance – and *remember* a great deal of what they had heard, remember especially the words of Scripture.

Aspects of 'establishment' culture – for example, the hierarchy's written Roman law, the university's latinate erudition, the prince's visual self-glorification – were irrelevant to the intellectual life of the late mediaeval and early modern city. The urban culture was primarily purveyed in the only truly mass medium then available, vernacular speech. It was purveyed by expressive preachers who depended for their effectiveness on their ability to reproduce and develop the moral, spiritual, social and political views of their audiences, views built up over centuries of Christian civilisation and preaching in Europe. The preachers were the natural spokesmen of urban cultural autonomy and though some of them, like Savonarola's rival, Fra Genazzano, appealed to a fashionable crowd with their accomplished Renaissance oratory, in the main the preachers provided a positive, fundamentalist and biblical alternative to the Renaissance values which supported the princely and national state, the chief aggressor against the city's independence. One of the most resounding challenges to the classical Renaissance came in Savonarola's dictum that a poor, pious old woman knew more about faith than Plato, an observation redolent of the irreverent populism of the streets.[44] To condemn the classical Renaissance in so brutal a fashion was to condemn in the process the Renaissance cultural support-system of the national sovereign state. True to its environmental origins, Christian radicalism found itself allied to municipal sectionalism or, in the case of Florence, urban patriotism. Religious dissent was not a force at all conducive to the building up of national monarchical states – though in a later chapter we shall see how the 'pluralistic' national state could gain strength from sponsoring religious toleration in multi-sectarian situations. For the moment, when we look at Europe between the end of the Middle Ages and the beginning of the modern period, we may adumbrate two hostile coalitions of forces: on the one side monarchy, nation and established church, with their cultural infra-structure; on the other city, religious sect and democratic culture.

It might in fact be possible to add one other factor to the 'anti-progressive' coalition of forces: regionalism. We have seen how the centripetal force of proto-nationalism, organised by royal governments, confronted the centrifugal force of sectionalism. The classic modern nation-state is unitary, and in language, law and administration a constant tendency has been evident in Europe to impose national uniformity in place of provincial diversity. The process of centralisation encountered considerable resistance in the early modern period. Did this resistance take a religious form or ally itself with dissenting religious forces? There is every evidence that it did. The English Pilgrimage of Grace was an expression of the separatism of the

North and its dislike of the modernising governmental methods and centralising policy of Thomas Cromwell in the 1530s. In the French Wars of Religion secessions of parts of France – Languedoc, for example – took place under aristocratic leadership. In the Revolt of the Netherlands the autonomy of the distinct provinces was a major issue from first to last. In Scotland in 1638 and in Ireland in 1641 violent measures were taken to throw off English control. In Germany throughout the Reformation the identity of each of the territorial divisions of the Reich was articulated through the choice by each territory, under its prince or magistrates, of its religion. Indeed, in all these cases, religion was a powerful partner of provincialism: in Tudor England the conservative Catholicism of the squires, tenant farmers and priests of the North; in civil-war France the Calvinism or Leaguer Catholicism of fissiparous provinces; in the Netherlands the developing Calvinism of the provinces of Holland, Zeeland and Friesland; in Stuart Scotland the inter-class solidarity expressed in the Covenant; in Stuart Ireland the nostalgic Catholic faith of gaelic tribalism. Yet in none of these cases can we say that provincial separatism was voiced in a *radical* religious form. The indispensable aristocratic and gentry leadership of rural protest ensured that provincial unrest would take a relatively conservative religious form, if it took a religious form at all: Catholicism of Calvinism.

Ought we, then, to disentangle radical religious dissent from the phenomenon of regionalism in the early modern period? Perhaps not altogether. Whether or not radical Christianity provided moral sustenance to provincialist movements, it remains the case that radical forms of Christianity were definitely associated with certain regions and became associated with them. South Bohemia, for instance, in the Hussite Reformation had a particular reputation for radicalism. In fifteenth-century England Lollardy became identified with distinct areas of the country – the Chilterns, for example – and both the Tudor and Stuart sectarians had an entrenched *point d'appui* in East Anglia.[45] Again in the English context, the first Quakers were readily identified with the North and the movement retained a northern base; the Quakers' preference for the first-person form of address may have been a reflection of distinctive northern usage.[46] In Reformation Germany a useful way of classifying the bewildering varieties of Anabaptists is to group them on regional lines. In Bourbon France the radical Huguenot Camisards were concentrated in the old heartland of French religious dissent, the Midi. Obviously the protection afforded by remote provinces helped keep alive non-establishment forms of Christianity, and this was as true of Lancashire Catholic recusancy as it was of the Waldensian survivals of Savoy, Piedmont and the Alpine valleys. In any case, whether or not province-based religious nonconformity was the conscious expression of regionalism, the existence of alternative forms of Christianity not enjoying government approval in particular parts of the national kingdoms acted as a major check to the development of the royal and national state, with its indispensable apparatus of the established church.

'Cujus regio ejus religio' ('the religion of the prince is the religion of his subjects'); 'une foi, un roi, une loi' ('one faith, one king, one law'); such formulae expressed the close affiliation in the early modern period between official Christianity and the emerging nation-state. The classical Reformation tended, sometimes heavily, to place its political loyalty at the disposal of the constituted prince, or when it was associated with protest to throw in its lot with dissident aristocratic elements. Supported by the 'national' church – the Church of England, the Gallican Church of France, the emphatically royal-controlled Spanish Church, the Evangelical Churches of Germany and Scandinavia – national and territorial states also received the cultural applause of Renaissance civilisation: the state's historical claims were underlined by Renaissance learning, its functions were explained and justified by Renaissance rationality, and its propaganda was delivered by Renaissance theoreticians, poets and artists.[47] The independence of the mediaeval city, surviving into early modern times, acted as a check to monarchical and national centralisation, as did the obstinate force of regionalism. To set against the officially approved academic, ecclesiastical and courtly culture, the city possessed a culture of its own, a culture with a religious expression, through the sermon, which guaranteed a widespread familiarity with the Bible. This scriptural awareness led in turn to a critical independence in the lay mind which helped cities like Ghent, Florence, Prague and London to conduct at least rearguard actions against princely statism. Dissenting and critical religious attitudes stood in the way of centralism and nationalism. Case studies like that of Reformation Nuremberg show how the artisan and workman, often possessing a modicum of education, were drawn both to political radicalism and democracy and to religious views well to the left of centre. But there were more positive reasons that religious radicals should exalt the religious role of the city. We considered earlier the attraction of the Augustinian metaphor of the church as the city of God. But Augustine's thought had more power than that of metaphor alone. Augustine's concept of election, especially as revived by Luther and Calvin, was at hand to reinforce perfectionist attempts to separate out the true from the false members of the church. John Tonkin has shown how Augustine never made absolute an identification between the church true and the church Catholic.[48] Christian churches have never resolved the ambivalence between catholic commitment to the world and elect sanctity. Radical religionists in the early modern period resolved it drastically by proclaiming a doctrine of the church as the body of the saints under the headship of Christ. Stated so absolutely, it was an ecclesiology that lent no support whatever to the authorised and profoundly statist notion of the church as being coterminous with the realm and made up of all members of a political society. Whether they rejected this ecclesiology on the basis of realised predestination or on the basis of adult conversions to Christianity, radicals like the Anabaptists and the English Separatists repudiated totally the idea of the comprehensive church, that main prop of the social order which helped the state to discipline the sinner and the criminal. Such social and national churches, with their orderly hierarchies and well-established forms of maintenance, were fully visible institutions. In comparison radical groupings lacked the actuality and inclusiveness of the fully developed church, although it *was* possible, on an admittedly limited geographical basis, to create visible yet radical formal church structures. The church of a whole realm was an absurdity to radical thinkers, but the church of a city might attain both visibility and perfectibility. Church visible and church true could be brought together in an urban framework in which a political society might be transformed into a true church. The ideal was difficult to realise, but it was within the bounds of possibility – through a political take-over of a commune by the godly, through enforced or voluntary exile of the godless, through discipline. These were the lines on which proceeded the relatively conservative urban reformations of Zürich and Geneva and the emphatically radical reformation at Münster. In these cases existing, historic cities were converted to godliness. In other, rarer, cases entirely new Jerusalems might be created out of virtually nothing but the Christian enthusiasm of the radicals involved: Tabor stands out as an example. But whether the godly city was converted from the world or was a new creation, its existence disclosed the possibility, at least on the local urban level, of reconciling church and society in a context in which discipline and control were humanly manageable.

Religious radicalism throve in cities because cities provided a religiously sophisticated and independent-minded laity able to understand and adopt radical perceptions of Christianity. Religious radicals also sometimes saw in the city favourable opportunities to realise an elusive yet desirable ecclesiology – that of the elect church visibly set up and made identical with a community. At the same time, religious radicalism ran parallel with and provided a rationale for urban political radicalism. To describe urban politics as characteristically radical or even anti-monarchist may seem surprising. The occasional demonstrative loyalty of London to the Tudors, of Paris to the Valois, of Antwerp to the Burgundian and Habsburgs may seem to contradict this assumption. But when we recall that Antwerp had to be taken by siege and cunning by royalist forces in 1585, that Paris rejected its king in favour of the Duke of Guise in the same decade and that London was firmly shut to its sovereign after 1642, we will gain a better insight into typical urban political allegiances, and realise the priority of religious over national affiliations. It is true that certain urban interests from all social strata had an economic stake in monarchy and were notable for their royalism, from the merchants and financiers of pre-civil war London, linked to the court through contracts and monopolies to the notoriously Tory bargemen of Charles II's capital whose livelihood depended heavily on transporting courtiers on the Thames. But in general terms republican and civic ideals survived most persistently in the cities of early modern Europe, for example in the Savonarolan popular party in Florence after the Medici restoration. These ideals retained their hold in those social elements wherein the republican creed would be reborn in the wake of the French and American Revolutions – artisans, craftsmen, small shopkeepers and tradesmen. And in just those urban social strata radical religious ideas, the product of individualistic thinking within the context of urban culture – the early modern religious counterpart of modern political dissent – most commonly had their currency.

CHAPTER 2

Religious Radicalism and Socioeconomic Change

When R. H. Tawney wrote *Religion and the Rise of Capitalism* he set out to modify the thesis originally advanced by Max Weber in *The Protestant Ethic and the Spirit of Capitalism*. Weber believed that the Calvinist theology impelled individuals in the direction of economic success. Calvinists, he thought, anxiously sought assurance of salvation and they found this assurance in the strict moral organisation of their daily lives, emphasising those virtues – frugality, thrift, sobriety, seriousness and honesty – which lead to wealth. The difference between Tawney and Weber was that, whereas Weber thought of capitalism as a 'progressive' force, Tawney, a Christian socialist, viewed the capitalist system as immoral. The capitalist system's emergence in Protestant countries, thought Tawney, had come about because Christian teachers had failed in their duty to speak out against it. Gradually, the moral scope of Christianity had contracted, until the details of economic life were considered to lie outside the sphere of Christian ethics. This was not the case, said Tawney, with the Catholic Scholastics of the high Middle Ages, nor was it the case with the major Reformers of the sixteenth century. Catholic economic ethics were somewhat relaxed in the late Middle Ages; a more pronounced relaxation of Protestant economic morality took place at a later date – in the late seventeenth and eighteenth centuries. The resultant Victorian Christianity which praised wealth was not a valid form of Christianity, but rather the victory of economics over morality.[1]

In this chapter, we will seek to apply Tawney's thesis to radical religious movements. We will explore Calvinism to see what guidance it offers on economic questions, and the extent to which, as a religious system, it offers encouragement to acquisition. We will see, along with Tawney, that not Calvinism, but a diminished religious sense provided what ideological impetus was necessary for the rise of capitalism. We will see how more radical forms of Christianity were affected by, and how they affected, capitalistic developments. And we will see how religious radicalism offered, sometimes, protection against economic change and, sometimes, protest against economic inequality.

First, though, we need to develop one of Tawney's contentions. This was to the effect that late mediaeval Catholic thinkers, notably in highly capitalised Italy, slightly relaxed the prohibitions that earlier mediaeval theologians had placed on acquisitive endeavour. We find that this relaxation of traditional strictures, which was evident in some late mediaeval Catholic thinkers, was not apparent in the protesters and reformists of the late mediaeval period. Such individuals took it for granted that moralists should speak on economic questions. Furthermore, in the actual content of their economic thought, individual reformists were fundamentalist and backward-looking. In short, the mediaeval reformists continued to insist that Christian laws take absolute priority over 'economic laws'. For example, the moral puritanism of John Hus deeply affected his consideration of economic questions. The changing economic situation in early fifteenth-century Bohemia presented landlords with many opportunities for enrichment, especially through increasing manorial burdens. Hus was asked his advice on one aspect of manorial exploitation – death duties – and in replying he left several key assumptions unquestioned: that a confessor should offer guidance on the details of economic conduct; that a Christian could be a landlord and that landlordism was lawful; and that the manorial system was basically Christian and acceptable. 'Since the taking of death duty or large inheritance is linked with covetousnes', he wrote, 'faithful Christians should diligently seek to avoid it, to be merciful towards their neighbours . . .' There was, then, good landlordism and bad landlordism, and, in upholding the conventional figure of the Christian landlord, Hus shared Catholic assumptions about the morality of the social system, shot through as it was with moral doctrine. The social system, with its fixed hierarchy, was divinely ordered, and therefore respect was due to the rights of social inferiors. The private property of a peasant, Hus pronounced, was 'the result of his labour and he is the owner of it'.[2]

In the rural world which Hus pictured 'covetousness' was a disturbing force, threatening the manorial order with dissolution. In urban society 'covetousness' and cash economics were the very motor of the social system. In speaking of 'covetousness' – *avaritia*, *cupiditas* – urban preachers, especially reformists, were forced to condemn, rather than try to uphold, prevailing economic structures. Hus, with his peasant background, imagined a rural society in which existence would be harmonious and neighbourly if covetousness were absent. Savonarola, with his thoroughly urban background, faced a world governed by cash relations. His estrangement from many aspects of this world did not prevent Savonarola from sharing Hus's view of the obligation upon moralists to go into the details of economic conduct. But it did impel him to see the possessing classes of Florence as people set at a distance from Christianity by the avarice that was implied in their social positions. So Savonarola admonished the holders of wealth for their obsession with their rates of interest. In Florence, as in papal Rome, *Giustizia* – social justice – was every day being flouted. Commercial and urban wealth allowed for luxury and display, which, in the condensed life of the towns, insulted the poor. The Church itself was caught up in these evils, and the Christian people, most injured by exploitation, would punish these moral and economic faults: 'When you see that God allows the heads of the Church to fall into wickedness and acts of simony, then the people's scourge is at hand . . . See how Rome is full of pride, of luxury, greed and simony.'[3]

Savonarola passed on the tradition of moral and economic criticism that the Protestant Reformers inherited. Whatever compromises the late mediaeval Church leadership had arrived at with the nascent 'spirit of capitalism', it is clear that the voice of popular puritanism, which Luther took up, remained anti-acquisitive. It is significant that, in denouncing indulgences, Luther blundered into a web of corruption involving senior churchmen and bankers. His denunciations of usury, his nostalgia, like that of Hus, for a well-regulated rural world, made him a foe of the developing financial and commercial capitalism of the early sixteenth century. In fact, we need hardly pause to consider whether or not Luther made a contribution to the 'rise of capitalism': he was rigidly anti-commercial. A discussion of the issue does arise, however, with regard to Calvin. After all, both Weber and Tawney believed that it was the Calvinist form of Protestantism that was particularly involved, or caught up, in the development of capitalism. We shall find that Calvinism was *not* a stimulus to economic growth – and yet the historical evidence seems to point in the opposite direction.

Let us briefly consider some of this historical evidence. In the second half of the seventeenth century evidence was mounting that Calvinists were to the fore in economic enterprise. In the case of France, from Toulouse in 1664, it was reported that 'nearly all trade of this country is in the hands of those of the Reputedly Reformed Religion', and in remarkably similar terms, from Rochefort two decades later, 'that the trade of this country is in the hands of the Religionists' (the Huguenots). In early eighteenth-century England, too, commentators agreed that Calvinists were rich. The ostentatious wealth on display outside London Dissenter Meeting Houses shocked conservatives, and the people of the streets put their finger on the identification: 'Down with the Bank of England and the Meeting Houses: and God damn the Presbyterians and all that support them.'[4]

Some cracks appear in the identification of wealth and Calvinism. It was based on popular prejudices and on stereotypes – some of which have passed into historical mythology. And within the association it was clear that only *some* Dissenters, and only *some* Calvinists – especially the Presbyterians – were believed to have great wealth. None the less, compensatory evidence of the link-up between enterprise and Calvinism seemed to come from looking at an officially Calvinist society, the United Provinces of the Netherlands. There indeed wealth and abundance seemed to have arrived with the adoption of the Calvinist faith. The Dutch had captured the world's carrying trade, made great advances in banking, established and profited from a vast overseas empire. Did their successes stem from their Calvinism? One of the most perceptive observers of the Dutch scene, Sir William Temple, scarcely mentioned Calvinism in his lengthy examination of Dutch economic success. Temple explained the Netherlands' wealth in terms of environment – his pet theory that the overcrowding of such a small country made for diligence. He explained Dutch prosperity on the grounds of the national character – 'the general humour, bent all upon industry'. Above all, Temple thought that the explanation for the rapid economic progress of the Netherlands lay in religious toleration. His analysis may have been wrong – after all, the Calvinist entrepreneurs of England and France did not enjoy toleration – but he was convinced that a major factor in making the Dutch wealthy was 'the general liberty and ease, not only in point of conscience, but all others that serve to the commodiousness and quiet of life; every man follows his own way, minding his own business, and little enquiring into other men's; which, I suppose, happened by so great a concourse of people of several nations, different religion and customs, as left nothing strange or new'.[5]

It was, then, the ambience of Dutch life that made the Dutch rich: not merely formal religious toleration, but a live-and-let-live attitude, respect for privacy and individual tastes. But we can see that this life-style owed nothing to Calvinism, which was censorious, conformist and disciplinarian – opposed not only to religious toleration but also to the kind of easy-going personal tolerance that Temple describes. If toleration made the Dutch rich, it was not Calvinism that made them tolerant. In fact, it was more likely that Dutch wealth was built on Dutch foundations, and that as far as these had to do with attitudes of mind, the attitudes and values went back beyond the Reformation, to the tolerant, enlightened Erasmian Christianity which Professor Trevor-Roper has examined. Great wealth could come only if the Calvinism of John Calvin was disregarded. For Calvin himself clearly inherited the prohibitive attitude to acquisition, the puritan emphasis on justice and charity which we saw in pre-Reformation reformers of the stamp of Hus and Savonarola. In Calvin's view work was to be

performed with the strictest honesty and without the aim of enrichment; if wealth came it was to put at the disposal of the poor: 'First,
Lord', runs Calvin's work-prayer, 'may it please you to assist us with
your Holy Spirit so that we may faithfully exercise our condition and
vocation without any fraud or deceit, but that we take care rather to
follow your laws than to satisfy the desire to enrich ourselves; but that
if it please you to prosper our work, that also you will give us the
strength to come to the aid of the poor.' Calvin in fact saw proverty as
an avenue to divine approval, forcing the individual back on the
resources of God's mercy. For the business of buying and selling he
evinced profound suspicion: 'One observes', he wrote, 'that these days
no commerce is conducted without lies and perjuries; that God's name
trips off the tongues of those who want to deceive; that it is not enough
for them to lie and to cover up, but they must also blaspheme the name
of God in the midst of business; we see the frauds that everyone adopts
to put one over on his partner; everyone seeks only to plunder and
enrich himself at the expense of others; we see the deceptions that are
carried out everywhere: this one oversells, this one offers no genuine
goods.' So, not only did Calvin suspect the global and usurious commerce carried out in centres like Antwerp and Venice, but he showed
stern moral disapproval for the everyday conduct of every market
town in the Europe of his day. Calvinism in its economic aspect means
other things besides a maximum 5 per cent interest rate; it involves a
fundamental suspicion of over-involvement in money-making, an
acceptance of inescapable poverty and a rejection of untrammelled
capitalism. If the word Calvinist is to have any meaning, it must mean a
Christian acting in conformity with the Christian religion as interpreted by John Calvin. If this definition is accepted, it is clear that the
wealth of the seventeenth-century Dutch Republic was not made by
observant Calvinists, but rather by men who modified their Calvinist
profession to suit their economic needs. Calvinism sat lightly on many
of the rich Holland Regents – men who preserved the secularist values
of the Erasmian period: tolerant, erastian and anti-clerical. Their
belief in religious toleration was not acceptable to the orthodox Calvinist clergy. Nor was that underlying attitude of personal liberalism,
which Temple thought lay at the root of Dutch commercial success.
None the less, the rigorous Calvinism of the Reformation was to be
found in Holland – as a powerful popular, enthusiastic, radical and
anti-acquisitive force. This was not the Calvinism that made fortunes,
but a more authentic version of the Reformation, to be found amongst
the small farmers, fishermen, preachers and schoolmasters of the
remote provinces. This bedrock Calvinism, uncorrupted by the compromises of Amsterdam, was fundamentally opposed to capitalist
acquisition. 'Calvinism in the Netherlands', writes Professor Hyma,

'retarded the development of capitalism.'[6]

Similarly in England and France, it was a relaxed Calvinism, a Calvinism remote from the spirit of Calvin, Beza, Cartwright and Perkins that allowed its laymen to build up treasures on earth. In both England and France Calvinism was distorted into unwonted channels: forced out of politics by political defeat and repression, Calvinists were permitted to do little more than trade. No doubt the structures of Presbyterianism allowed dominant commercial laymen to impose their commercialist values on many preachers, writers and congregations. But what was true of some urban Presbyterian groups was not true of the whole of European and English Calvinism, and certainly not true of religious radicalism in general.

Calvin contributed greatly to the thought, if not to the structures, of the radical reformation. Those Calvinists, in Holland, England and France, who prospered through dedicated attention to self-enrichment were only in the most formal sense Calvinists at all. In Holland, for example, the old reality of acquisitive individualism clearly survived under a veneer of 'neo-Calvinist' forms. Furthermore, those who prospered through luck, speculation, opportunism, risk, and government and war contracts owed nothing at all to the reputed Calvinist virtues of caution, thrift, industry, and so on: those virtues do not bring great wealth. If Reformation Calvinism did not lead to capitalism, the more radical forms of the Reformation did not either. Certainly, Anabaptism was not a religion to make men rich. Far from being possessed of a restless or anxious Protestant impulse to economic success, these Christian radicals were, observers agreed, characterised by 'contentment', and the hostile Bullinger noticed how they reproved 'covetousness'. Reproof, discipline and social control were, as with pristine Calvinism, the main features of the Anabaptist system, but these traits did not make men wealthy. Rather, these characteristics were part of the inheritance of anti-acquisition that the religious radicals shared with the early Calvinists as their legacy from the late mediaeval reform movement. Needless to say, the Anabaptists, as an integral part of their lay religion, placed a high value on work, but it requires more than work to produce riches. In fact, the hard work of Anabaptist workers may have made others rich. Perhaps this was the reason that they were given limited religious toleration in early eighteenth-century France, for they were regarded there, as they were in Poland, as industrious and skilful tillers of the soil – and not at all as moneyed men. In general, in rural societies Anabaptism seemed to keep its moderately prosperous peasant-communitarian character. In some rural areas, and in towns, the craftsman character of the movement was strongly apparent. Professor Littell explains the attractions that Anabaptism had for dispossessed skilled workers: 'the Anabaptist craftsman transformed social misfortune into a religious vehicle, and glorified in "living loose from the world" '; industry and poverty were the main characteristics of the Anabaptists – they were 'a poor, unpromising people that have to do their daily work' – but group organisation provided employment and a sense of place for the uprooted. In the Anabaptist refuges of Moravia craftsmen were highly valued. Just as church discipline controlled the moral behaviour of the community, so it regulated its economic life. Individual economic impulses were discounted and, as in any mediaeval guild, output was subordinated to community controls and needs. Predictably, the industry of the Anabaptists brought individual and group prosperity; Anabaptist products were highly sought, and Catholic priests had occasion to complain at their parishioners' buying Anabaptist wares, even on the Sabbath. By the early eighteenth century, and in certain promising locations, the Anabaptists' economic activities were becoming diversified. In Amsterdam and Hamburg, a few Anabaptists, favoured by local toleration and by the business opportunities on hand in geographically well-situated cities, rose to considerable prosperity. None the less, there was always a religious pull away from profit-making. There were regular levies for church purposes and in both Hamburg and Holland the communities paid frequent donations, especially for church buildings and for religious refugees. At the same time, church principles and discipline acted as a check on profit-making. Like the English Quakers, the Strasburg Anabaptists ruled against the manufacture of 'unChristian' clothing, and the Hamburg Mennonites carried their Christian pacifism – again, like the Quakers – to the point of refusing to arm their merchant vessels.[7]

Despite communal restrictions on profit-making, some Anabaptists flourished economically. In the most favoured location of all – Amsterdam – there is evidence of the frank enjoyment of the fruits of wealth: 'there are some', a Lutheran minister noticed, 'who are attracting attention by using periwigs and other indications of worldliness'. In the easy-going Dutch city, in fact, all the perils of acculturation and toleration became apparent in the mid-eighteenth century, when some of the most assimilated Mennonites began to accept civil and military office – and to leave the church. Long before that, these prosperous, individualistic Mennonites had ceased to be Anabaptists in any acceptable sense of the word. However, Amsterdam was clearly no more representative of the development of Netherlands Anabaptism than it was of the development of Dutch Calvinism. In the provinces, where, as Temple reported, Anabaptists remained in the 'lower ranks of the people, mechanics and seamen', a much more rigorous and puritan faith was to be found.[8]

The same kind of distinction between an élite and a general membership was to be found in English Nonconformity. On the one hand, we find a prosperous element, many of whose members conformed to the ideal type of capitalist Dissenter. Such individuals – many of them Presbyterians – were especially to be found in such centres as Bristol, Nottingham, Norwich and London. Naturally, their wealth attracted comment, much of it hostile. They provided an important motive for the dilution of Reformation economic principles. But whilst some hostile commentators spoke about the Dissenters' wealth, others, without apparent contradiction, referred contemptuously to the poverty and to the lowly educational and social condition of most Dissenters. In fact there was no contradiction at work here. The majority of Dissenters, particularly the majority of the more radical Dissenters, were rightly identified with manual trades and skills. The association of dissent with weaving was in England as old as Lollardy. So was the popular caricature of the man – or woman – of the lower classes presuming to preach and minister, as in this lampoon on a Baptist lay-minister:

> A Shoemaker a Dipper was,
> and left off stitching leather,
> Ye duckt poor fooles to purge their sins,
> like silly sots together.

Such caricatures were grounded in facts. In Bedford, John Bunyan's 'Anabaptist' congregation consisted of the 'meanest sort', led by a heel-maker and a hatter; in fact, hatters, cobblers, cordwainers and maltsters made up the bulk of the Nonconformist congregations in Bedford. In Oxford the picture was similar, though there the socio-educational differences between the Presbyterians, led by a former master of Pembroke College, and the more radical Baptists-Independents, taught by a tanner and a miller, were well brought out.[9]

Groups like Bunyan's congregation were highly disciplinarian and anti-individualistic. Bunyan spoke for his congregation in his profound distrust of great wealth. He compared the soul of man to a town like Bedford, to 'a Market-Town, and a Town that delights in commerce . . . let Mansoul be taken up in much business, and let them grow full and rich, and this is the way to get ground of them'. This suspicion of wealth echoed the views of small craftsmen whose hope of survival lay in the retention of mediaeval collectivist guild and corporate restrictive legislation. Thus the economic puritanism of the Reformation and the pre-Reformation remained embedded in the thinking of a typical Dissenting group. It is clear that individual entrepreneurs in the late seventeenth and eighteenth centuries would have to relax Reformation principles if they were going to pursue wealth without inhibitions.

As we saw in the case of Holland, wealthy and socially integrated Mennonites often left their Church. In England, many Presbyterians moved back into the Church of England in the later seventeenth century, and in the eighteenth century others moved into Unitarianism – much to the horror of more fundamentalist popular elements within the congregations. A relaxation of Reformation orthodoxy, even departure from the church-group, these tendencies characterised some of the individuals and families within European religious dissent who achieved great wealth in the early modern period. As we shall see, the uninhibited pursuit of wealth, the hoarding of profits and income and the personal enjoyment of wealth were prohibited by the most radical of the post-Reformation religious groups. Nor were work and profit to be pursued for their own sakes. Rather, those most characterised by capitalist values – single-minded dedication to profit, acceptance of risk, use of accumulated wealth to reinvest or to acquire social mobility – faced church censure, or found themselves isolated from the rank-and-file church membership.[10]

The moral legacy of English puritanism, including a suspicion of 'enterprise', was inherited intact by the Quakers. The Quakers were an anti-acquisitive group, putting moral before economic considerations. This may seem a strange remark, in the light of Quaker economic success, but we shall see that capitalistic success was an aberration from the Quaker norm and that those who prospered dramatically did so in despite of Quaker principles. The tone of Quaker economic casuistry was in fact set by George Fox at the beginning of the movement's history: care for the poor, personal austerity and a suspicion of the profit motive. From Fox the Quakers took their repudiation of acquisition for its own sake, or for purposes of self-indulgence, and their renunciation of opportunist business conduct and of speculative operations. Some Friends, indeed, came under suspicion of involvement in such nefarious capitalistic activities as smuggling and slaving. But all such activities came under the ban of a religious society which insisted that it had the right to pronounce on the everyday conduct of business, and to submit business to Christian ethics. The greatest possible caution in business was the Quaker norm – even if this meant passing over opportunities for profit; strictly legal methods, only moderate attention to one's trade and careful avoidance of risks were the Quakers' guiding business principles. The advice of the Yearly Meeting built up over a number of years ran as follows: 'that none overcharge themselves with too much trading nor break their promises or contracts therein, but be careful to keep within the compass of their own substance in the management of their affairs to prevent failures and breaches, and avoid all indirect and unwarrantable methods, both in trade and merchandise, whereby the government may be defrauded of its due'. If the 'spirit of capitalism' means the single-minded pursuit of gain, in the Quaker code it was expressly set aside in favour of spiritual priorities: 'That all take heed and beware of covetousness, over-reaching and oppressing of any, and be watchful against an earthly spirit getting up in any, for that will bring forth a slighting of and neglecting their testimonies in keeping to first days and weekdays meetings and bring a decay of their strength and zeal for God and his truth.' These general principles were consistently applied by Quakers. Thus, in 1699 in the prosperous port district of Lancaster a committee of weighty Friends was appointed to investigate the extent to which local Quakers were 'overcharging themselves in trade etc.'. For Quakers debt, though it is obvious now that it was the lubricant of trade, especially with the colonies, was what usury was for the rigorous Calvinists of the north-east Netherlands – an illicit and reprehensible condition. Those who ran their businesses on the lines of credit and debt were, however solvent they were, disowned by the Society – as was the case with William Godsalve of Lancaster, who, though he protested that he had means to pay all his creditors, and hundreds of pounds to spare, was disowned by Lancaster Monthly Meeting in 1708 because his fellow Quakers feared the prospect of his failing in business and because he kept loose company in pursuit of his business.[11]

Why did Friends fear business failure in the midst? It might be argued that their caution was a purely economic and prudential one: excessive debt simply does not make good business sense. This may be true, though it ignores the role that credit and debt played in the commercial revolution. But Friends did not criticise indebtedness on economic but rather on moral grounds – that debt 'occasions divers honest people to suffer loss'. With their old-fashioned views on credit, the Quakers were undoubtedly naïve about the hard facts of trade in the late seventeenth and early eighteenth centuries: the facts that money lent to a man of enterprise was necessarily lent at some risk, that investment was a form of gambling, that the possibility of failure was the price to be paid for the likelihood of success – as was the case with the enterprising Quaker undertaker of the new port of Lancaster at Sunderland Point, Robert Lawson, who failed simply because his credit would not stretch far enough. Further, entrepreneurs like William Godsalve came under censure because, as a necessary part of their business, they entered into socio-commercial relations with those of 'the world' – drinking, entertaining and all the other early modern apparatus of opening and concluding transactions. In other ways, too, Friends' avenues to opportunities for profit were closed to them by the fundamentalist principles of their Society: they were forbidden to adopt the prudent measure of arming their ships, they were advised, most uncapitalistically, to retire early from business, and they were counselled to observe the greatest caution with regard to the rich harvest of the public funds. Honest Christian dealing precluded some promising manufacturing opportunities – such as the 'making, selling or wearing striped cloth shifts or striped silks or any sort of flowered or figured thing of different colours' – and it certainly put an end to the possibility of certain dubious profits: 'all Friends who are concerned in transporting people into foreign parts take care not to crowd them together in ships so as to prejudice of their health and danger of their life'. All in all, the constant application of Christian ethics to business, the ceaseless calls that the Society, its government and charity made on the time and means of its members, the attitude of reserve towards 'the world's people', and the deep spirituality and austerity of Quaker religion, all conspired to counteract the opportunities for acquisition that were open to Quakers. Undoubtedly such opportunities did exist: Quakers, like English and French Calvinists, were channelled out of politics and the professions and into trade; their reverence for work gave them obvious advantages; the fact that many of them became urbanised – perhaps so as to ease the burden of tithes – brought them into favourable locations for business. Clearly some Quakers – though they occupy too much historical attention – became very rich indeed. The long litany of Quaker entrepreneurs stands as a solid testimony to the economic appetites of some Friends: Fry, Cadbury, Clarke, Rowntree, Lloyd, Barclay, and so on. It is clear, though, that in conditions of prosperity the edge was taken off the religious commitment of some Quakers – to a point where the Quakerism ceased having any real content and, in some cases, became merely ancestral, or fell away. The youthful experiences of Elizabeth Fry, in an environment of innocent and civilised worldliness, show how far some prosperous Georgian Quakers had travelled from the puritan austerity and egalitarianism of George Fox: 'I took a lesson in dancing, and spent the day quietly. I went to Meeting in the evening . . . I called on Mrs. Siddons, . . . then on Mrs. Twiss, who gave me some paint for the evening. I was painted a little, I had my hair dressed, and did look pretty for me . . . I own, I do love grand company. The Prince of Wales was there . . . I did nothing but admire his Royal Highness.' The tone of this passage, with its conformity to the sociability, the triviality and the rank-consciousness of late Georgian feminine life, is entirely different from anything we might find in early women Quaker diarists. By the late eighteenth century, indeed, capitalist Quaker families, like the relaxed and affluent Gurneys who influenced the young Elizabeth Fry, were no longer, except in the most formal sense, Quakers at all. Indeed, as with the wealthy Dutch Mennonites, the climax of social ascent, which we see in the worldly ways of the young Elizabeth Fry, was reached when families and individuals joined the establishment completely: the banker Samuel Hoare, two of whose daughters joined the Church of England, renounced Quaker pacifism, and the banker Barclays enthusiastically joined the established ministry and the armed forces. It is, though, highly significant that successful capitalists left this radical movement, for the movement did not encourage great accumulation. A few spectacularly prosperous Quaker families did not typify the Quaker movement or the attitudes of the majority of its less wealthy members, with whom the old puritan other-worldly spirit continued to reign supreme. A gulf of life-style, education, means and outlook opened up between the 'aristocracy' of wealthy Quakers, many of whom were speedily moving out of the Society, and the ordinary membership, whose social and economic views continued to be echoed in the minutes of Quaker Meetings on all levels. In part the élite put themselves outside the Quaker network of friendship: they moved upwards out of the close Quaker social circle. The gulf that separated the small élite of capitalist Quakers from the petit-bourgeois and lower-class membership resembled the cleavage between the formally Calvinist mercantile magnates of Amsterdam and the rigorist peasant farmers and fisherman of Friesland and Groningen. In the British Isles, as in the Netherlands, the dividing line in the sects was geographical as much as it was social: on the one hand Edinburgh, Norwich, London and Bristol, on the other hand south-west Scotland, Yorkshire, Ulster and the Lake Counties.[12]

For all this, it is undeniable that Quakers – like Anabaptists and Calvinists – were disproportionately to be found in industry and commerce. Indeed the very existence of a large corpus of Quaker business casuistry illustrates the economic preoccupations of so many members of the group. But the merchants, who formed an important bloc of the Quaker membership, were not always capitalist merchants, but more often only small shop-owners and craftsman-manufacturers. Certainly mercantile activity within the Society was not allowed to run its own course or to follow its own laws. In eighteenth-century Quakerism, the high value placed on apprenticeships, the insistence (which we also found in Hutterite society) on communal control of products, and the sense of the individual's responsibility for the group and the group's responsibility for the individual, all these profoundly anti-individualistic traits remind us strongly of the mediaeval craft guild. Within the cocoon of protection, the Protestant individual – Calvinist, Anabaptist or Quaker – was fortified within a religious system which held poverty at bay. The Reformation religions we are discussing held work in high regard. They provided an educational system for the laity. Care for time, the practices of Bible- and tract-reading, journal-writing, daily moral accountancy – all these encouraged the growth of a full individual consciousness, of concentration, analysis, recollection and attention to detail – valuable assets in a life of work. But these virtues did not in themselves lead to spectacular capital accumulation. As far as the sixteenth, seventeenth and eighteenth centuries are concerned, Samuelsson is right: 'great fortunes are . . . the product of "fortunate speculations", of vast profits from vast risks and vast luck' – and, we might add, from patronage and perquisites and from relentless dedication to making great fortunes. The wealth that came to nominal Calvinists – to a de Geer, a de Witte, a d'Herwarth – was not likely to come the way of a convinced Quaker who conscientiously observed the religious principle 'that none overcharge themselves with too much trading'. This advice was intended to 'prevent failures' – that is, bankruptcies – but it was also unlikely to result in outstanding or immediate economic success. However, it might lead to the steady accumulation of modest capital over a number of generations. The Protestant economic virtues, though they were not those that would make their practitioners very rich men, are not without significance in economic history. No doubt care with money produced the thousands of anonymous small savers whose investments assisted the take-off of industrialisation in the eighteenth century. But for members of religious groups like the Quakers, the chief fruit of their economic morality and discipline – their warnings against overextension of business and credit, their guarded attitude to other businessmen, their contentment with modest gains – the result of all this was economic survival in difficult times. Protection, not *laissez-faire* capitalism, was the theme of Quaker economic ethics. As a result of this protection, not many Quakers became very rich, and of those who did many, significantly, lost their Quakerism. Modest sufficiency was the goal of the Friends' economic code – though not even this limited goal was reached by all Quakers and in the eighteenth century Quaker philanthropy was heavily involved with the Society's own poor. In a religious group like the Quakers extremes of wealth and poverty were to be found, but a tendency was apparent in such groups for wealth to gravitate towards the middle. A tendency was also apparent in such groups for the social élite and the 'capitalist' to fall away from membership: wealth bought social mobility – that is the chief function of wealth – but membership of a socially unacceptable religious group acted as a check on upward mobility. The hiving-off of the moneyed élite allowed Quakerism to maintain its economic fundamentalism, and also to retain its remarkably homogeneous, modest bourgeois socioeconomic base. In the Society of Friends wealth was encouraged to move towards the middle by the Society's internal philanthropic provisions, which were intended to pull in towards the centre the extremes of abundance and indigence. Through generations Quakers had no hesitation in prescribing in great detail how income was to be gained and how expended.

Their meticulous discipline resembled the activities of a lay consistory. There was no scope for those prerequisites of a capitalist market economy, freedom to acquire and to spend. Nor was there any of the easy-going *laissez-aller* attitude that Temple saw as the secret of Dutch wealth. The Quaker discipline was unlikely to produce Quaker capitalists who maintained their Quakerism intact, but it did afford psychological and material protection to the small farmers, shopkeepers, skilled workmen, shepherds, schoolteachers, clerks, housewives and widows who made up the membership of typical provincial Quaker Meetings. Protection, discipline and charity helped such people to stay afloat in stormy pre-industrial economic seas – to survive the capitalist revolution, if not to make it. But as well as offering protection against economic change, the groups of the radical reformation offered protest against economic injustice.[13]

Radical Christianity provided the intellectual resources for social revolution. This was so because the source-book of Christian radicalism, the New Testament, constantly emphasises the need, not only for charity, but also for justice among men. For this reason, the insurgents in the German Peasants' Revolt adopted the 'evangelical law' as the warrant for their demands for social justice. As well as proposing justice within a system of property, the New Testament also offers alternatives to private property. First, the Gospel extols indifference to private wealth: 'Take heed, and beware of covetousness: for a man's life consisteth not of the things which he possesseth.' Secondly, the New Testament proposes community of goods, arising out of this indifference towards property: 'And all that believed were together, and had all things common; and sold their possessions and goods, and parted them to all men, as every man had need.' Such passages can of course be explained as counsels of perfection, for the attainment of special merit on the part of spiritual élites. This explanation lay behind the official institutionalisation and restriction of holy poverty to the approved monastic and mendicant orders within mediaeval Catholicism. Similarly, perfectionist ethics may be appropriated by perfectionist sects: for example, after the Reformation, the Hutterites practised communal life as a sectarian peculiarity, while the Quakers have sometimes shown a tendency to regard the refusal of oaths, and even the peace testimony, as a sect privilege. This tendency to minimise the significance of New Testament ethics by restricting them to perfectionist groups has often been checked by the mandatory tone of the New Testament itself: its obligations are laid on *all* Christians. The attempt to limit the profession of poverty to the orders of the Church failed in the Middle Ages, and holy poverty was an embarrassment to the propertied Church of the early fourteenth century. So, because of the promptings of the New Testament itself, the protests that the New Testament registers against materialism, exploitation and economic individualism have continued to have meaning for Christians beyond the groups that might at any time have seemed to appropriate perfectionism to themselves.[14]

The Scriptures offer a norm from which economic injustice can be scrutinised and condemned. So does religious prophecy and religious illumination. Earlier we saw how Savonarola condemned financial exploitation. But usury and avarice permeated the Italy of his day. The very source of religious authority was riddled with greed – the papacy, the custodian of the Scriptures. When the formidable magisterium of the church was put at the disposal of *avaritia*, the people's preacher had to claim a countervailing prophetic authority – a divine mandate to rebuke social sins. The scriptural stereotypes were familiar – Haggai, Jeremiah, John the Baptist. However, prophetic authority did not derive from Scripture but was rather seen as valid because it came from God Himself: 'Believe me, Florence, that it is not I but God who speaks these things.' Savonarola's prophetic authority came from dreams and visions and was authenticated by the political course of events in Florence in the mid-1490s. On the basis of this authority the Florentine preacher claimed the traditional right of Italian moral reformers to speak out against the abuses of those in high places, but to speak with exceptional vehemence because of the prophetic authority of his source.[15]

This same sense of utter prophetic certainty, totally inverting the accepted order of human institutional and intellectual authority, was to be found in the South German 'Drummer of Niklashausen' and was used to uphold a simple ethic of love and equality. The 'Drummer' – Hans Böheim of Niklashausen – identified himself with a source of transcendent power – the Virgin Mary – so as actually to hereticate the established clergy and to call for a reversion to equality of work and property: 'Item, the priests say that I'm a heretic, and they want to burn me, but if they knew what a heretic was, they would discover that they are the heretics, and I am no such thing . . . Item, that the fish in the water and the game in the fields shall be in common. Item, that the princes, spiritual and temporal, as well as counts and knights, should have just so much: it must also come about that the common people have enough to give us all an equal sufficiency. Item, it will come about that the princes and lords must also work for a daily wage.'[16]

The proposals in the Niklashausen manifesto for universal work and a redistribution of land to the peasants violated the social order in which peasants themselves had been conditioned. However, German peasants, both in the Niklashausen movement, and later in the great Peasants' Revolt, were able to see that social order as, in varying degrees, unacceptable. As we have seen, a source of social criticism, and especially criticism of socioeconomic inequality, was on hand in the New Testament, which was becoming increasingly available to a mass audience in the Reformation period. To reinforce scriptural critiques, prophecy and claims to direct illumination were called in. In the Reformation period the Protestant Reformation itself provided another source for theories of emancipation and equality. First, the Reformation made possible social emancipation because it rejected the awesome authority of the Catholic Church. In the wake of this revolution, all authority was, for a time at least, called into question. More specifically, Luther's doctrine that all true believers were priests set up an expectation of equality and freedom. Luther's theology was one of freedom won through Christ. Christ's death set men free from the necessity of works. In proclaiming this, Luther was echoing his mentor Paul. As Paul had taught that Christ's death freed men from the tyranny of Jewish laws, so Luther saw that it freed men from the burdens of Romanism. This doctrine of freedom was interpreted by German peasants in 1524–5 as freedom also from unjust manorial and feudal burdens. No one, Luther had announced, could impose a burden on a Christian without his consent.

Being a Christian made a Christian free. This notion was abroad over much of Europe, in the early Reformation especially. In England the idea was current that being English made Englishmen free. The myths of the common law and of Magna Carta convinced many Englishmen that their liberties were the product of their history. But if being English made Englishmen free, being Protestant and English made them doubly so. Religious dissenters, in conflict with the authorities, took their stand on their English liberties. Thus, in the 1590s Puritans, harassed by the Anglican leadership, took issue with the legally dubious 'ex officio' oath. In the seventeenth century oppressed Quakers made much of their rights as Englishmen. In 1667, at the Lancashire Assizes, George Fox argued the technical illegality of the charge against him and the Swarthmore Quakers took exception to tithe actions against them because they were not conducted with due process. For the Quakers, William Penn put forward a view of the fusion of English and Protestant liberty: 'Let us confront our ecclesiastical matters with the plain text of holy Scripture; this is Protestant: and let us compare our civil transactions with the ancient Laws and Statutes of the realm; this is English.'[17]

The Reformation made an already free people freer. Rome, from which the Reformation had cut England adrift, stood for the Jewish law of works in the New Testament and for the Egyptian bondage of the Old. So a national and a spiritual sense of liberation were combined. Reading England for Israel, the English were seen as a chosen people in a unique relationship with God which was confirmed in the way their history providentially endowed them with freedom and with religious illumination.

But, in the fusion of Reformation and English institutions, did the laws of England really play a part in making all Englishmen free? Perhaps the laws of England made only some Englishmen, the proper-tied, free – as conservatives argued in the debates within the Par-liamentarian army in 1647. Precisely because they emerged from history – that is, from in the mediaeval days of Catholic and 'Norman' rule – the laws and liberties of England provided only liberties for a few – and enslavement for the many. As for the Tudor Reformation, Nonconformists, oppressed by Laud's church, did not feel that it liberated men. To radicals, the Church of England, and its temporary successor the broad-based national religious establishment of the Commonwealth and Protectorate, did not measure up to the standards of religious liberty and Reformation. Such churches were maintained by traditional methods – tithes – and continued to use recondite academic theology. The key to emancipation, civil and religious, lay in breaking free of the bonds of history as development, and in forsaking tradition in favour of a drastic reunification of the present with the scriptural past. The laws of England were imperfect seen from this point of view, and so was the uncompleted Reformation of the six-teenth century. Yet England had still, many thought, a special part to play in the working out of the divine plan for human freedom. This is how George Fox rebuked the junior officers of the Parliamentarian army for their failure to carry out a freedom crusade in Europe: 'had you been faithful to the power of the Lord God which first carried you on, you had gone into the midst of Spain . . . to require the blood of the innocent that there had been shed, and commanded them to have offered up their Inquisition to you, and . . . knocked at Rome's gates before now and trampled deceits and tyrants under'.[18]

Thus, while Fox gave Englishmen a special role in initiating change, he, like Milton, made freedom and the Gospel a European property, available by virtue of the Scriptures to all Protestants. This required the specific national historical content of the doctrine of freedom to be deleted. As far as social justice went, the long centuries of the development of English fundamental law were an interval between the Apostolic Age and the new realisation of its principles in the present age: 'And amongst the Christians of the first age there was a man's meeting set up at Jerusalem to see that nothing was lacking, which was the gospel order according to the law of Jesus, and this continued as long as they lived in the spirit, life and power of God; but when the apostasy came in, and the true church fled into the wilderness, which was to continue there 1260 days . . . and then all things went out of order, and everything was wanting in the time they worshipped the Beast, and the devil made the world like a wilderness; but now the judgment of the Great Whore is come, and of the Beast, and with them the false prophets and dragon who shall be cast aside into the lake of fire. And the true church come up out of the wilderness and the manchild which was caught up into heaven come down again to rule all nations with a rod of iron. And the marriage of the Lamb is come, and the Lamb and the saints shall have the victory, and the Everlasting Gospel shall be preached as was amongst the Apostles, and the Gospel order shall be set up as was among them, and a man's meeting as was at the first conversion, to see that nothing be lacking in the church.'[19]

The climax of his millenarian dream, derived out of the Book of Revelations, and perhaps from the Joachimist tradition, was the end of poverty for Christians: 'Then all is well, so there is not a beggar to be among the Christians . . .'

The theory of liberation was gradually being extended in its scope. For Fox, freedom, justice and the gospel belonged to 'the Christians'. English laws applied to Englishmen; the Reformation of the sixteenth century was, at best, only a beginning. But the social and religious fruits of the re-connection between the Gospel and its renewal in the present could be made available to Christians – and men could be made Christians through mission. Revived Christianity was to be propagated from its base in revolutionary England throughout Europe, throughout the territories of European dominion, to the Jews and indeed throughout the world. The early Quakers conducted a vigorous mission which took them, audaciously, to Rome and to the Turkish Empire. A 'second-generation' Quaker expressed the same sense of mission with all its pristine force: 'But yet methought I saw that the Lord will call upon the nations to repent, by sending forth his servants, as verily He is doing in this our day . . .'[20]

Through mission, the Gospel, and the freedom and equality it implied for radical Protestants, could be carried to all. All men were free by virtue of the Gospel. Christian liberation was a broader concept than English or Protestant liberation. But it was not as extensive in its scope as was the idea of human liberation. Whereas Christian liberation derived from the New Testament, human liberation was traced back by some to the Old Testament – to Genesis. Richard Overton explained human freedom and equality as the legacy which all men owed to their common mythic ancestor: 'for justice is my naturall right, my heirdome, my inheritance by lineall descent from the loins of Adam, and so to all the sons of men as their proper right without respect to persons . . . For by natural birth, all men are equally and alike borne to like propriety, liberty and freedome, and as we are delivered of God by the hand of nature into this world, every man with a naturall innate freedom and propriety . . . even so are we to live, every one equally and alike to enjoy his Birthright and privilege; even all whereof God by nature hath made him free . . . Every man by nature being a King, Priest and Prophet in his owne naturall circuite and compasse . . .'[21]

Overton universalised freedom and gave it an entirely natural base. Men shared a common ancestor and were for that reason equal and free. This explanation of liberty cut it free from its restrictive English, Protestant and Christian bases and made it possible, for radicals, to speak of the rights of Irish Catholics and heathen American Indians.[22]

Men were free because of their descent from Adam. The myths of Eden and Adam are a Judaeo-Christian version of the myth of the golden age, a time of plenty, simplicity and innocence. The concept of sin reduced freedom. If man was indeed deeply sinful, restraints had to be put upon him. If, on the other hand, the natural man – Adam – was innocent, he could safely be given his natural freedom. In the Christian tradition an awareness of the force of sin runs alongside a realisation of man's freedom from sin through the death of Jesus. Though Luther stressed the freedom bought by the Atonement, he, like all the other major Reformers, retained an acute sense of the power of sin in human life. The mystics, however, seemed to break away from the shackles of sin in their quest for a reunification of man and God. 'The life of man', wrote the Silesian mystic Jakob Boehme, 'is a form of the divine will, and came from the divine inbreathing into the created image of man.'[23]

Man, then, was by virtue of his divine creation, naturally good. So was the universe. If man was Adam, the world was Eden. 'Thus this world', the author of the *Theologia Germanica* wrote, 'may well be called a Paradise . . . and in this Paradise, all things are lawful, save one tree and the fruits thereof.' The world, indeed, was more than a godly place. It was a place of religious instruction and a reflection of its Creator: 'this world is verily an outer court of the Eternal, or of Eternity, and specially whatever in Time, or any temporal things or creatures remindeth us of God or Eternity; for the creatures are a guide and a path unto God and Eternity'. Boehme – whose heady radicalism appeared dangerous to both Peter Pett and John Wesley – echoed the *Theologia*'s optimistic view of the universe: 'The visible world with its host of creatures is nothing else than the emanated Word which has disposed itself into quantities . . . this visible world with all its hosts and beings is nothing but an objective representation of the spiritual world, which spiritual world is hidden in this material, elemental world, like the tincture in herbs and metals.' If the universe was a book, it was worth while learning how to read it. Perhaps science provided the key. The Lutheran Reformation emphasised the value of the study of botany, for God was to be studied in the perfection of plants – a point which George Fox took up. But in fact the book of nature, which provided the highest knowledge of God, needed no special training to read, and was open to all men, even the most unlettered.[24]

We saw earlier that radical Christianity offered protection to under-privileged groups. It also provided protest – against economic inequality and injustice, and against servitude. By progressive extensions of the conceptual scope of the idea of freedom, men were seen as being free and equal, because they were English, because they were Protestants, because they were Christians, because they were sons of Adam, because they were creatures of God, and because they were innocent. The world, far from being fatally corrupted by sin, was good, and taught men immediately and directly the highest truths. Thus the last bonds were to be severed – the intellectual bondage to theologians and savants. Until this intellectual revolution had been accomplished, the English Revolution was incomplete. Before the political revolution John Lilburne knew that the key to the truth lay in the contemplation of nature – and of himself: 'the learning which made the Apostles famous, was not human learning (for none of them had it but Paul, and he renounced it), but it was heavenly learning, which came from God, being the gift of his Holy Spirit . . . And though my Adversaries are learned in the Phariseicall, Philosicall, deceiuable learning of the world . . . yet in one sixe moneths, in a Prison and fettered condition: I have got more true spiritual learning and knowledge, in the mysteries of Godlinesse, then is amongst them all.'[25]

Thus untutored individuals, free of academic pride, had access to the most highly prized truths. Radical Christianity meant an overturning of all accepted intellectual and educational hierarchies: the poor possessed the truths of religion. Not only did the poor have special access to the truth, but radical thinkers insisted that they had a special and highly favoured place in the divine economy. Hanserd Knollys saw that the poor had played a crucial role in all the major decisions in the history of the church: 'The voice, of Jesus Christ reigning in his Church, comes first from the multitude, the common people. The voice is heard from them first, before it is heard from any others. God uses the common people and the multitude to proclaim that the Lord Omnipotent reigneth. As when Christ came at first the poor received the Gospel – not many wise, not many noble, not many rich, but the poor – so in the reformation of religion . . . it was the common people that first came to look after Christ . . . The voice that will come of Christ's reigning is like to begin from those that are the multitude, that are so contemptible, especially in the eyes and accounts of Antichrist's spirits and the prelacy . . .'[26]

Knollys went on to predict that the traditional political classes would carry through necessary change, after the 'poor' had initiated it. However, radical movements arose in England during the revolutionary decades which showed that the 'poor' were no mere agents in a struggle fought for the ultimate goals of the landed classes. The most significant of these popular movements was the communitarian Digger movement. But such phenomena did not arise merely out of the revolutionary ferment in England, but out of the libertarian and egalitarian ideas which, as the radical reformation rediscovered, lie at the core of Christianity. A prerequisite for the full accomplishment of social revolution was the intellectual revolution we have been discussing. Social emancipation and freedom from deference – as with the Quaker use of the egalitarian 'thou' and the refusal of 'hat honour' – came through the restatement of the simple principle of the equality of men in the sight of God; the same principle, linked to the application in politics of the Separatist ideal of democratic church government, produced demands for political equality; in economic life, the ideal of Christian justice, the vision of the equality of Eden and the recollection of the New Testament all led to demands for equality of property. But the inequalities of early modern English and European society were especially marked in the intellectual field. Illiteracy was widespread and education an expensive privilege. Social emancipation therefore necessitated a recognition of the *intellectual* rights of the common man. The Digger writers were aware of the close interdependence of the hierarchies of power, property and intellectual authority: 'since human flesh . . . began to delight himself in the objects of the creation more than in the spirit Reason and Righteousness, . . . selfish imagination, . . . working with covetousness, did set up one man to teach and rule over another . . . And hereupon the earth, which was made to be a common treasury of relief for all, both beasts and men, was hedged into enclosures by the teachers and rulers, and the others were made servants and slaves. And that earth that is within this creation made a common storehouse for all, is bought and sold and kept in the hands of a few . . . From the beginning it was not so . . .'[2]

'In the beginning it was not so' was a Quakers' formula for condemning corruptions and human inventions, tithes, for example, which broke the divine law of nature. For the Diggers, a simple view of history made it possible to condemn, specifically, enclosures of land and, generally, the system of private property according to which enclosures were justified. In part, Winstanley and Everard criticised private property because it broke the observed rational laws of creation: communal property was to be deduced from the very nature of the universe. But along with 'Reason', the Diggers used history – Scripture history – to back up their case. 'The beginning' was Eden. The laws that *ought* to govern human society were written for all men to read in the account of Eden given in Genesis – just as the laws of economic equality were intelligible from any observation of nature. But the Digger vision of equality, though it remained simple and immediately intelligible, as well as resting on a golden age myth and on 'rational' observation, had a specific Christian source – the life of Jesus and the New Testament, which linked the mythic ideal to the millenarian realisation of human equality and perfectability. The life of Jesus renewed the primitive paradise and reminded man of God's egalitarian plans; the next renewal would come with the Second Coming when 'Jesus Christ . . . will dwell in the whole creation, that is, in every man and woman without exception'. Most important, all men could know that inequality among men could not be justified in God's name. All men could readily know God and his design for human society. Simple men could apprehend the Father through His creation, the Son through the Scripture, and the Spirit through the equality of prophecy. In these ways radical religious perceptions offered an alternative to social, economic and intellectual inequality.

CHAPTER 3

Religious Radicalism and the Protestant Reformation

In 1518 Martin Luther saw to the publication of the late-mediaeval devotional work, the *Theologia Deutsch* (German Theology). Luther was interested in the discovery and re-issue of such mediaeval religious works, especially when they had a Wyclifite or Hussite origin which might establish the existence of a tradition of religious dissent throughout the centuries of papal dominance.[1] Luther's problem was that, alone, he seemed to be challenging many centuries of Catholic belief. The answer to this charge was to turn history against the orthodox by producing the pedigree of religious nonconformity. Research into ecclesiastical history with the aim of proving that the Protestant Reformation had roots deep in the mediaeval past became a preoccupation of Reformation scholarship and resulted in master-pieces of Protestant historical writing, such as Flacius Illyricus *Magdeburg Centuries*. But the efforts of Luther and his disciples, especially with regard to the publication of mediaeval religious works, brought to light not only the existence of mediaeval dissent but also the vitality of mediaeval lay religion. This lay religion provided a seed-bed for the growth of religious radicalism, but its emergence was also an achievement of the mediaeval Church, whose constant missionising, preaching and publishing had their effect in creating a pious Christian people.

The formation of the devout laity was the work of the institutional Church. Clerics acted as influential urban preachers; they wrote some of the most widely read pious treatises; they acted as chaplains to guilds, beguinages and confraternities. Above all, as confessors, writers, preachers and authors, clerics acted as highly responsible mediators between official doctrine and the religious needs of the laity. In this last function university-trained clerics, such as Meister Eckhart, popularised the doctrine and philosophy of the Church. This work of popularisation was performed in part by simple, but sometimes inspired, translations of Latin technical terms into their vernacular equivalents. Thus the Latin term for the concept of the 'spark' of divinity in the human soul – the *Scintilla* – was rendered into German as *Seelenfünklein* – literally 'little soul spark' – a key term in the vocabulary of later mediaeval German mysticism. But successful spiritual counsel on the part of clergymen necessitated more than the invention of a new vocabulary. What was required was a fusion between the mind of the counsellor and those of his auditors and readers. The popularisation of religious thought in response to the needs of lay, conventual and semi-conventual people – apparent, for example, in the Rhineland and the Low Countries – helped produce a flowering of mediaeval mysticism and pietism. In this context lay people, or individuals enrolled in semi-regular order like the Beguines, could themselves assume the initiative from their spiritual guides and produce authentic works of devotion and mysticism. This lay and vernacular piety was a major contributing factor in the enlargement of the individual consciousness, which is a key feature of late mediaeval and early modern European civilisation.[2]

We can now begin to describe some of the elements of this movement of piety. In the first place we find a nurture of the psyche and of the consciousness and emotions. The scrupulous examination of conscience, the quest for felt contrition, the systematic encouragement and appeasement of anxieties over salvation; these were aspects of the new devotionalism. In the monastery Martin Luther underwent all these experiences, but found that monastic disciplines were inadequate for dealing with his psychic condition; indeed, as Luther found, in common with many of his contemporaries, the pious lay life of work and family was more deeply religious than the obsolescent forms of monasticism.

Connected to the emphasis in the lay piety movement on human personality and emotions was a stress on the humanity of Jesus. The quest, which was evident in the early Middle Ages, for the apostolic life had led up to the ideal, adopted by Francis of Assisi, of a Christlike life. This tradition is enshrined in the very title of the most enduringly popular mediaeval devotional work, *The Imitation of Christ*. The *dévot* was to model himself on Christ, but Christ Himself approached the human soul in the sense that greater emphasis was given to His humanity and to His life and death. This emphasis led to characteristic late-mediaeval cults, such as that of the Five Wounds, which summed up the actuality of Jesus's humanity; another manifestation was the realism of late mediaeval religious art, notably in depictions of the Passion and Crucifixion.

Not only the death of Jesus, but death itself became a preoccupation of the late mediaeval devotional tradition. It is possible to relate this concern to the alarming incidence of death, especially in the century of the Black Death. This is a useful insight as long as it does not see religious ideas as simple functional responses to material conditions. Awareness of death's religious significance, echoed for example in the testamentary provisions of a group of fourteenth-century English knights, though probably having a good deal to do with the appalling unpredictability of death in the late mediaeval period, must also be seen as part of the enlargement of the religious consciousness itself.[3]

The other main features of this lay piety were moralism, private prayer and devout reading, religious associations, close contact with confessors and spiritual advisers, and some emulation of regular disciplines and ascetic practices through movements like the Franciscan tertiaries. As to the last point, it is not quite correct to castigate the adoption by the laity of ascetic practices as the mere transposition to non-clerics of the particular styles of the religious orders.[4] The point about such practices as the hair shirt and fasting, when they were taken up by the laity, is that these pious habits were adopted in a lay environment, satisfied an evident lay need, and provided, to borrow Max Weber's term, an asceticism within the world. So the main features of lay devotion were specifically lay, and were successfully integrated with family life through the medium of family prayer and religious nurture, as in the household of Thomas More.

A further area of exploration of the lay devotion is its authors and its literature. The masters of spirituality included Gansfort, Ruysbroek, Groote, Suso, Tauler, Eckhart, Rolle and Hilton; the literature consisted of psalters, books of hours, lives of the saints and manuals with titles like *The Scale of Perfection*, *The Cloud of Unknowing*, *The Prick of Conscience*, *The Ancrene Riwle*, and so on. However, taking priority over all these 'secondary' works was the Bible. Some of the authors of the piety movement – notably Suso and Eckhart – came under suspicion of heresy. In fact, though, in the devotional and mystical movement which we are considering there was no necessary heretical tendency. Indeed the devotional movement displayed orthodox characteristics and depended heavily on the sacraments of the Church, especially Penance and the Eucharist.[5] In fact, far from exhibiting heretical tendencies, mediaeval lay religion was in general non-dogmatic. None the less, lay religiosity, partly because of its biblical source, was moralistic and critical. Evangelical moral norms provided a vantage-point from which to watch the progressive decline of the late mediaeval Church. Lay moralism led to a discriminating attitude towards the clergy. In fact, distinctively lay work values were often applied to clerics. The requirement of actual work to be done on the part of priests can be seen in the establishment by members of the pious laity of preaching foundations, the endowments of which sometimes specified the number of sermons to be delivered by a stipendiary preacher. The setting-up of these preacherships did not necessarily mean a devaluation of the sacraments in favour of the preached word, for the sermon also occupied a high place in official Catholic thinking. But in the endowed preacherships we do see an emphasis on the quality of clerical performance, to be evaluated by the devout laity. The standards that the laity used in judging the clergy were typically lay. Characteristic expectations were that a minister of religion be educated and use his education in teaching and preaching. With regard to morals, typical lay expectations were that a cleric be chaste – or even married – and that he observe public decorum and sobriety. The emphasis was on respectability and satisfactory performance, and this shows some importation of the values of the lay world of work into the religious sphere. This process of evaluation of work may seem to conflict with the traditional Catholic view of a priest as being unimpeachable as an effective priest because of the objective sacrament of ordination. However, the Church leadership had itself paved the way for the lay scrutiny of clerics; for example, the earlier mediaeval Hildebrandine reformers had suspended the holy orders of simoniac priests. So lay moralism and criticism were not intolerably unorthodox. These features, along with scripturalism, and devotion to the Eucharist, were present on the conservative wing of the Hussite Reformation, and that movement was typical of the lay devotion in being doctrinally orthodox.[6]

However, the Hussite Reformation was unorthodox because of a question of organisation – because it sought a separate identity. The Hussite Reformation was a national movement, but on a small scale all over Europe the Church and the lay religious movement disagreed over laity's quest for a separately organised religious life. Sometimes the Church was able to accept and accommodate these lay forms of organisation, as with the Lombard *Humiliati* under Innocent III; sometimes lay groups were completely repulsed, as with the Waldensians; at other times a lay formation was alternately favoured and suspected by the Church, as with the Beguines. In the case of the last-named, official disapproval arose with regard to the distinctive organisation of the group.[7]

It was inevitable that informal groupings, concerned with mutual edification and pious conversation, would evolve among lay men and women of highly developed piety. Such informal groupings could develop into fully fledged associations – religious societies, within the greater society of the Church, and able to satisfy certain basic human impulses, as well as conforming to Christian norms, especially to the scriptural model of the church set out in the Acts. The human needs that religious voluntary societies catered for included social aid, service, self-esteem, a sense of place and a feeling of community. However, in so far as they broke free of priestly control, the tendency of a highly hierarchical organisation like the mediaeval Church was to disapprove of lay religious associations, and this tendency became pronounced in the Counter-Reformation.[8] Official suspicions increased in proportion as a lay organisation sought to break loose from formal clerical supervision – that is to say, in proportion to its aim of being fully lay. Essentially the mediaeval Church held to the assumption of a society organised on simple lines: generally speaking men were members of a single society in its two manifestations of state and church. Urban man did not fully fit into this order, for he belonged to secondary vocational and political organisations, and this urban habit of association received religious forms of expression. The Church's attitude, seeing men as members of the simple society of the Church as the people of God, did not allow the pious laity all the scope they clearly needed to form autonomous societies within the Church – *ecclesiolae*. In fact the mediaeval official reform movement had run counter to the institutional emancipation of the laity. Innocent III's disciplinary reforms necessitated the concentration of power in a central clerical bureaucracy. This process was underlined by the subsequent work of lawyer and administrator popes. Of course this work was never completed; in fact, from the second half of the fourteenth century to the Counter-Reformation, power over the Church was devolved to the national kingdoms. Yet the administrative and fiscal preoccupations of the later mediaeval Church, and the remoteness and formality of its government and discipline, even on the national level, left the Church unable to satisfy the widespead lay impulse towards the formation of socio-religious associations.

On the eve of the Reformation the hierarchical Church was not travelling the same route as the lay piety movement. In particular, the Church left partially unsatisfied the lay demand for a Bible religion. The Church was even more deficient in upholding the strict moral standards demanded by the religious laity. With regard to discipline, official late mediaeval Catholicism provided only a formal and, indeed, mercenary system which fell short of the standard of community discipline through mutual counsel and reproof. Specific heretical movements had come into existence as a reaction to the Church's failure to encourage lay religion in its full associational form. The Free Spirit heresy arose out of the orthodox but suspect Beghard movement; in the case of Hussitism, little or no heresy was present initially: in the case of the Waldensians, a stereotype of heresy was imposed on the movement by the Church; in all these cases, the suspicion, hostility and censure of the hierarchical Church pushed the groups in question out of the orbit of the institutional Church. On the other hand, falling short of outright heresy, on the eve of the Reformation an indeterminate mass of lay Catholic opinion, ostensibly at home in the Church, continued to express aspirations towards a less clerical, less superstitious, more evangelical Christianity. This lay audience, not inclined to dogmatic unorthodoxy, provided the Reformers with their mass constituency. Could the Protestant Reformation provide them with the lay religion, and especially with the appropriate forms of association, which they sought?

Many of the services provided by religious associations are sanctioned by scriptural Christianity. Communal discipline, the settlement of disputes, fellowship, sharing and aid, all feature prominently in the church of the New Testament.[9] The prominence of these features in the primitive church may have had something to do with the situation and the social needs of the first Christians – in the main socially depressed and isolated individuals in the cities of the Roman Empire. Thus a fusion is apparent between religious ideals and social needs. We might say that, *mutatis mutandis*, social pressures in early modern Europe acted on individuals in the same way as did the social problems of the Roman Empire in the Apostolic and sub-Apostolic periods. It is clear that there are certain historical situations in which the need to form human protective associations is particularly pressing. Such a situation was present in the sixteenth century. The ingredients of the situation were urbanisation, new technologies and a rapid pace of political, social and religious change. In these circumstances, individuals and families were uprooted from protective and familiar rural backgrounds, new crafts and skills were brought into existence, larger industrial units were developed, and the rapidity of change created feelings of anxiety and insecurity about the future. Large-scale capital accumulation, abrupt price increases, the instability of employment and the reliance of whole sectors of populations on single industries, the mushroom growth of cities and the risk of epidemics; these were part of the familiar picture of early modern change and they impelled its victims to form protective associations, which took a religious form. In turning to religious associations, the victims of change in the sixteenth century were not turning to religion as a simple opiate. Nor were they forming reformist organisations on the lines of modern trade unions. There is, however, this resemblance between a nineteenth-century trade union and a sixteenth-century religious association: that the religious group acted as a benefit society, as an institution in which the dispossessed could find a social role and a sense of purpose and belonging. We have seen that, tied as it was to its own clerical structures, the mediaeval Catholic Church failed to accommodate fully the laity's need to form autonomous associations. At first sight the Protestant Reformers seemed able to provide a lay religion, decentralised, democratic and congregational in its organisation, allowing scope for

the group enforcement of moral discipline, and providing the fundamental scriptural Christianity which was at the heart of lay aspirations.

The promise of such a Christianity was held out by Luther in popular
works such as the 1520 pamphlets *Bablyonian Captivity of the Church*
and *Freedom of a Christian*. Luther's Christianity echoed many of the
religious aspirations of the late mediaeval laity. The doctrine of the
priesthood of all believers followed naturally on Luther's theology of
salvation by faith alone. The idea that all true Christians were priests
provided, for the lay adherents of Luther, a vindication of their striving
for religious equality with the clergy. Luther had become disenchanted
with the exclusively clerical and monastic concept of vocation and he
turned away from this narrow definition of the calling, to proclaim
instead that a religious vocation lay in all forms of work, service and
family life. Thus the spiritual content of lay life was enormously
expanded in Luther's thinking. At the same time, Luther placed faith
above the sacraments; he drastically reduced the number of the sacraments; he discounted the sacrificial character of the Mass; and he gave
a personal encouragement to the clergy to marry. In all these ways, and
especially by reducing the priestly character of the clergy, Luther
shortened the distance between clergy and laity and diminished the
mysterious and elevated position of the pastor. Indeed, the ideal type
of Lutheran pastor corresponded to the long-standing requirements of
the pious laity. The good pastor was to be an educated, preaching
minister. Just as Luther transferred the traditional clerical concept of
vocation to the laity, so he applied to the clergy itself his ideal of the
calling. The minister of the word was evaluated on the basis of performance and service – specifically lay criteria, raised by Luther to a new
level of religious significance.

Anti-clericalism was rife in late mediaeval Europe. As part of the
Protestant Reformation the status of the clergy was often sadly
weakened. In England the financial maintenance of clerics was
reduced; in many German and Swiss Protestant cities clerics were not
considered full citizens.[10] Nevertheless, it was not a necessary part of
lay religious aims to abase the clergy. Rather a different relationship
was sought between cleric and layman. In this relationship the minister
was given no automatic superiority over the layman by virtue of the
conferment of priestly office only. Greater equality of ministers and
congregational groups was a necessary part of lay religion. Luther
envisaged the church as a number of congregational associations of the
pious faithful, in which the laity took the lead, and in which the pastors
were primarily preachers and counsellors: 'Therefore all teachers
should and must be subject to the judgement of the hearers, and so
should their teaching . . . Accordingly, we should have no doubt that a
congregation which has the gospel must and should choose and call

from amongst itself someone to teach the Word on its behalf.'[11]

Luther, then, articulated the long-standing lay Christian demand for a more lay-controlled church. It is clear also that Luther envisaged the 'discernment' and evaluation of ministers by congregation. This was possible because Luther, in common with countless pious lay people, viewed religion not as a professional mystery, but as a matter of the greatest simplicity – a matter for the 'layman' in our modern sense of the word. Immediate intelligibility was considered to be the essence of true Christianity. This was because of Christ's words about the need to be childlike; it was also because of the nature of God, who was not to be controlled by any professional corps of theologians. 'God', wrote Luther, in the preface to the *German Theology*, 'always refuses to choose fine, pompous and brilliant preachers for his words, but as it is written: "Out of the mouths of infants" – by the mouths of the inarticulate and sucklings you have proclaimed your praises best of all.' This theme was taken by as a rallying call in the German Reformation: the religious sovereignty of the common man was emphasised and the idealised peasant ('Karsthans') sensibly arbitrated the theologians' controversies.[12]

In preferring the ignorance of the common man to the sophisms of academic theologians, Luther brought to a head an important aspect of the Christian laicism of the later Middle Ages. He was, however, himself a highly skilled scholastic technician, and so it might appear that his disparagement of learning was a self-condemnation. Indeed, Luther found the intellectual tradition in which he was raised barren. Like Eckhart and Cusanus before him, he demoted intellectuality because of his low view of mere humanity. But the most obvious reason for Luther's disrespect for 'that harlot reason' was that religious truth was immediately to hand, without the tortuous processes of theology, in the form of the Scriptures. In exalting the Bible, Luther put himself at the head of the lay devotion. He had particular reasons for his exclusive stress on Scriptures. At a debate at Leipzig in 1519, Luther's orthodox antagonist Eck had forced him to repudiate all other sources of truth apart from Scriptures. In fact, though, Eck forced Luther to face up to, and state, his already fundamental scripturalism. Luther had found in 'the word of God', in Paul's Letter to the Romans, the answer to all his spiritual anxieties, in the words 'the just shall live by faith'.

Bible Christianity – an uncluttered, immediately intelligible religion – was proclaimed by Martin Luther, and it supplied a response to an established lay religious need. But Luther provided a further service to lay spirituality in translating the Scriptures into German. This was a monumental achievement. Earlier vernacular translations into European languages had been imperfect from various points of view: they were not translations of the Bible in its entirety; they were generally derived not from original languages but from St Jerome's translation into Latin; or they were not rendered into a generally acceptable form of a national language. Luther's version was free from all these faults, and in its printed form this Bible equipped the literate lay German with an encyclopaedia of his religion, for reading in home and family.

Many themes of mediaeval lay religiosity, then, were taken up and expanded by Martin Luther. He developed a Bible religion; he exalted mysticism and private prayer; he spoke of congregational autonomy and a levelling of the difference between cleric and layman; he exalted work, marriage and family life and gave them all a religious and vocational significance. However, the key to Luther's success or failure in canalising the lay devotional movement lay in the realm of church order. Could the Lutherans really produce a form of church government in line with lay aims – that is to say, allowing lay people to play a full part in the government of the church, its educational, disciplinary and philanthropic activities, and its teaching and preaching? The appropriate structure would need to be both decentralised and democratic, allowing lay people to hold such offices in the church as would enhance their sense of control over, and involvement in, their affairs.

At the inception of the Lutheran Reformation, the possibility existed of a plurality of autonomous churches. A number of Reformers, not all of them entirely dependent on, or in agreement with, Luther, operated on a local, and particularly an urban level. Such were Wenceslas Linck, Andreas Osiander, Johann Agricola, Caspar Hedio, Johann Brenz, Wolfgang Capito, Johann Oecolampadius, and others. Some of the 'lesser' Reformers were particularly concerned with reformation on the congregational level. Zwingli in Zürich emphasised the religious value of the congregation (*Gemeinde*), and in his ministry of the French church in Strasburg John Calvin was the chosen pastor of a voluntary congregation. In the very heart of the German Reformation, in Wittenberg, during Luther's exile after the Reichstag of Worms, the city briefly adopted a local reformation, which contained possibilities for the religious and social self-fulfilment of lay people.

However, most of these early possibilities of diverse reformations, partly directed by the ordinary laity, fell away with the spread of Protestantism. The need for uniformity grew as the Evangelical movement became embattled with a Catholic reaction. At the same time the Lutheran movement fell increasingly under the control of civil oligarchies and of the princes. A symbol of the latter was the Visitation system, first erected in Electoral Saxony in the late 1520s. This system, with its supervisors appointed by the territorial prince, did not conform to Luther's early vision of the church. In the territorial system in so far as the laity took a hand in the running of the church, it was as members of the princely order, or as civil servants appointed by the princes. In these circumstances, the task of conserving the congregational principle fell on radicals like Thomas Müntzer and Andreas Carlstadt, both of whom became local pastors to congregations, with whose religious and social life they sought to identify themselves. Similarly in Zürich, Zwingli's congregational polity got lost in the growth of the magistrates' intervention in church affairs. It was no accident, though, that Anabaptism, with congregationalism at its heart, grew up in Zwingli's Zürich in the mid-1520s.[13]

Much could be expected from the Calvinist system in terms of involving the laity fully in the affairs of the church. Calvin's theoretical ideal of the church, based on Paul's Letter to the Corinthians, was of a society in which the talents of all would be pooled for the good of all.[14] Through such New Testament offices as the deaconship and through Calvin's emphasis on the individual church as a medium for Christian charity, the human drives to organise, to work voluntarily for others, to receive a measure of recognition, could be taken up and employed by the congregation. Within the limits of catholicity Calvin also recognised the right of individual churches to have variety in unimportant matters of worship. However, in the crucial matter of the government of the church the rank-and-file laity was in fact given insufficient scope. At Geneva itself the clergy and city council were too much involved in discipline for discipline to be truly congregational. In Calvinist churches like that of Lyons the laity who were prominent in the church were the notables of local society. In France generally, because of the need for protection, the nobility quickly assumed the lay direction of the church, just as in England the most prominent and useful lay elements in the Calvinist puritan movement were from the gentry and nobility. Calvinism satisfied many established lay religious appetites. It was scriptural; it accorded a high place to lay work and to the family; it created – notably in England – a system of sensitive moral advice and counselling; it emphasised preaching, reading, discussion and education; its worship was simple and comparatively flexible. But despite these advantages, Calvinism fell short of the tradition of lay religion inherited from the late Middle Ages. First, Genevan Calvinism was both too clerical and too concerned with theological accuracy. Secondly, it was too involved in the social hierarchy, and accorded too much influence in church matters to men of rank and power. Thirdly, its discipline and purity of doctrine relied excessively on police power and on enforcement. Fourthly, its structures were centralised and undemocratic. In France in particular the Calvinist church formed a pyramidical structure which reduced the independence of local congregations. Such formal structures affected the self-regulation and internal democracy of individual churches. Classical Calvinism inherited the view of the layman as a subject of the church and in terms of structure it disappointed lay strivings. For this reason many lay Christians turned away from the classical Calvinist mode. They sometimes resorted to societies which combined religious and industrial functions in an associational form, such as the Printers' Guild at Lyons; sometimes they turned back to the devotions of reformed Catholicism; or they moved into non-Calvinist and non-Lutheran forms of the Reformation; or, notably in England, they sought to combine Calvinist orthodoxy with non-Presbyterian and congregational church structures.[15]

A good example of a Reformation movement maintaining the lay religious traditions of the late Middle Ages is Anabaptism. In this movement we see a middle, lower-middle and artisan class composition; a cult of the Scriptures, devotional reading and mysticism; a relative indifference to theology; an elimination of the distinction between clergy and laity; an absence of central organisation and a stress of the local congregation; the functioning of the local church as a social group operating voluntary structures of aid and discipline; in short, we see the fulfilment of the lay religious impulse.[16]

The same features characterised English Separatism in the Tudor period. The local Separatist congregation was a voluntary gathering of the elect. Its members might confirm their association by a contract – a church covenant. Churches were separated not only from the 'false worship' of the Church of England, but also partly from other 'true' churches. No professional clerical caste arose, but only congregationally approved leaders. A quest for a caring discipline was one of the strongest motives for leaving the national Church, and it was to the forefront of the activities of the community.[17]

Perhaps these themes in the life of English Separatism were inherited from the pre-Reformation Lollard tradition. Whether they were or not, they were certainly passed on to the life of Independency in the sixteenth century. In both Separatism and Independency we see an original striving to retain Calvinist orthodoxy, while at the same time evolving a democratic, laicist and localist form of the church, with voluntary and effective discipline. The development of lay religious associations was particularly vital in England in the 1640s and 1650s. Quakerism represented a highly developed form of lay associational religious life, and it emerged out of the traditions of Separatism, Independency and 'the sects'. Thus we may consider how Quakerism satisfied human and religious needs, both those of a permanent kind and those peculiar to the conditions of pre-industrial England.

Relief against material hardship is, of course, a permanent human need. It is to the fore in Christian ethics, and the mediaeval Church had, with varying degree of success, tried to cope with the problems of hardship and poverty. However, Catholic methods of poor relief could be criticised on the grounds that they sometimes took on the character of doles from a clerical corporation to an indigent laity. This would apply, for example, to the food rations given out by the sixteenth-century Spanish monasteries, or to the doles handed out by the mediaeval monks of Furness in the North of England. Ideally, Christian poor relief has in it an element of sharing. Thus a community of Christians can be brought together in relief activities, and fellowship, as in the Acts, can be expressed through the pooling of surpluses. On the material level, early Quakers took care of the problems of poor relief. Payments of money were made to widows, to the old and the sick; financial help was provided for educating the children of poor Quakers and even of poor non-Quakers; and, in line with Reformation principles, ambitious plans were drawn up to eliminate poverty through creating work. But beyond these essential material aims, Quakers unconsciously performed psychological functions of community aid. The Quakers involved all their members in poor relief; sums of money stipulated to be collected from each member, carefully graded according to his or her means, allowed all Friends, even the less well off, to share in group responsibility for the poor. Of course, particular Quakers concentrated on philanthropic work – as financial clerks, administrators of charity trusts, and so on. It should be said that Quaker charity was never fully bureaucratised, and much scope was provided for spontaneous giving. None the less, and following Paul's principle that the church should employ the special talents of its members, certain Friends – typically those with business backgrounds, free time and organising experience – were used in the administration of aid. In looking at the career of a typical Quaker amateur administrator, William Stout of Lancaster, we can see how involvement in church government, especially in relief work, gave the individual's life a depth of meaning and importance that it would otherwise have lacked. Across early modern Europe oligarchic developments in town corporations and guilds deprived many lower social elements of political participation in urban affairs. In England after 1660 these oligarchic tendencies were underlined in the Corporations Acts, which restricted borough office to communicating members of the Church of England. The law now deprived petit-bourgeois Nonconformists, like the shopkeeper Stout, of any opportunity to take part in the government of their town communities. Men like Stout had many qualifications for service: literacy, practical intelligence, shrewdness, energy, leisure from relatively undemanding businesses. The urge to work in a local group, to occupy small offices of dignity, to bring order to group affairs, to sit on committees, to plan and direct, all these were put at the service of the church group.[18]

Discipline is prominent in the life of Christian church groups. It obviously answers the Christian need to maintain ethical standards. But it also performs an anthropological function, especially in periods of rapid change, particularly urbanisation. The operation of discipline, through the machinery of counsel, warnings, reprimands and the ultimate sanctions of the ban and excommunication, reminds the individual that his moral conduct is not a matter of indifference. It is essential to the human operation of church discipline that it be enforced within and by the local group. The criticism made of traditional Catholic discipline was valid: that it treated sin as crime: that it was mechanistic and pecuniary; that it was ineffective; that, by putting a tax on sin, it even had a vested interest in immorality. Most of these criticisms also applied to the disciplinary system which the Church of England inherited from its Catholic antecedents. Formal, legal ecclesiastical discipline simply opened the gap between the individual and the authorities who governed his life. Discipline maintained by a church court, handled by a bishop's commissary or chancellor, had no real elements of concern or counsel. Like ecclesiastical philanthropy it was operated *upon* communities, not operated *by* them. By contrast, local congregational discipline provided inexpensive and speedy ways of settling disputes within a community; it directed the conduct of youth and supported the family as an instrument of moral nurture; and it provided moral oversight of individuals – a surrogate form of kinship control – in otherwise impersonal urban areas. Quaker communities, in the sphere of discipline, functioned like large and censorious families; in doing so they safeguarded otherwise rootless and unsupervised individuals, especially youth and rural immigrants, from some of the typical features of early modern urban life: alcoholism, bankruptcy, prostitution and crime. The discipline strikes us as being oppressive and meddlesome, but it suited the disorder of much of early modern English town life.[19]

G. F. Nuttall tells us that one of the characteristics of Independent groups in seventeenth-century England was 'fellowship'. We can develop this concept to cover companionship and civility, a dissolution of loneliness, and intellectual and emotional stimulation. Clearly 'fellowship' corresponds to human needs, which arise particularly in times of mobility and change. For early modern Quakers fellowship meant a sense of belonging to an interlocked national society; it meant the removal certificates which provided Friends migrating to new districts with immediate social contacts upon their arrival; it meant the equality and simplicity of a Quaker Meeting.[20]

Democratic church life was guaranteed by the structures of Quakerism. Formal arrangements for church order greatly affect the degree of majority lay control of the affairs of an individual church. As we saw, the pyramidical system of classical Calvinism tended, over much of Europe, to exclude popular elements from church government. It was apparent that the best guarantee of congregational democracy lay in the establishment of a loose type of church federation, though preserving the ultimate theoretical unity of the church. Thus in English Independency the autonomy of the individual church was seen as the precondition of its democracy. Quakers too had a decentralised and democratic organisation. The basic Quaker unit was the Particular Meeting, often a small and very intimate union of a few families. It is true that a supervisory authority existed in the Yearly and Quarterly Meetings, but local Meetings frequently dissented from decisions arrived at in the 'superior' bodies. The sources of Quaker authority – private judgement and Scripture – were open to all. Universal participation in Meetings was made possible by the drastic reduction in the distinction between ministry and clergy and by the absence of a sacramental system. All were allowed to speak – men and women – and the restrictions on this right, governing prolixity and pomposity, only confirmed everyone's access to speaking rights. Quaker puritanism with regard to dress and consumption helped to conceal social differences, at least until the appearance of the wealthy 'gay Quakers' of the eighteenth century. Books and lending libraries were available in great profusion, and from 1690 Quaker schooling chalked up great successes in turning out a literate and intellectually independent Quaker membership. All members were involved in the affairs of the church community. It is true that certain prominent individuals – 'weighty Friends' – did emerge, and yet every effort was made to give each member of the Society a useful task in line with his or her means and abilities; the tasks ranged from representing districts at the Yearly Meeting and conducting negotiations with governments, to taking food to imprisoned Quakers and conducting visiting Friends around remote districts.[21]

Seventeenth- and early eighteenth-century Quakerism adequately satisfied the human need for association, and frequently did so in places and in circumstances where social provisions were few and where the individual and the family were faced with anonymity and isolation. However, in the religious sphere, congregational associations operated above all to guarantee the development of lay religious life. Free lay association was vital to the maintenance of the radical core of Christianity, and of the essentials of traditional lay devotionalism. The organisational preconditions for the development of the lay devotion were not catered for by the magisterial Reformers – Luther, Zwingli, Calvin, Cranmer, and the others. Without appropriate and independent forms of organisation, lay religion, as we defined its characteristics at the beginning of this chapter, found it difficult to develop intellectually; and therefore, in forms such as Anabaptism, Separatism and Quakerism, pious lay people formed their own associations; these associations had a primary purpose in fostering religious life and thought, and an important secondary purpose in creating human companionship. However, though the magisterial Reformation did not encourage associations of the laity, it did foster religious ideas which were taken up by lay Christians. Luther especially was a medium for the transmission of the 'Catholic' lay religiosity of the late Middle Ages to the piety of the early modern period. As we saw, Luther's main emphases – on the centrality of Scripture, on the priesthood of all believers and on justification by faith alone – gave intellectual support to long-standing lay desires for a less elaborate, more evangelical, more lay-oriented religion; Luther exalted prayer, preaching and personal piety; he respected the lay calling; he put Jesus and the Crucifixion at the centre of his religious world-view; he expressed his thought in the ordinary German language; he demanded a puritan morality, with good works flowing from faith; he upheld – in his own life – the ideal of a working clergy; he disparaged intellectual sophistry. In these ways Luther took over the lay tradition, but he also built on it and developed it in significant ways. Thus Luther was the fountainhead for many aspects of the radical reformation.

Let us briefly examine some aspects of the radical Luther. Luther considered, as we saw, that the Bible had sovereign authority for Christians. In this he would seem to echo those groups – for example the Waldensians, the Lollards and many of the Anabaptists – who sought complete fidelity to the Scripture. It is easy to see why such groups lived under the shadow of the Scriptures. Indeed for all Christians the Bible, and especially the New Testament which records the words and actions of the founder, possess unique authority. The Bible also took on some of the authority that belonged in the late mediaeval and early modern periods to all sources that derived from the past. As in literature, politics, the arts and philosophy, so in religion it was the past, and especially the classical past, that possessed authority, and, no doubt, the Scriptures acquired some of the authority that belonged automatically to an ancient text. Dissident Christian groups turned to the Bible also because it provided them with an alternative authority on which to base their dissent from established churches. So, for all these reasons, the Bible was an infallible guide for many groups of lay Christians. Indeed many groups remained in a rudimentary biblicist stage, and never developed beyond scriptural literalism. The English Lollards were probably in this category. It is true that bizarre, sceptical and ingeniously heretical ideas were found amongst the 'Lollards' of late mediaeval England, but the authorities used the term 'Lollard' to describe heresy in general. The Lollard movement proper was based on a repudiation of all Catholic practices not explicitly found in Scriptures, and this was how the Catholic observer Bishop Pecock saw the movement; Lollardy also meant a highly reverential attitude towards the text of Scripture, and we can see this attitude in the visit which a group of Lollards paid, with their ancestral Bible, to Robert Barnes in 1527. Lollardy, perhaps because of geographical remoteness and intellectual isolation, did not for the most part progress beyond the Scriptures; in the main Lollardy offered a negative critique, based on the Bible, of Catholic developments and traditions. Other groups who, like the Lollards, experienced geographical remoteness, also failed to develop beyond strict biblicism. Such movements represented not religious development, but antipathy to development – a highly fundamentalist basic Christianity in which intellectual and liturgical change were condemned according to the static norms of Scripture. Certainly the majority of Lollards never seem to have taken up a relative attitude to the Bible. Such an attitude involves looking at the Bible as a book to be read with special spiritual insights; or as a book possessing authority alongside other books, or other sources of ideas; or as little more than a book, and merely historic. Such attitudes to the Scripture were to be found during the religious ferment of the English Revolution. These attitudes often came to the fore when magisterial churches tried to appropriate the authority of the Bible to themselves, as was the case with the attempted Presbyterian establishment in England in the 1640s, or with the conservative wing of the Hussite movement in early fifteenth-century Bohemia. The downgrading of the Bible as a source of authority was probably a consequence also of a proliferation of alternative religious literature; this was the case in Revolutionary England, and with the Quakers. Radicals were heard to say that the Bible represented the illumination of the Spirit in the past, but that, as revelation could be available in the present, its recipients were as authoritative as Paul, John, Moses and all the other scriptural writers.[22]

The superiority of the inspired Christian to Scripture, the Christian's ability to evaluate Scripture, to prefer one passage over another, to consider the historical circumstances in which Bible passages were written: it would hardly seem that such a biblicist as Luther could have had sympathy with such radicalism. In fact, Luther himself arrived at a relativistic view of the Bible. It is true that he relied on the word of Scripture, for he found, as we saw, the kernel of his theology of salvation in it – in the Letter of Paul to the Romans. However, when Luther turned to the Letter of James he found a different version of salvation, one which threatened the certainty he had found in Paul. James's words were no less absolute than Paul's: 'faith, if it hath not work, is dead'. Luther's reaction to the difficulty of reconciling these conflicting texts was characteristically brusque: 'I do not regard it as the writing of an apostle', and he went on to emphasise the 'Jewish' character of the Epistle. Indeed, there were long-standing scholarly objections to the authenticity of James; but Luther repudiated the Epistle primarily on the basis of his developed individual faith – something akin to the selective 'inner light' approach to Scripture characteristic of religious radicals. It is well known that after 1520 Luther denounced external ecclesiastical authority in favour of the primacy of Scripture. But even the primacy of Scripture could be set aside in favour of a reading of the Bible that conformed to personal religious and psychic needs. Luther in fact advanced the principle of selective, subjective and inspirational Bible-reading, a principle that lies at the heart of the more developed forms of religious radicalism in the Reformation period.[23]

Luther heralded this approach. He was also the father of the radicals in other ways. Faith was at the centre of Luther's religion. But faith, in the sense of assent, can clearly only be the property of conscious adults. When applied to the sacraments of the church – essentially, for Luther, Baptism and the Eucharist – the requirement of faith weakens the automatic or 'magical' working of sacraments. With regard to the Eucharist, Luther for a period hovered uncertainly between a concept of Christ's presence depending on personal faith and, on the other hand, an objective corporeal reality. The same difficulty arose over baptism. If the efficacy of the sacrament depends on the recipient's faith, how can an unconscious child receive it? Luther got round this difficulty by appropriating to the child the faith of its faithful sponsors, but this was not a satisfactory solution from the point of view of his own thought. Anabaptism, which insisted on adult baptism, was a natural outcome of Luther's insistence on faith, and in that sense Luther was the author of Reformation radicalism.[24]

Luther appears in the character of a radical by virtue of some of his statements on religious toleration and relations with the state. Toleration is usually associated with such radical individuals and groups as Sebastian Castellio, the continental Anabaptists and the English Separatists. But Luther anticipated them in his idealisation of tolerance and the separation of church and state: 'For it rests on the conscience of the individual', he wrote in *Vom Weltlicher Obrigkeit* (1523), 'how he believes or does not believe – a fact which subtracts nothing from the temporal power, which should be content, look after its own business, and let anyone believe this or that as he is willing and able, and constrain no-one by force.'[25]

Similarly, it is clear that Luther anticipated the radicals – the Anabaptists and Quakers, for example – in his pacifism. For Luther, state, law, power, and force were the opposites of Gospel, spirit, love and self-surrender. In particular, force, because it was entirely dissimilar from the Gospel, could never be used on behalf of the Gospel. Luther thus seems to be the author of the passivity and pacifism that lay at the heart of the radical reformation in all its authentic manifestations: 'the Christian law', he writes, 'is not to strive against injustice, not to stretch after the sword, not to protect oneself, not to avenge oneself, but rather to give body and property, and let whoever wants to steal it steal it'.[26]

No doubt we could go on listing the areas of similarity – or indebtedness – between Christian radicals and Luther. Christian libertarianism, for example, and the sharp distinction between law and Gospel, which we find in the antinomian Johann Agricola and in other expressions of antinomianism, can be traced to Luther's *Freedom of a Christian*. However, we should pay attention to Luther's method when he writes of such matters as Christian freedom, the election of pastors and all the other 'radical' topics. Time after time Luther prefaces his remarks with words like 'therefore' and 'accordingly', and when he does this he is drawing out the implications of texts from the Old Testament, from the Gospels, from Paul and from other Epistles. Luther was thus the medium for the transmission of the radicalism of the New Testament, but he was by no means an indispensable mediator; in fact his power as a transmitter depended much more on his having made available a German Bible than it did on his work as a biblical scholar and commentator.

Let us consider again the points where Luther seemed to initiate radical standpoints: the logic of adult baptism; Christian simplicity; tolerance; pacifism; indifference to the state; all these attitudes are to be found in the Scripture, in the Gospels above all, and they derive not from Luther but from Jesus. However, if the Gospel had binding force it would maintain Christians in permanent and static obedience to itself, and this, as we have seen, did not characterise the more radical groups after the Reformation. Neither did over-deference to the literal Bible characterise Luther, for he chose his emphases in his reading of the Scriptures and he read the Bible in the light of his personal needs and anxieties. In this sense the radicals who took a relative view of the Bible seem to have been in Luther's debt. However, anti-literalism in approaches to the Bible has a long history, predating Luther. The twelfth-century Calabrian Abbot Joachim, for example, had looked forward to an age of the spirit, characterised by a heightened, supra-literal and inspirational reading of the Bible.[27] But beyond Joachim, the Scripture itself seems to stress its own limitations. John's Gospel emphasises how *little* it contains of the truth about Jesus (John 20: 30, 21: 25). Throughout the Gospels Jesus Himself speaks of the illumination by the Spirit who is to come after him, and the Spirit does indeed inspire the Apostles in the Acts. The theme of direct revelation is continued by Paul's exaltation of spirit, prophecy and freedom above law, sin and letter. So the Bible itself encouraged a non-literal approach to Christianity. The Scriptures do this because they are a diverse source, with internal inconsistencies, which can be reconciled by private illumination. But above all, the Bible is relative in its authority because it is not the revelation, but a partial account of the revelation of God; for Christians, Jesus. Freedom from the Bible is implicit *in* the Bible, a point lost to scriptural literalists, but one seized on by many advanced Christian radicals. The Bible can function as a potent source of radical and spiritual Christianity, as material for contemplation. Naturally this contemplation can be conducted privately. Even more the 'leadings' of Scripture may be followed in group contemplation by a congregation, and this is the real importance, from the religious point of view, of the free associations of the laity which we have been considering. Such associations are an ideal framework for 'ongoing' Christian exploration. The concept of the Spirit, with His gifts of prophecy, healing and discernment, is vital to Christian discovery – free, if necessary, from the very letter of Scripture itself. But, as we saw at the beginning of this chapter, the lay devotionalism, many of whose characteristics passed into post-Reformation radicalism, was concerned with the central figure of Jesus. How was Jesus to be apprehended in a Christianity set free from its scriptural moorings? The literal meaning of the New Testament with regard to Jesus is material. The Gospels deal with the physical reality of the incarnation, death and resurrection of Jesus; similarly, given a literal meaning, the words of the institution of the Eucharist imply a 'real presence' of Christ in the sacrament. With regard to the latter, cracks opened up in the fabric of faith through the thought of reformers like Zwingli, who gave the words of institution a symbolic, commemorative and spiritual meaning. This line was taken up by radicals. Sebastian Franck took an entirely spiritual view of Scripture: 'The letter is also no teaching or light for the outer man, because God means and seeks something quite different from what the bare letter can show and do.' This inner reading of the Scripture both spiritualised and universalised Christ: 'The inner, truly living, natural and almighty word of the Father, which in recent times has become flesh, and is taken to be the seed of Abraham and named "Christ" in the New Testament, is that which goes forth directly from the mouth of God . . . through which everything is created . . . God must himself utter it in our soul and heart so that the word may also become flesh and Christ be born in us.' Franck's Reformation emphasis on the godness of God seems to lead him also to develop a major theme of the lay piety – the humanity of Jesus. In so far as lay Christians shared, as they obviously did, the humanity of

Jesus, so they might share with Him the word of God and be 'godded' in exactly the same way as He was. The non-literal interpretation of key scriptures – the Resurrection, for example – the spiritualisation of Christ – these processes diminished the historic uniqueness of the Word-made-flesh, but made possible the divinisation of the religious adept. Just as the Bible itself was seen, not as a unique revelation but only as part of a revelation given anew in each generation, so the spiritualisation of Jesus put Him on a par with the pious radical lay Christian. The culmination of the process was the entry into Bristol, in imitation of Jesus's entry into Jerusalem, of James Naylor in 1656.

But this was not the end of the process. Spiritualising the Eucharist, universalising Jesus, these processes meant the end of faith. They implied a view of spirit and matter as two separate categories, each incapable of transforming or affecting the other. This is what is meant by the end of magic in the Reformation, but obviously it was taken much further by the *radical* reformation. The disconnection between spiritual and material meant the end of miracle, and the end of miracle meant the end of faith. The dissociation of material and spiritual meant even more than this: it led to a secular society. The relative lack of Christian standards and sanctions in the public life of modern indus- trial societies can be explained in several ways: for example, by refer- ence to religious toleration and pluralism, making it impossible for the standards of any one denomination to be imposed on society at large. But radical religion is also responsible for the secularisation, the de- Christianisation of modern society. First, because it envisages a model of Christian organisation as a voluntary association, not as a public and inclusive church; secondly, because it establishes on a secure footing the de-materialisation of religion and the de-spiritualisation of the material. The divorce, the duality, make it impossible to conceive of a Christian society.

CHAPTER 4

Religious Radicalism and Religious Toleration

At the beginning of the sixteenth century the intellectual preconditions for religious toleration were favourable. The areas of scholarly inquiry were being broadened out; the German humanist Johann Reuchlin, in the teeth of opposition from Dominican conservatives, but with the full support of progressive intellectuals, fought to establish Hebrew and Judaism as proper topics for Christians to study. The Dominican Order stood for the principle of Catholic intellectual certainty; not only did the Order dominate the Inquisition, but its principal ornament in the Middle Ages was the 'rationalist' philosopher-theologian Thomas Aquinas. The mainstream intellectual tradition of the Dominicans was that, below the level of faith, the mind can attain to a high degree of knowledge, and that the Church can uphold and enforce such truth. This characteristically high mediaeval confidence in the ability of the human intellect to possess truth and in the right of the Church's tribunals to impose it was at a low ebb when the sixteenth century opened up. Aquinas's system – Thomism, as it is called – shared in the disfavour with which the most advanced minds viewed mediaeval Scholasticism – seen as a barbaric, hair-splitting system of human mental inventions. The Inquisition – the institutional expression of the belief that religious truth could be accurately defined and imposed – had for some time been running up against considerable lay and middle-class opposition, especially in northern Europe[1]. Finally, the Dominicans, the trustees of Thomism and of the Inquisition, justly or unjustly shared in the unpopularity which attached to the religious orders in general at the close of the Middle Ages.[2]

So the philosophic and institutional basis for organised religious intolerance was much weaker at the end of the Middle Ages than it had been in the thirteenth century. Confidence in the human mind's ability to arrive at certainty was eroded by a growing appreciation of God's majestic omnipotence, and of the consequent insignificance of the human intellect. The tendency among thinkers was to dismantle rather than to construct. Thus, one of the most imposing intellects of the fifteenth century – the tolerationist Cusanus – praised 'docta ignorantia', 'learned ignorance' – and Lorenzo Valla, in confirming Cusanus's doubts as to the authenticity of the Donation of Constantine, undermined the Church's claims to temporal power. In these ways philosophic scepticism and scholarly criticism, rather than philosophic assurance and scholarly assertion, were becoming the rule in the most fashionable intellectual quarters.

This was the mental climate in which Erasmus developed. It is worth noting that Erasmus worked within strict, self-imposed intellectual limitations. His work has four principal characteristics: literary scholarship; social and ecclesiastical criticism; moral counsel; and style. The first category is represented pre-eminently by his Greek New Testament, by his patristic editions and by his work on secular classical authors; the second category is represented by popular satirical works like *Encomium Moriae* (*In Praise of Folly*) and the attributed *Julius Exclusus* (*Pope Julius shut out of Heaven*); the third category is represented by edifying works like *Enchiridion Militis Christiani* (*Christian Soldier's Manual*); and the fourth characteristic is present throughout the Erasmian corpus. We should note that in all of Erasmus's vast output there is nothing approaching an intellectual system. There is an attitude, a cast of mind, but it is minimalist: to what minimum and original elements can we reduce Christianity? The search for the origins took Erasmus to the New Testament and to the Church Fathers; the quest for the universally accepted human wisdom took him to the classics; his emphasis on the certainties of conduct rather than the vagaries of credence led him into social criticism and moral counsel; and style lent dignity to the commonplace. This whole anti-system led, directly and indirectly, to tolerance: directly because Erasmus consciously saw tolerance, linked to love, as the essence of Christianity, indirectly because his reductionism raised the level of rational criticism but futher lessened the possibilities of rational assent.

It is arguable that, while Erasmus recognised the necessary connection between tolerance and Christian charity, he fundamentally misunderstood the nature of the Christian religion if he believed that it was a religion of tolerance. The essence of the Christian religion is to be dogmatic and intolerant, to seek precise and exclusive confessional formulae. This is the case historically: the story of St John's flight from the Ephesus bathhouse[3] to avoid the dangers of heresy casts doubt on the popular idea that credal authoritarianism came as a late and corrupt development in Christian history. Christianity is also essentially, as well as historically, intolerant – as befits a religion relying on faith for salvation. We cannot even say that the ethical content of Christianity bypasses the need for exact definitions of belief, for acceptable ethics are themselves seen as being founded on correct thinking. The tendency for Christianity to stress the need for orthodoxy of belief increased in the Reformation, for the insistence on faith *alone* as the means of salvation underlined the need for correct faith.

The decline of systematic theology which was summed up in the career of Erasmus was a false start to that most astoundingly theological and dogmatic century, the sixteenth. The century saw a revival of Catholic Thomism spreading out from the Spanish universities; it saw the development of Evangelical and Reformed scholastic systems; above all it saw from Calvin's pen a majestic statement of systematic Augustinism, the *Institutes of the Christian Religion*. With the renaissance of theology, with the revival of belief in the capacity of the human mind, albeit through revelation, to be correct, came a revival of intolerance. The first victims were 'charity' and the civilised personal relations which Erasmus exalted. The virulence of Luther, the vindictiveness of Calvin and Paul IV towards theological foes are surface signs that in the decades after 1517 Erasmian values – the preference for ethics over dogma – were not regarded highly. The careers of some of Erasmus's intellectual disciples show how his programme of peace and toleration fell in ruins: Zwingli, with all his Erasmian Greek learning, turned violently against the Anabaptists; Calvin, whose edition of Seneca had established his Erasmian credentials, sought to suppress all dissenters; Thomas More and Reginald Pole put aside their Erasmianism to act as agents of Tudor persecution. If the Erasmian ideal was deserted by scholars, it was even less honoured by princes. It is true that, when it suited them, kings posed as humanist monarchs – founded schools, repressed superstition, sponsored learning; however, when the ideal seemed to conflict with reasons of state, no monarch ever heeded an Erasmian plea for peace or toleration. In politics and intellectual life genuine tolerationists went into short supply in the decades after the division of Christendom. After mid-century the irenicists were reduced to theologically illiterate survivors of an earlier age, like Catherine de'Medici; or ambiguously placed Catholics like Michel de L'Hôpital and Emperor Maximillian; or *politiques* like Queen Elizabeth and William of Orange.

In these circumstances, with the climate for Christian variety growing less favourable with every decade, radical religious dissent rose to the surface with a vitality unparalleled since the fourteenth century. How could religious radicalism possibly survive? Clearly the sixteenth century witnessed the achievement of formal measures of civil toleration, most notably the 1555 Peace of Augsburg in Germany and the 1598 Edict of Nantes in France. However, although Erasmian ideas may have been borrowed to adorn such concessions, measures like the

Augsburg truce and the Nantes Edict were imposed upon political authorities by political necessity and military main force. Acts of toleration, these measures were not acts of tolerance, but rather the outcome of exhaustion and political weakness. Such measures of toleration – in the German Reich, in France – followed paralysing civil wars, which had been commenced, but which had failed, to end religious disunion within national communities. These major European internal treaties of religious peace, because they recognised stalemates based on force, never conferred any advantage on radical groupings. In Germany the religious peace of 1555 recognised the right, not of individuals, but of territories and estates, to adhere to the Catholic or Evangelical religion only; in France the religious peace of 1598 recognised the inescapable right of the Huguenot coalition to exist. How little of tolerance there was in the Nantes Edict, how much it admitted the temporary weakness of the state, is shown by the determination with which the resurgent Bourbon monarchy sought in the seventeenth century to undermine, and finally to cancel, the Edict's provisions.

The major public toleration treaties, then, emerged out of state weakness, and gave permission for no more than two, relatively conservative, forms of Christianity to exist in a given state. However, another political possibility of religious toleration began to emerge with the rise of the modern state. This possibility lay not so much in treaties between monarchies and autonomous, religiously oriented political and military estates; the possibility lay rather in grants of toleration on the part of states towards informal religious groupings. These concessions, though they recognised political necessity, could work in such a way as ultimately to strengthen the states which granted them, to secularise those states and, in making them religiously comprehensive and neutral, to modernise them, to broaden their bases and to free them from the sectarian insurgency which was the chief bane of European political societies in the sixteenth century. It is a striking fact that some of the more effective of early modern European states – Brandenburg-Prussia[4] and the Netherlands, for example – offered relatively generous toleration terms to a variety of religious communities. In the Dutch Republic we see that quite radical groups – the Mennonites, for instance – were beneficiaries of the Toleration clause (XIII)[5] of the 1579 Union of Utrecht – the state's constitution – and we may argue that this republic was confirmed in its existence by conferring toleration on a number of religious denominations which were, in the process of being tolerated, induced to endorse the state. Thus the possibility of a highly authoritative impersonal state presiding over a number of pacific religious groupings in a pluralist society may seem to have been latent in the establishment of the Dutch Republic. In that republic religious toleration was the expression of a profound, and perhaps Erasmian, reluctance to signal clerical dominance over the state by carrying out the policies of repression which the Calvinist ministry demanded. In the long run religious toleration in the United Provinces was the guarantee of the stability of the republic, although initially the grant of toleration was a consequence of the insecurity of the polity, for this new and illegitimate state was threatened from birth by the world's greatest military power, Spain, while only a minority of the republic's population adhered to its official confession, Calvinism.[6] For that reason even the Roman Catholic element in the Dutch population had, tacitly, to be indulged. In that sense the religious toleration established in the Dutch Republic in 1579 was, like the religious truces of Nantes and Augsburg, an expression of the fragility of the state; none the less, through securing the support of the religious communities by defending them from repression, the Dutch Republic purchased political stability; by treating the members of the religious communities as innocuous, the Dutch state converted them into harmless citizens. This is evident in the terms on which Catholicism survived in the Netherlands. Traditionally, Catholicism was accustomed to a public, 'church-type' existence, and its liturgy reflected the established position it had enjoyed everywhere in the West before the Reformation; the clandestine Catholicism of the Netherlands lacked the demonstrative and triumphalist ritual of baroque Catholicism, but this liturgical mutilation signified the transformation of North Netherlands Catholicism from a church into a sect or a denomination; the members of this denomination did not in the early modern period enjoy full civil rights and were thus disabled from giving the state their full service or unequivocal allegiance, but neither were Dutch Catholics, for all their numbers, given the motive that sixteenth-century Huguenots had for taking arms against the state so as to secure either religious toleration or confessional ascendancy.[7]

It is necessary to appreciate the limits placed upon religious toleration in the United Provinces. Popular and clerical forces apart, the States General and local magistrates sometimes suppressed unorthodox books, while local magistrates banned religious radicals.[8] The Netherlands had a vital mediaeval tradition of piety, and in the seventeenth century this tradition continued to produce separatist movements, though this process conflicted with the drive of the Dutch Reformed Church to occupy the position of a national establishment of religion. This conflict between a national, state-supported church and purist Christian movements was also to the fore in England, where, the Separatists complained, the socially inclusive nature of the state denomination muted the godly discipline which was the hallmark of a true church. In this way, national churches, observing relatively lax and average ethical standards, necessarily engender dissident fundamentalist movements, though, of course, the fundamentalist movements are also bound to conflict with the basic aim of the all-inclusive state church. In the same way Jansenism was a separatist protest against the generally acceptable moral standards and confessional discipline with which the Jesuits equipped the restored public Catholicism of Bourbon France.

We ought to consider post-Restoration, and indeed post-Revolution, England as a state rather like France in its basic assumptions about the relationships of state, church and Dissent. A public and exclusive church was, for many, not just in France, but in England and the Netherlands too, a guarantee of the holiness and safety of the state. Unable as yet to justify its existence in merely human and material terms, the English state, after 1689, still took action against the forces of Dissent, blasphemy, heresy and non-Christianity which, it was believed, threatened society's good standing with regard to a deity who was still generally viewed as being intimately concerned with daily human affairs. Because the early modern English state was, from our vantage-point, primitive, because it lacked adequate natural legitimation and relied on Christian sanctions to keep subjects in order, for these reasons the English state was obliged to support the Christian religion. By the Toleration Act of 1689 it might appear that the state freed itself from its exclusive commitment to the Church of England by adopting a generalised form of the Christian religion as the approved confession. Certainly 'the Toleration', as contemporaries labelled it, was not to be construed as a measure permitting non-Christianity; indeed some public moralists felt that most of the Protestant varieties of the Christian faith upheld the moderate and civilising morality that society required. Therefore, subjects 'of tender conscience', though freed from the traditional requirement of attending Anglican services, were directed to attend the Meeting Houses of their choice,[9] and in that sense the Toleration Act actually gave the backing of the law to the Dissenting churches. It would seem, then, that under the Toleration English Nonconformists as a body came together to form what the Roman Empire would have known as a *religio licita*, a cult licensed by the state. In return, it has often been said, the Dissenters became quiescent citizens and rid themselves of the frictional and politically unacceptable characteristics of their Stuart ancestors. And yet the Dissenters were very far from being absorbed into the mainstream of post-Revolution English life; they remained, in name and fact, Nonconformists – dissenters from the state-supported Establishment, membership of which was vital to qualify a person as a complete English citizen. The Toleration Act upheld the exclusion of the Dissenters from the full benefits of citizenship. First of all, and like all laws, the Toleration had to be interpreted, and many law officers, regarding the measure as a temporary licence for schism, chose to put a strict interpretation on the Act – refusing, for example, to extend its benefits to new Dissenting growths like the Methodists in the eighteenth century. Secondly, although the state after 1689 gave guarded approval to variants of Protestant Christianity, it was *only* the Protestant Trinitarian, Christian religion that was indulged, and state and church retained both the right to define Protestant Christianity and the power to withhold the Act's concessions from groups not qualifying as Protestant Christians according to the official criteria; from that point of view it is true to say that the Toleration Act gave the state the right to persecute for religion.[10] Thirdly, and most important, the Act did not lift the barriers to the Dissenters' enjoyment of basic civil and educational rights and its very title emphasised the fact that it set out merely to exempt 'their majesties' Protestant subject dissenting from the Church of England from the penalties of certain laws.

The grudging and circumscribed nature of the provisions of the Toleration Act reflected the fact that the measure was passed at a time of acute crisis for the state in the aftermath of a revolution in the succession to the throne. The Puritan faction had revealed its military and political power between 1642 and 1660, and nearly thirty years of repression since the Restoration had failed to destroy this 'alien' force in English society. Certainly the new Williamite regime had to outbid the late King James for the support of the Dissenters, but the Toleration Act was not, unlike the Union of Utrecht, with its ingenuous toleration clause, the founding charter of the state; rather, like the Edict of Nantes, it marked a nadir of political instability and the notorious fact that for the second time in forty years the English had rid themselves of a king. It was likely that, as in the French case, the slow recovery of political stability in England would be attended by attempts to revert to religious homogeneity in the commonwealth. If the Revolution, and its concomitant the Toleration, symbolised political fragility, it was not surprising that proponents of authoritarianism should seek to minimise both the Revolution and the Toleration. Of this school of thought, in the conservative reaction under Queen Anne, Henry Sacheverell and Francis Atterbury were leading spokesmen.[11] We might think that these ideologues were wrong, and limited in their thinking: they thought that an effective state could endorse only one church, whereas it appears to us that a neutral state, upholding civil equality for all, is more soundly established, less open to question, in all more 'modern', than a state tied to the apron strings of a monopolistic church. This is true: the deliberate religious objectivity of the United States had been a major factor in ensuring the remarkable degree of American political stability over the last two centuries. But if religious toleration is to underpin a government such toleration must be granted rather than exacted, and is only appropriate in a modern, non-traditionalistic type of regime. Thus, the late Stuart and Georgian opponents of religious toleration, who were also proponents of forceful government as they saw it, showed some understanding of the highly traditionalistic nature of English institutions in the pre-modern period. At least they realised that a religious monarchy governing a stratified rural society was effective – on a woefully low level from a modern point of view – for as long as it preserved religious unanimity, and that consequently measures like the Toleration were deplorable admissions of momentary state weakness. Like republican government, religious toleration was a leap in the dark, cutting the state adrift from its mediaeval traditions, sanctions and limitations, though in fact making possible the erection of the literally absolute modern state. When English life and institutions were transformed in the nineteenth century, an almost total degree of religious toleration was handed out by a state unimaginably more powerful, for all its liberalism, than any of its predecessors. The modern leviathan, self-sufficient, omnicompetent, entirely secular, is effective enough to guarantee religious and ideological diversity and derives some of its effectiveness from the guarantees it is able to maintain. In comparison, early modern monarchies – even the monarchy of Louis XIV in all its splendour – were puppets of mediaeval tradition and of clerical and popular religious enthusiasm.

How bound the eighteenth-century state was by inhibiting conventions is shown by the accepted view that it could not employ many categories of citizens. Governments were generally tied to the employment of a hereditary caste, defined in part religiously. A conservative like Swift found it an absurd proposition that the state should employ religious Dissenters: 'As if places would go a-begging, unless *Brownists*, *Familists*, *Sweet-Singers*, *Quakers*, *Anabaptists*, and *Muggletonians*, would take them off our hands.'[12] The Baptists, of course, remained, with the Independents and the Presbyterians, one of the three main pillars of Georgian Dissent; the Muggletonians maintained an existence of a sort down to the twentieth century; but for many it was the Quakers who most authentically and most numerously represented the old, mid-seventeenth-century tradition of extreme enthusiasm. Plans, albeit abortive, for ecclesiastical comprehension in the late seventeenth century had been in part designed to detach radicals like the Quakers from 'respectable' Dissenters, especially the Presbyterians. Such radicals did not share the reasonable placid Christianity which liberal Anglican advocates of toleration presupposed; whether the Quakers were Christians at all was at best an open question; weighty Anglican opinion, not restricted to demagogic zealots like Henry Sacheverell, and not limited either to the time of Tory-

Anglican reaction under Anne, considered the Quakers – the largest and best organised of the surviving radical puritan groups – to be outside the pale of toleration.

In 1722 Parliament debated a measure, which was actually successful, to relieve Quakers of the burden of civil oaths. The clerical contribution to this debate in the House of Lords is deeply illuminating: it tells us that the attitude of mind necessary to make the formal Toleration work in practice was withheld by the most senior Church leaders from the Quakers. Even White Kennett of Peterborough, who went out on a limb to defend the Quakers' right to affirm, was capable of describing these sectarians as 'Reprobates'.[13] The two primates were much more consistent that White Kennett in their attitudes to Quakers. Dawes of York may be discounted as a strident Anglican supremacist, though his views enjoyed large-scale clerical support, as an anti-Quaker petition from London clergymen shows: 'the Quakers', said the London ministers, '"pretend to deny the payment of Tythes upon a Principle of Conscience, and therefore . . . may be under strong Inducements to ease their Consciences in that Respect by violating them in another'. This was in fact a traditional Anglican attitude to Dissenters: tender conscience, it was believed, was a convenient mask for self-interest; in particular the Quakers were not the moral and truthful people they claimed to be – 'their Interest', thought Archbishop Wake of Canterbury, 'only will clash with their Veracity'.[14]

The unbridgeable gap between Quaker and Anglican thinking was that Quakers, albeit unconsciously, were agitating for a purely secular state and society, while Anglicans cherished the ideal of a sacral commonwealth, attended by constant supernal endorsements; thus the London clergy found it an intolerable proposition 'that Justice may be only administered, and Government supported without the Intervention of any solemn Appeal to God'.

Society was Christian, Quakers, in their mendacity, did not uphold a Christian social morality, and, if this were not enough to put them beyond the bounds of tolerability, they were not judged to be Christians; taking baptismal orthodoxy as a criterion which the Church possessed in ruling who was, and who was not, Christian, the Quakers were held to be 'a Set of Men, who renounce the divine Institutions of Christ; particularly that by which the faithful are initiated into his Religion, and denominated Christians, and who cannot . . . be deem'd worthy of that sacred Name'.

Presented in these ways before England's highest tribunal, the views which Anglican ministers took of a typical radical religious movement, the Quakers, can be described as stereotyped and deeply prejudiced. Both junior and senior clergymen insisted that the Quakers were not Christians – not 'recognised as amongst the gatherings of Christian people' – and therefore hardly covered by the Toleration: 'as they renounce the Institutions of *Christ*, so have they not given the Evidence by Law required of their Belief in his Divinity'. It followed that the argument that Quakers were 'well affected to the Government' was 'a Position of which we have some doubt', for the Quakers were viewed as 'a particular Sect of Men who refuse to serve the State either as civil Officers or Soldiers', who, if they were further indulged, would 'become as bad Subjects as Christians'.[15]

This last point was, at least in part, a serious one. Though the state's need to press the involuntary into military service was an index of its still rudimentary moral and financial effectiveness, it was a serious charge that Quakers refused to serve – though the experience of the Dutch Republic with the pacifist Mennonites showed how this problem could be circumvented through fiscal means. As for the point that Quakers 'refused' civil office, few Anglicans would countenance such a relaxation of the Test and Corporation Acts as would allow the Quakers to serve. Given that England had a non-Anglican minority, the public service, especially in the borough corporations, was impoverished before 1828 by the deliberate refusal, thoroughly supported by Church opinion, to enlist Dissenters. But public and military service was only part of the problem, the other part of which was the Dissenters' attitude to government and society which penal laws and prejudiced official opinion called forth. The more victimised and execrated a religious group was, the more estranged it was in its view of the civil and religious establishment. Thus the Anglican doubt that the Quakers were 'well affected to the Government' was, in fact, well founded, though of course disaffection, an inert but basic Quakers stance, was a reaction to the official view of the movement as inherently disaffected. The primary expression of Quaker disaffection was permanent hostility to the Church, though as the laws made it plain that this Church was inseparable from state and society, so state and society were necessarily involved in the Quaker repudiation of the Establishment.

Just as majority Anglican opinion retained a hostile stereotype of the Quakers, so Quakers preserved a highly unfavourable image of the Church of England. In neither case was the stereotype completely inaccurate. Anglican opinion was right in seeing the Quakers as a perverse, un-neighbourly, anti-social, alienated and disaffected sort of people: the laws and institutions of England made them so. And Quaker views of the Church as a bitter, exploitative, coercive, impersonal, proud and unyielding institution were close to the mark: the institutions and laws of England – and especially the 'Alliance' (to use Warburton's term) of church and state – forced the Church of England into forms of behaviour most befitting a department of state. All the same, the Quakers spoke of the Church as if it were a religious institution – though not truly a Christian one. Fox's language about the Church was deliberately dismissive and deflationary – the church building was a mere 'steeplehouse' – but a tendency arose for such language to become customary and formal. However, new life was breathed into the Quaker anti-Anglican vocabulary by persecution after the Restoration; in 1675, for example, the Lancaster Monthly Meeting, which covered a wide area of north Lancashire, denounced 'the priests of Baal, bloody lords who have their hands in the blood of our brethren and who is the cause of all this banishment of our brethren and hath spoiled so many of their goods, casting into prison . . .'. This is an indication of the scriptural source of Quaker anti-Anglican language and thought: if the Quakers viewed themselves as the true Israel of old, – in 1675 Lancashire Quakers compared themselves to Abraham among the Egyptians and Canaanites – then the Church was analogous to the idolators and oppressors ranged against the chosen people; on the other hand, if the Quakers chose to see themselves as the new Israel of Christians in the New Testament, then the Church was the Jewish priesthood which persecuted Jesus and the martyrs. Now it might appear that this thought and language was appropriate to the Quaker view of the Church of England in the period of the 'great persecution' between the Restoration of the monarchy in 1660 and the Toleration Act of 1689. It might seem, on the other hand, that in so far as the Toleration Act brought recognition to the Quakers, and their consequent adaptation to English life and society, so such vituperation was decreasingly appropriate. As we have seen, however, the Toleration Act made only small adjustments to the position of radical Dissenters, and yet the view of this statute as a watershed – on the one side oppression, on the other acceptance – is still sometimes advanced. A modern historian of Quakers believes that after the Toleration Act the Friends benefited from a 'religious liberty that came to them with the new eighteenth century, offering the Society a place in English life . . . a greatly strengthened position before the law'. As a consequence of this toleration Quakers moved into a tranquil relationship with state and society and were de-radicalised: 'they were no longer the prophets of the common man . . . their social note was muted . . .'[16]

John Sykes is saying, then, that the lot of Quakers improved with the Toleration, and the eighteenth century. As a precondition of toleration the world's hostility towards them dropped away, and in return their hostility to the world and their social radicalism disappeared. Now these generalisations may indeed apply to a small minority of London-based Quakers, and to the progressive circles in which they moved. However, we have seen that, deep into the eighteenth century,

Anglican opinion remained unreconciled to the Quakers. We shall see that lay opinion remained anti-Quaker too; and we shall see that, both in the aftermath of the Toleration Act, and into the eighteenth century, Quakers – and with good reason – remained bitterly hostile to the world around them.

For Dissenters in general and Quakers in particular neither the Toleration Act nor the dawn of the eighteenth century achieved very much in mitigating the underprivileged position of the sectarians. Indeed, the early eighteenth century witnessed political measures, such as the Occasional Conformity, and Schism Acts, which were frankly designed to extirpate Dissent. Meanwhile, whether or not the Church party – the Tories – were in power, there was no intention, either in the Toleration Act or in subsequent political discussions, to restore to the Dissenters the political rights that had been taken away from them by the 1661 Corporations Act. It is true that during the years of the Whig ascendancy in English politics evasions of this Act were permitted, though with less frequency and generosity than is sometimes imagined.[17] Above all, evasions of the Corporations Act were backdoor measures, unacceptable to the exact Nonconformist conscience, and they were attempts to get round a statute kept on the statute book precisely to point out to the Dissenters their inferior legal condition. Exclusion from English social life was also the official rule for Dissenters in such matters as legal capacity, higher education, professions, the armed forces and the trading corporations. Indeed the special position of the Church was carefully explained and justified to the Dissenters – by so liberal a thinker as Bishop Burnet[18] – in terms which demonstrated, albeit obscurely, that their own precarious position in the national life would be completely destroyed unless they respected all the rights of the Establishment. Thus, though the eighteenth-century state could guarantee to do nothing for Dissent beyond what was done in 1689, Dissenters were expected fully to support Anglicanism as citizens. They were expected, for example, to observe Anglican holy days. Above all, Dissenters at large were required to pay to maintain *Ecclesia Anglicana* through the tithe levy.

In putting forward proposals for toleration in the later seventeenth century the Independent spokesman John Owen agreed that the financial maintenance of the Church would have to be a reserved item.[19] Similarly, in the eighteenth century, it was clear that amongst the desiderata for any successful application for easing the position of Nonconformists there would have to be total respect for the finances of the Established Church. Though acceptance of tithing was expected from Dissenters in general, it can hardly have been given whole-heartedly, and for Quakers it was a concession never at any point made. Tithes made up the central area of collision between the Quakers community and a state which throughout the eighteenth century remained essentially committed to the principle of a formal, non-voluntary and universal maintenance of the national Church. Quakers appreciated that there were particular high points in persecutions for tithes: the year 1705, for example, was 'a time of great suffering and spoiling of goods with many'; but in point of fact the 'old and grand oppression of tithes' was never lifted in this period and tithe prosecutions went on throughout the century. We need to appreciate that in speaking of tithe actions as 'sufferings' Quakers were not using exaggerated language: failure to pay could result in imprisonment, and imprisonment had been known to result in death. But in fact tithe levy involved injustice at every turn: damage was done to property during distraints, levies, especially of livestock, were sometimes higher than the 10 per cent allowed by law, excessive costs were granted against Quakers in the courts, and vital household, shop and do.nestic manufacturing goods were confiscated in lieu of trivial tithe sums. Tithes, then, were onerous, and the processes attending on their levy had the effect of demonstrating to Quakers that every man's hand, or at least every powerful man's hand, was against them. Among the lay tithe impropriators who burdened Lancashire Quakers in the early eighteenth century were some of the North's leading landlords: Lord Brandon, the Duke of Devonshire, Lady Clifton, Lord Dunmore, Lord Molineux, and so on. Such an array of grandees showed the Quakers that their enemy was not always the Church of England, but – because of the numerous tithe impropriations that had taken place, especially in the North, at the Reformation – the landed nobility and gentry of England, the very leaders of politics and society. Some of the Lancashire Quakers' opponents on the tithe question were lay impropriators of tithe, like Lord Dunmore, MP for Wigan, and Sir William Lowther of Holker Hall, MP for Lancaster between 1702 and 1705. Some Quakers hoped 'to make interest with the Members of Parliament' to ease their burdens. However, even from the point of view of their economic interests as landlords, Members of Parliament like Lowther and Dunmore were diametrically opposed to the Quaker position.[20]

It was because the law, the Church interest and the economic concerns of the landed classes upheld tithes that Quakers, certainly in the first half of the eighteenth century, could expect no effective relief from these burdens. Indeed it was clear that on this issue the very law of England set its face against them and maintained injustice – as Israel Fell of Lancashire found in undergoing four years' imprisonment for a shilling tithe.[21]

The laws, the law enforcement agencies, the gentry and nobility of England conspired to make Quakers pay a heavy and degrading levy which, in origin and still in main part, supported the Church of England. Quakers responded, first of all, by attacking the Church, using an unmeasured and, indeed, subversive language. Their attitude to the Church of England, the main sacral and ceremonial prop of a highly religious society, was neither cordial nor tolerant, but was a response to the Establishment's intolerant attitude to the Quakers. In condemning the Church, Quakers were condemning the vital bond of an hierarchical society; they went on, as we shall see, to condemn that society. As for the Church, Lancashire Quakers felt that its constant demands for tithes stood to its condemnation. These exactions upheld 'the Antichristian ministry of our age', a ministry made up of 'hirelings and such as woe was pronounced against'; the Anglican clergy was an order 'such as God never sent nor commanded, who make merchandise of souls and follow the way of Balaam'. Quakers made extensive use of this kind of scriptural language to attack the Church, and in particular they employed the New Testament's polarity of law and freedom to castigate the Church: a 'Levitical priesthood abolished by that of Christ'; above all, Quakers used an apocalyptic language in their repudiation of tithes and the Church: tithes were 'of Antichrist, and altogether contrary to a Christian principle now in these gospel times . . . that popish institution will in time be taken off . . . a free minister is come, to wit Jesus Christ . . . tithes ought not to be paid in this glorious dispensation we are under, I being in some measure made sensible that He is come who is the substance of all'. Thus tithes and the Church stood condemned from the radical vantage-points of eschatology and Christian liberationism; the Establishment was also found wanting from the point of view of church history: the pre-Reformation origin of tithes was pointed out – they 'had their rise in the night of apostasy and time of popery' – but, even more corrosively, Quakers thought that tithes destroyed the cherished identity of the Church of England as a church of the Reformation: 'an antichristian custom introduced by the Pope in the dark night of apostasy, and continued by those who, notwithstanding their specious pretence of Reformation, are found in the same spirit with them who set up these idolatrous practices by the spirit and power of Antichrist'. Indeed, so far from being a reformed Church, the Church of England was not a church at all, but rather 'that formal worship and house called the church' or the 'church so-called'.[22]

There were important differences between the Anglican perception of the Quakers and the Quaker perception of the Church. The official view of the separatists was founded on tradition, law and political conservatism. The Quaker view of the Establishment was based on Scripture, private illumination and an appreciation of the social injustice of tithes. Yet, despite these differences of approach, there was this similarity between the opinions which each of these rival religious societies held of the other: while the Churchmen denied that the Quakers were Christians, or proper beneficiaries of the Toleration, the Quakers denied that the Church of England was a church. The Anglican attitude was based on the fact that Churchmen were still monopolistic and exclusive in their aspirations, and instinctively unreconciled to the development of a pluralist society in which a number of mutually tolerant denominations might coexist harmoniously. On the other hand, the Quakers, like other sects,[23] were deeply intolerant of the official Church, were alienated from the laws and government which upheld the Church, and were in general estranged from the social order whose values the Church expressed and supported.

Since the Restoration the Quakers had been a world-rejecting people, and their sense of hostile isolation easily survived the Revolution and the Toleration. Their social exclusiveness governed most of their thinking: the purposes of schooling, for example, was that 'youth may be preserved from the corruption and looseness that is in the world'. Ethics were a matter of avoidance of the world, for immorality came from 'following the vanities of this present world', and the lesson was 'neither to have fellowship or a familiarity with the world's people'. In fact, the sense of withdrawal from the world received conscious sectarian expression: in Lancashire 'all young people of our sect' were warned against 'fashioning themselves according to the customs and ways of the world'. Such basic suspicion of the social world continued up to the end of the seventeenth century, and into the eighteenth century the old biblical image of estrangement – Israel in Egypt – remained vivid: 'if we partake with them of their sins we shall partake with them of their plague'.[24]

The basic Quaker stance of hatred of the world was clearly expressed in the Society's vigilance over mixed marriages. Through impure marriages not only did the Friends suffer contamination from the sinful world at large, but they also submitted themselves to the ministrations of the hated Church of England: 'married by a hireling priest, who for money can in unrighteousness join people together', was a typical accusation against those 'marrying out'. Hatred for the world certainly did not preclude mission to it; indeed world-hatred was the stimulus for a missionary assault on society. In turn, the Quaker missionary imperative made Anglicans more suspicious of the Quakers: it was feared that statutory ease for the Friends, 'granted to a People already . . . too numerous, may . . . contribute to multiply their Sect'.[25]

The fear that Quakers were energetic proselytisers was not completely unfounded – Friends retained a lively sense of mission – though the Anglican fear that easement would increase the flow of conversions was illusory. It may seem strange to say that such an aloof group as the Georgian Quakers preserved a missionary drive, but Christian mission has nothing to do with human agreeability and the Quakers, in their historical reflections, associated mission to the social world with repudiation by the major part of that world. Nor was it surprising that the Quakers were spurned. Blunt and spikey, in an age of stylised social behaviour they upheld an aggressive incivility that was neither quaint nor acceptable. They deliberately abstained from popular sports, feasts and recreations and so sometimes appeared to be bad neighbours. But this social introversion was the expression of the fact that when Quakers considered the world – and especially the tradi- tional hierarchical village world of squire, parson and populace – they had before their eyes a picture of animosity and, indeed, of savage persecution. In the 1690s – in the very shadow of the Toleration – Quakers decided to recall the origins of their movement, and espec- ially to dwell on the climate of antagonism in which 'Truth' took root. Reviewing the first planting of their faith in uncouth areas like Furness in north Lancashire, they recalled how the 'rude multitude', egged on by justices of the peace, army officers and parsons, dealt as roughly with the Quaker missionaries as, a century later, the village mobs were to do with the early Wesleyans. Looking back on the earliest history of their movement, post-Toleration Quakers emphasised the general hostility that greeted its inception and took the opportunity to restate their loathing for the ritual centre of their English world: the 'evil worship' of the Church of England.[26]

Conflict with the world was thus imprinted on the Quaker memory and it remained fundamental to the Quaker outlook. Crowning that society which the Quakers shunned was the Church, which they abhor- red, and the state, which they suspected. We saw how it is often taken for granted that the Toleration Act and the coming of the 'age of reason' between them emancipated the Quakers. Against this view we must appreciate that after the passage of the Toleration Act, and well into the eighteenth century, Quakers encountered conflict with the state over religious oaths. For Anglicans, oaths, like tithes, were the badge of a Christian commonwealth. The ideal of a Christian society collided with Quaker perfectionism and separatism, and oaths were a focus of the collision. *Was* English society Christian? If so, religious oaths had real value. If it were not – if no whole society *could* be Christian – oaths were a blasphemous misuse of sacred sanctions. These were issues – concerning the very nature of civil society, whether it was sacred or secular – which underlay the dispute over oaths that was carried on between the Quaker community and the English gov- ernment and church for more than thirty years after the 'Toleration'. The successive forms of affirmation offered to Quakers by Parliament in the immediate post-Revolution period and down to 1722 were unsatisfactory to the general membership of the Society of Friends in that, however watered down these affirmations were, they resembled oaths in that they involved the deity in civil transactions. An indication of Friends' radical obduracy with regard to what the state had to offer is the frequent refusal to have any Affirmations Act at all – a clear indication of a refusal to compromise with the state over a point of religious principle. Some Quaker Meetings in Lancashire found Scripture literalism more compelling than any pressure to arrive at an accommodation with the government which, after all, upheld the Toleration: 'the form of sound words layed down by Christ instead of an oath is that which we ought to stand by and to, and not go from it'; the mood of Lancashire – though not alone – was unaccommodating, fundamentalist and confrontationary: 'That "yea, yea" and "nay, nay" ought to be stood by and too, and that nothing more be offered or accepted to or from the government to ease from the burden of oaths but what truly is commanded with Christ's command.'[27]

There is in this sort of Quaker thinking an intractability, a refusal to enter the arena of give-and-take, which marked the Quakers out as difficult subjects. Their wish to suffer, essential to their New Testament Christianity, made them seek new opportunities for collision with a government which remained understandably nervous about the loyalties of its subjects. In 1708, in a statement which could easily have been read as an expression of disloyalty, Lancashire Friends ruled that the Abjuration Act, designed by means of an oath to test the loyalty of office-holders to the Protestant Succession, 'was not safe for Friends to accept of', and they went on to repudiate the compromises which their more accommodating London agencies were proposing to accept from the government. The willingness to undergo hardship rather than to give full support to the government was stronger in Lancashire than it was in the London-based Meeting for Sufferings, but the martyr complex was stronger in the provinces in general than it was in the metropolis. Sufferings, indeed, established Christian credentials and identified Georgian Friends with the martyr-heroes of the first period: 'Friends', said the Lancashire Quaker women in 1721, 'are clear, and suffer as formerly.' Their highly guarded attitude to the establishment, their exaltation of conscience above citizenship, were amply repaid by a government which, in attitude and action, continued to regard them – and rightly – as unsatisfactory and unreliable subjects. Clearly the Christian egalitarianism of their behaviour – the refusal of 'hat-honour', the levelling 'thou', practices challenging the hierarchical values of Georgian society – cannot have endeared Quakers to governments, but the main objection to Quakers had to do with the nature of English government and concerned the Quakers' repudiation of the state's Church. In arguing against the repeal of the Test and Corporation Acts which excluded Dissenters in general from political office, Sir Robert Walpole, often considered a liberal statesman, put forward his view 'that all men should be excluded from executive positions who think it their duty to destroy' the Established Church. We might think that Walpole's view of the Dissenters was false and out-of-date – that it would have been appropriate only to the militant Puritanism of the sixteenth and seventeenth centuries. However, the very fact that Dissenters were agitating for a repeal of the restrictive laws was proof that they did intend to 'destroy' the position of the Church as the only fully acceptable form of religion in England. Walpole's public view of the Dissenters as a whole – one of latent suspicion – was conditioned by his membership of the Church of England, which he made plain in speaking against the relief proposal in 1736: the first minister said he was 'a sincere member of the Church of England' and – clearly taking up the convention that Dissent was schism from the true national Church – he only wished the Nonconformists would be converted to it. Why did Walpole speak as he did – failing, it seems, to grant to the Dissenters the right to the integrity of their profession? The traditions of Walpole's party were pro-Dissent, he had given them benign assurances and their support had been invaluable to him in general elections. No doubt, as with Archbishop Wake of Canterbury, it could have been said of him that 'in his personal dealings with nonconformists . . . he always showed a spirit of comprehensive charity'. The answer to the puzzle is that the first minister's 'personal dealings' had nothing to do with the case, but that he occupied a formal public position which resembled that of the bishops in that it obliged him in his public capacity to support to the hilt the privileges of the Church. As Walpole himself put it, he believed that the exclusion of Nonconformists from public life was vital for the protection of the Church, which in turn upheld the stability of the government. If this were true, then it made sense to bar from public service the mass of Dissenters, who were unreconciled to the Church, and the Quakers in particular, who by their words and deeds proved themselves to be diametrically opposed to the special position – indeed to the very existence – of the public confession. And it was true that the state relied on the Church. Burke went so far as 'to lay it down as a fundamental of the Constitution, that the Church of England should be united and even identified with it'. Burke's historical and political theory assumed a self-evident fact of Georgian Whig politics: that successive regimes depended on the Church. They did so because of the myths of popery and the Revolution, and because bishops helped achieve majorities in the Lords and assisted with electoral work in the constituencies. But above all eighteenth-century governments toed the Church line because most English people belonged to the Church and because many preserved an atavistic loyalty towards it. We can see this in the large-scale and violent popular opposition against measures designed to make a small niche for Jews and Roman Catholics in English life; we even see it in the hysterical outcry against a calendar reform which gave the country a 'popish' dating system. Whether we look at George Fox's autobiographical recollections of popular persecution in the seventeenth century, or at the treatment doled out to many Methodist preachers in the eighteenth, we are aware of spontaneously generated popular hostility, and especially rural popular hostility, to dissident preachers. The hostility of the rural populace to evangelists may have arisen from simple fear of strangers and outsiders; but, in addition to this response, rural hostility to religious novelty – popular intolerance – was the expression of some degree of commitment to the Church of England as a defender of familiar folk ways and traditions; in opposition to these traditions both Quakerism and Methodism were rightly identified as variants of the persistent puritan offensive against the customs, recreations, rituals and work habits of rural England. Hanoverian governments learned that they had to defer to these manifestations of popular feeling. In doing so the English state revealed its inability as yet either to re-educate or police the community, its incompetence in creating the preconditions for orderly religious variety; in short, the state showed its responsiveness to the crudest expressions of popular prejudice and thus demonstrated its real fragility.[28]

The expression of the compact between governments and the Church was the retention on the statute book of discriminative legislation intended to remind the Dissenters of their second-class citizenship. The effect of such discrimination on most Dissenters was not very grave in practice, though the absence of equality before the law for a large minority of Englishmen was a disability for the state. On the other hand, and even after the grant of an acceptable oath in 1722, Quakers, as we have seen, continued to experience an actual oppression – from tithes – and the government, because of the weight of conservative and Anglican opinion, was unable to relieve this oppression. Under-privileged groups, when they secure no assistance from the normal and secular mechanisms – the law, the state – for the correction of grievances, frequently turn to supernatural sources and, more specifically, to millenialism. Arising out of a sense of 'blockage' millenialism is, then, a reflection of the alienated, and indeed revolutionary, condition of a group. In the High Church reaction late in the reign of Queen Anne, it should not surprise us to see the

Quakers – with the routes to the solution of their problems closed by the hostility of the authorities – resorting to explicit millenial hopes. In what was a time of 'great suffering in many places', 'a bowing time to many', Quaker eschatology rose to the surface in a vision of 'the coming of Christ in the flesh, the Saviour of the world'. In fact, though, persecution, and the expectation of persecution, was not confined for Quakers to the High Church reaction of the last years of Anne, but was rather their permanent condition before the law, subject, as they remained, to the harassment of tithes. With the government, from whom alone they could expect relief, closed to their entreaties by its commitment to Anglicanism, the Quakers' sense of civil frustration continued to issue in an authentically seventeenth-century language of alienation, enthusiasm, egalitarianism and radical eschatology: 'We have cause to say that the arm of the Lord is not shortened at all, neither is His ear heavy that he cannot hear, but He is the same that ever He was unto His bowed-down people who are putting their trust in Him and waiting for His arising. He it is that bringeth down every exalted thing and raiseth the poor out of the dust, [cf. Luke 1: 51, 52] blessed be His name whose living presence hath been among His waiting ones at this time.'[29]

With regard to the Quakers, the state was losing an opportunity to enlarge its scope by dealing with the just grievances of a section of the community. The official attitude, articulated by Walpole and the bishops, was to view the Dissenters as dissidents, and the actions, or inaction, that flowed from this view turned perception into reality. Religious monopolism – the theory and practice of a state church – evoked an attitude of political and social dissent. The state and society which supported the claims of a monopolist church were involved in the disdain with which religious dissidents viewed the public confession. At the same time, the state's patronage of a single Christian communion invited other communions to challenge the privileged position of the approved church. Through treating religious dissenters as inferior citizens – especially by excluding them from public office – the state lost the service of Nonconformists, and it also failed to secure their complete loyalty to itself. Monopolistic religious laws were upheld, especially in France and England, because each of these countries, in the sixteenth or seventeenth century, had undergone a religiously motivated civil war in which the survival of the traditional religion and regime had been endangered, or temporarily destroyed, by religious disunion. The initial precariousness of the post-civil war regimes demanded, as Bishop Barlow argued in the case of England, a minimal degree of cultic toleration, at least until such a time as the state was effective enough to revoke such concessions made in a time of impotence, and revert to the exclusive maintenance of the publicly endorsed variant of Christianity, whether Gallico-Catholic or Anglican. In fact, the revival of religious monopolism, by perpetuating into the eighteenth century mediaeval assumptions about religion and society, and by extending the Reformation period's atmosphere of internecine war, restrained the state, impeded its growth. Shackled by irrelevant historical recollections of a single church, the national state, particularly in France and England, did not, before the end of the eighteenth century, move into the position of impartiality and supremacy which the recognition of religious pluralism affords the modern state. Sacral sanctions and their expression, legal intolerance, acted as a check on the development of the effective state, and governments that persecuted the religious conscience, especially in response to public opinion, were fundamentally insecure. It was for this reason that in the seventeenth century the proponents of modern, impersonal, rational and scientific government methods, for example, Locke and Pett, advocated toleration. In France Louis XIV's revocation of the Edict of Nantes was dressed up in all the garb of baroque absolutism, but it was in fact an act of obscurantist piety rather than act of state and it was for this reason that a professional statist of the stamp of Vauban deplored it. In the Dutch Republic statism and Erastianism went together with a belief in economic priorities as the political ideology of the conservators of the state, the *Regenten*. These men of affairs had considerable difficulty in holding at bay the intolerant clerical forces which commanded fanatical popular support and they found in the Reformed church a troublesome internal opposition to the progress of state-building. In France and England regimes existing 'by divine right' were much less effective than the purely natural and functional state organisations that came fully into being in the late eighteenth and early nineteenth centuries. Official, established churches *seemed* to endow national states with valuable rhetorical support and they conferred on states preternatural authentication; they appeared to consort best with kingship, though in fact they limited monarchy's scope, for they sometimes made rival *jure divino* claims which challenged those of monarchy itself. Thus the support which established churches gave to early modern states was bought at a heavy price, for the state was sometimes forced to follow clerical leadings, to accept moral restraints on its freedom of action and, above all, to act against innocuous, and indeed valuable, groups of subjects as if they were insurgents. Why then, did early modern western European states accept such inconvenient bargains with national churches? The answer is threefold. First, there is the fact that early modern statesmen preserved primitive assumptions about the divine direction of human affairs and felt that society's religious character guaranteed its preservation; such views were no doubt especially current in religious monarchies like that of England, where 'headship of the church' imposed strict limits on the monarch's actions. Secondly, churches in the Western states articulated mass popular religious feelings and superstitions to which the still insecure state had continually to defer; in late eighteenth-century Scotland a modest measure of relief for Roman Catholics had to be withdrawn because of popular feeling against it but in 1855, though the climate of popular anti-Catholic protest was still intense, the government was effective enough to secure the restoration of the Catholic hierarchy in Britain. The third part of the answer to the question about the apparent necessity for religious repession is that Dissenters were perceived to be enemies of civil concord. Indeed, for as long as Dissenters were viewed as subversives, and harassed accordingly, they were insurgents, battling, as the French Huguenots battled, against the state if necessary, for the right to exist. Granted the right to exist, to share civil and educational opportunities, to be free of the burden of supporting established churches, sectarian groups – markedly in the nineteenth and twentieth centuries, and pre-eminently in North America – have generally given complete support to the religiously neutral state. Toleration is a two-way process, and the government that tolerates religious variety is repaid by recognition of its secular demands on the part of religious sectarians. Indeed, it has probably been the goal of Christian radicals since the Reformation to erect the kind of religiously neutral state, with total separation of church and state, that has existed in the United States since its inception; thus in the area of politics it is certainly true to say that Protestantism – and in its most advanced form, separatism – carries out the de-sacralisation of human existence. If this has been the case – that Christian separatism leads to true pluralism – then the persecution of Dissenters, even of the kind built into England's Test and Corporation Acts – was based on the kind of false analysis of Dissent contained in Walpole's 1736 speech: that is to say, the stereotype that all Nonconformists were religious supremacists who threatened order through their ambition to impose their exclusive faiths on a recalcitrant commonwealth. Had this assumption remained valid, as in the high Reformation era it had been true of most orthodox Calvinists, it might have justified repression on the grounds of civil peace: 'You may be what devil you will there', wrote an observer of the Dutch Republic, 'so you be but peaceable.' In fact, political tolerance, which freed the state from the leading strings of clerical zealots and bigoted democracies, and which converted even Roman Catholics into placid donominationalists, also helped to distil out from the religious radicalism of the Reformation period its real quiescence with regard to the state – separatism's willingness to accord the modern impersonal liberal state its full rights by pursuing the policy of rendering to Caesar the things that are Caesar's.[30]

CHAPTER 5

Conclusion

The end of the Middle Ages saw a revolution in the religious life of Europe. This revolution was more complex than the simple setting-up of Protestantism alongside Catholicism. The religious revolution in fact involved the establishment of a number of different Christian churches. Earlier in Christian history alternatives to Catholicity had been put on an established footing. Such were the Donatist church, which flourished in North Africa in the fourth and fifth centuries, and the Albigensian or Cathar church of southern France in the Middle Ages. However, these established dissenting churches had been annihilated: the Donatist church eventually by Moslem conquest, and the Cathar church by a Frankish Catholic crusade. In the sixteenth and seventeenth centuries, on the other hand, new churches were founded, having before them a durable life-span. These new churches included not only the classical forms of the Reformation, such as Lutheranism and Calvinism, but also churches with a more fundamentalist and sectarian character. For example, in the sixteenth century Anabaptism, and in the seventeenth century Quakerism emerged as definite and enduring forms of Christian radicalism and sectarianism; indeed, even the radical millenarian group, the Muggletonians, preserved a shadowy existence from the mid-seventeenth to the twentieth. The sixteenth century witnessed the end of Catholicity; in the Middle Ages the single church for Western Christendom had encountered a number of protest movements: with the establishment of the Hussite Reformation in Bohemia in the fifteenth century a protest movement arose as a new church. The acceleration of that trend in the sixteenth century permanently affected the Catholic Church itself, for in losing its catholicity it joined a number of new churches which enjoyed control over limited areas of the West. Such new churches assumed the traditional position of the Catholic Church in areas of Europe, such as England, Scotland, North Germany and Scandinavia, which had been won for the Reformation. But, as we have seen, the Reformation was not a simple division of Catholic against relatively conservative Protestant. Radical Christianity also entered the interstices of the religious divide and throve in the crevices of Christian disunity. However, in those parts of Europe where Reformed and Evangelical churches were set up in succession to the papal Church, their clergies also inherited from their Catholic predecessors the problem of religious dissent. This was the case because, in assuming the obligations of catholicity within a limited area, the new Protestant churches repeated many of the compromises which the mediaeval Church had made with 'the world'. Above all, these were compromises with states – compromises which inevitably impeded the realisation of evangelical goals. Thus, for example, the bishops of Elizabethan England found that the relationship with the crown which they had inherited from Catholic times made it difficult to attain the goal, which Archbishop Grindal had before him, of making the country 'godly'. The inadequacies and compromises of the Reformation churches made the resurgence of sectarian protest inevitable. How were the Reformation churches to deal with such protest? The question itself breaks down into two: how were churches to regard dissenting movements, and how were they to proceed against them?[1]

When we consider both the attitudes and the actions of major Reformation churches to religious dissenters, we must be aware of the precedents that they had before them, in particular the precedent of the treatment of dissent by mediaeval Catholicism. The mediaeval Church established its attitudes to dissent in institutional forms, the form of bishops' courts, but above all the form of the Inquisition. It seems that the institutionalisation of the campaign against dissent was originally the result of an attempt to protect heretics from popular lynch-law. Be that as it may, it is clear that episcopal inquisitorial tribunals were less effective at detecting heresy than was the formal papal Inquisition. Many bishops were too preoccupied with politics, or too theologically uneducated, or too indolent or absentee, to take effective action against heretics in their dioceses, and in fifteenth-century England, where the Inquisition was not introduced, the campaign against Lollardy was not intensive. The Inquisition was a more specialist, and in some ways more effective, body. It was staffed by trained members of the regular orders and it had legal procedures designed to detect and convict: anonymous accusation; ignorance of the specific charge on the part of the accused; absence of defence counsel testimony from categories of persons not qualified to give evidence in more customary procedures; use of torture; and a general presupposition of guilt. Equipped with such legal advantages, the Inquisition – as a spiritual tribunal – was sometimes all too effective, as, in the person of the inquisitor, the character of the police detective came to take over from that of the pastoral confessor and reclaimer of souls. As ecclesiastical policemen inquisitors were sometimes over-concerned to trap their subjects, and they were capable of detecting heresy where none existed. Thus, when the devout Poor Men of Lyons came to seek official ratification in 1179, they were tested for their orthodoxy and asked by the ingenious Walter Map whether or not they believed in the Mother of Christ; their pious affirmative left them open to a technical charge of heresy, for the theologically correct answer to the question would have been that they believed in the Mother of God. An even more extreme example of inquisitors inventing heresy was the detention of the ultra-orthodox Ignatius Loyola on a charge of 'judais-ing' tendencies because of his cultivation of Saturday as a day set aside for the honour of Mary.[2]

The legal procedures and assumptions of inquisitors were a reflec-tion of their intellectual attitudes to heresy. These attitudes can be deduced from the actual conduct of inquisitors in the field, and from inquisitorial handbooks like Bernard Gui's fourteenth-century *Prac-tica*. Inquisitors viewed heresy as a diabolic conspiracy against the Church. Because it had malevolent supernatural support, special legal measures against it were justified. Heresy was believed to be especially attractive to the uneducated and to women, and thus 'excessive' religiosity in these groups was itself suspect. Heresy of course from the point of view of the inquisitors could have no source within Christian-ity – such as in the New Testament – and therefore it had to be brought in from outside, could be transported almost like a tangible commod-ity, but was also likely to recur in certain identifiable locations where, exactly like a virus brought in from outside, it had earlier appeared.

Such in brief were some of the characteristics of the mediaeval Church's, and especially the mediaeval Inquisition's, view of heresy. Essentially, those who specialised in the treatment of heresy took a thoroughly intellectual and academic view of it, in accordance with their training. Heresy was to be diagnosed, tabulated, categorised, named and made as specific and articulate as possible – hence the articles of belief which were extracted from dissidents to be presented to them for revocation. It ought to be said that the clinical approach of inquisitors to heresy involved a clash of attitude between them and their subjects. The official Church thought in terms of formal confes-sions of faith – creeds like the classic Apostolic and Nicene creeds. Many heretical movements, because of their individualistic, inspira-tional and scriptural character, lacked such definite statements of belief. Even more so, heretical groups were out of sympathy with the highly developed official theology of the Middle Ages. Rationally deduced doctrines and formulae, such as Purgatory and transubstanti-ation, were in a sense too advanced for most fundamentalists and they rejected the scholastic techniques that had helped evolve such theories. Thus, when grilled on transubstantiation, an English Lollard answered that he would not be drawn into a discussion of Aquinas's dialectic. On occasions like this the specialists appeared to be not so much specialists in heresy as in theology.[3]

The problem of heresy which had confronted the mediaeval Church was passed on to the new Catholic Church of the Counter-Reformation and to the new Protestant churches. Catholicism revived its Inquisition in the sixteenth century, but in many respects the methods of the new Protestant churches were more lenient than the approach which the old Church reaffirmed in resurrecting the Inquisition. Evidence for Protestant leniency is not lacking: Martin Bucer and Wolfgang Capito tried to inject toleration into the Reformation at Strasburg, Philip of Hesse's Lutheran state mitigated harshness to Anabaptists, and Anabaptists were measurably less ill-treated in German Evangelical than in German Catholic lands. But a less hesitant treatment of the problem of heresy by Protestants is evident in the case of Calvin and Geneva. In trapping the Spanish unitarian Michael Servetus, Calvin actually collaborated with the Inquisition at Vienne in France; this, as well as the way that Servetus after his arrival and trial in Geneva was 'relaxed' to the secular arm for burning, reminds us that Calvinists faced the same problem as their Catholic forerunners and tried to solve it in much the same way. Indeed, in some Protestant countries investigatory tribunals, like England's High Commission, could be compared with the original Inquisition, if only because they used abnormal legal procedures. However, the central area of similarity between the treatment of heresy by Catholic and conservative Protestant clerics lay in their inability to understand the phenomenon. Where heresy was continuous, Protestant analysts sought to make it appear recurrent; where dissent was elusive, Protestant diagnosticians tried to make it seem specific.[4]

Heresy was continuous in the sense that it was part of the Christian tradition, always deriving validation from its scriptural source. But like their Catholic predecessors, official Protestant spokesmen tended to see the heresies they confronted as recurrent outbreaks of the same alien virus. Thus Zwingli immediately recognised in Anabaptism a recrudescence of Donatism which, it seems, required the repetition of baptism for converts from Catholicism; the Zürich reformer went so far as to approve for the Anabaptists the punishment of drowning which the code of Justinian had specified for the original Donatists. With equally irrelevant scholarship a series of late Elizabethan English pamphlets proved that the Separatists were true Donatists. Zwingli's scholarly approach to Anabaptism also characterised his successor Heinrich Bullinger who, like Zwingli, took on the task of imposing a kind of catholicity in a limited area – the city of Zürich and its *contado*. Like Zwingli's, Bullinger's view of Anabaptists was distorted by historical learning and he likened them to Cathars, but Bullinger was also misled by a theologian's instinct to classify. His taxonomy, which purported to reveal the existence of seven distinct categories of Anabaptists (including the 'Abominable Anabaptists'), took no account of the shifting, amorphous nature of the movement, within its common scriptural moorings. Bullinger's number of seven distinct variants of Anabaptism was too high in that it failed to appreciate the common denominator of Scripture in the movement; and too low in that it failed to realise the almost infinite possibilities of individualism within this and other fundamentalist movements of the Reformation period.[5]

We must appreciate the problems of the Reformers, especially of the urban Reformers of the type of Zwingli and Calvin. Not only did they assume traditional obligations to maintain the Christianity and the unity of whole political societies, but under the pressure of Reformation ethics they sought new levels of 'godliness' in those societies – work and thrift, marital fidelity, civic concord, sobriety, the authority of the family, frugality and abstinence from pleasure. Unanimity of belief in the church blessed the commune with unity, but from the point of view of doctrine and of conduct the enemy of society was the individualist. Classical Reformers rightly viewed as individualists those outstanding heresiarchs, like Castellio or Servetus, who devised highly personal – sometimes rationalist, sometimes spiritualist – theologies. But *groups* of separatists could also justifiably be considered to have individualist tendencies. The paradox of separatism in the Reformation period is that within intensely communal churchly structures personal freedom of opinion flourished. This is indeed not so much of a paradox, for in fact the high degree of 'fellowship', which we find, for example, in English Independency, could be maintained only if allowances were made for the autonomy of the individual's credal conscience. There were, of course, limits in radical Christian groups to the freedom of doctrinal opinion that was permissible. Conduct was of higher importance than belief, but there were occasions when differences of belief involved major differences of conduct. However, it remains true that the schisms that did arise in radical Christian groups tended to arise over questions of practice, emphasis and personality, rather than over questions of doctrine properly understood. Separatist groups were notoriously liable to fission over personalities. This is hardly surprising, not least because typical radical religionists lived in social isolation from the wider world but in close proximity to one another; clearly the over-heated personal atmosphere often put a strain on fellowship – as we can see from the tussles within the *émigré*

English Separatists' community in Holland at the end of the sixteenth century, when the community split apart over such apparent trivia as the extravagances of the wife of the pastor, Francis Johnson. Similarly, it was a struggle of powerful personalities between George Fox and James Naylor and a difference of emphasis over the proper place of enthusiasm that tore the nascent Quaker communities apart in the mid-1650s. Later in the history of Quakerism – in the 1670s – it was not 'theology' that caused division in the Wilkinson–Story separation, but rather exclusively practical questions of organisation and behaviour. 'Theoretical' disagreements were of course possible – as in the exiled English Separatist groups over baptism and re-baptism – but by and large radical groups were free of the basic theological disputes that divided the major churches – over grace and election, over transubstantiation, consubstantiation or a commemorative Eucharist, and so on. It is true to say of Anabaptism, and of Quakerism, for example, that they lacked theologies as the major churches would have understood the term. For Anabaptism, the 1527 Schleitheim Articles have often been seen as a credal formulary, but in precision and technicality they are in no way to be compared with, say, the Augsburg Confession of the Lutherans; the Schleitheim Articles must be seen as an attempt to reach a denominator of agreement, but are concerned with Scripture, behaviour, excommunication, withdrawal and other practical and ecclesiological questions. For Quakerism, it might appear that with the appearance of Robert Barclay's *Apology* Quakerism itself acquired a theology, and Barclay has been credited with importing the Calvinist preoccupation with theological nicety into Quakerism. If this is so, then Barclay was but a single figure in a movement lacking other theologians, but in fact Barclay himself was at pains to exalt Scripture and relegate 'philosophy' in matters of religion. The lack of precise doctrinal formularies in these radical movements was the precondition for internal intellectual tolerance within them – though standards of behaviour were exactly specified. With regard to credal questions, it is true to say that in many radical movements every individual was his own church, for the principle of the inner light which was enshrined in movements such as the Anabaptists and the Quakers gave ultimate sovereignty in questions of belief to the individual. It was of course difficult to hold up the process whereby individualism in belief led to individualism in conduct. We saw earlier that group controls were the essence of the life of early modern radical sects. Jonson's Zeal-of-the-Land Busy is a caricature of a censorious radical puritan, with his obsession with the 'brethren' and the 'saints', condemning out of hand all aspects of the turbulent life of Jacobean London. But beyond the caricature lay the reality of earnest religious groups setting a *cordon sanitaire* between themselves and the moral chaos of the unregulated towns – like London or Antwerp – in which they were so notably to be found. However, the maintenance of group discipline was always threatened, though not always destroyed, by a basically personal attitude to faith. Quaker discipline required a complete detachment from the Church of England, epitomised, as we have seen, in a blank refusal to pay tithes. In what was admittedly a rare, if not unique, instance of a principled refusal to accept the group's code, at least one post-Restoration Quaker said that he found his inner guidance told him tithe-paying was actually permissible. On another matter of ethical control – that of dress regulations – a single Quaker could oppose her scriptural belief in freedom to the strict and detailed code of the church: 'Christ Jesus saith', wrote Margaret Fox, 'that we must take no thought of what we shall eat, or what we shall drink, or what we shall put on, but bids us consider the lilies, and how they grow in more royalty than Solomon. But contrary to this, we must look at no colours, nor make anything that is changeable colours as the hills are, nor sell them, nor wear them; but we must be all in one dress and one colour. This is a silly poor Gospel.'[6]

The importance of such challenges should not be exaggerated. Normally groups like the Hutterite Anabaptists retained the ability to make moral legislation for the individual; if the individual did not accept the discipline, he or she left, or was expelled from, the group. But in radical Christian groups autonomy of belief was a corollary of their characteristic lack of exact theology and their equally characteristic and consequent idealisation of intellectual toleration. However, the preference which we find in Separatist groups like the Anabaptists for ethics over beliefs was, ultimately, a false preference, because beliefs always have behavioural consequences. Usually in radical groups the moral consequences of dissident beliefs were successfully concealed, precisely because Separatist communities were groups of people who were agreed on the observation of certain moral standards. But there were occasions when individualism in the realm of ideas was carried over into the most disturbing kinds of behaviour. In the early 1600s, the English Separatist teacher John Smyth, along with other Separatists, and perhaps under Mennonite influences at Amsterdam, evinced doubts about the validity of his original baptism in the 'popish' Church of England. It is probably true that Separatism logically does require a second conferment of sacraments, especially baptism, after withdrawal from the church which originally conferred them, but in English Separatism this insight had long been concealed by the necessity to dissociate the movement from Anabaptism proper, which had a dangerous reputation in England. Free in Holland of English constraints, Smyth allowed his doubts and beliefs to lead him into a course of action that was more sensational in the context of the time than any sacramental conduct of the Anabaptists; in re-baptising himself, Smyth implicitly rejected all churchmanship, or rather made of himself a church. In fact the damage was soon repaired, for Smyth betook himself to the Amsterdam Mennonites for church baptism. But Smyth's act of self-baptism had signalled in a vivid way a victory for something like a modern principle of individualism. The individual, cultivating his own conscience, conducting his own reading, following his own 'leadings', disparaging priesthood and academic learning, able to leave and join churches, was master of his own mind, and he even showed his autonomy in *voluntarily* joining religious associations which, however authoritarian they were, he himself had chosen to accept. It may be argued that religious sects in this way have made *some* contribution to the emergence of modern man, atomised and free, believing as he lists, choosing, by and large, those associations of which he will be a member. But because of its tendency, albeit concealed, to individualise morality – because it individualised religious belief – religious dissent can be said to have contributed to the individualisation of morality encountered in modern societies.

Throughout this book it has appeared that the established Protestant churches of the Reformation inherited, in their local areas, many of the functions, obligations and assumptions of the mediaeval Catholic Church. Typically, an established Protestant church was entrusted with, and accepted, the obligation to impose some degree of Christian morality on a national or territorial society – for example, the Kingdom of Sweden, or the Electorate of Saxony. Like the Catholic Church before them, the 'magisterial' Protestant churches, whether they worked in a large-scale national framework like that of England, or a small-scale civic context like that of Geneva, insisted on a church membership coterminous with that of a civil society. For the Church of England Bishop Hooker defended the coincidence of membership of secular and ecclesiastical society with an assurance that might have been envied by some mediaeval Catholic apologists. The relationship of state, church and society envisaged both by Catholics and by magisterial Protestants was essentially conservative. The state was seen in varying degrees as a Christian agency which the church ought to support; churchmen and certainly lay church members could lawfully be employed in civil capacities. One of the features that made Christian radical groups radical was their general refusal to enter into the relationship with the state which the Protestant churches took over from the Catholic Church. The implicit demand of mediaeval dissenters for a separation of state and church, for a clear identification of the pure in church associations of their own, was made more explicit by the radical sects of the sixteenth and seventeenth centuries. The vision which the sectarians had of pure churches was resisted by conservative spokesmen because the implied divorce of church and society would make it impossible to impose any fixed moral standards or discipline on society as a whole. Separatism thus appeared as thoroughly irresponsible to a host of Protestant opponents, from Bullinger in the sixteenth century to Thomas 'Gangraena' Edwards in the seventeenth. In its social position, and in its attitudes to religious dissent, a territorial church like the Anglican Church resembled the mediaeval Catholic establishment. However, after the seventeenth century Anglican opponents of religious dissent were able to count on a large measure of popular support and, indeed, as we saw earlier, political projects for toleration often had to be shelved in the face of popular protest. On the other hand, in Catholic days religious dissent in the cities had been a popular force, arising out of a popular verbal culture, linked to democratic traditions and ideas of social equality, and helping to express popular religious culture. Why was it, that whereas in the fourteenth and fifteenth centuries, religious dissent was a popular force – for example, in Savonarola's Florence and Želivský's Prague – by the eighteenth century popular forces had turned against dissenting Christians, as in the example of the action of English mobs against Nonconformists in Georgian England?[7]

The answer lies first in the resurgence of the countryside in early modern Europe. Many cities grew rapidly in the sixteenth, seventeenth and eighteenth centuries. London provides a good example. In its progress to becoming the largest city in Europe, London took in and often wasted vast numbers of men and women: it has been estimated that one in every six English people in the period 1650–1750 had experience of life in London. Now many of these new urbanites may have adjusted to urbanisation by gravitating towards voluntary church groups. But many others doubtless remained unreconstructed countrymen, unadjusted to town culture and religion. Now part of Anglicanism's inheritance from Catholicism was an appropriateness to rural life: in their seasonal liturgies and their ceremonial and symbolic approaches these churches were well-suited to the outlook of country people. When the first generations of country-dwellers moved into growing towns, they often brought with them their inarticulate religious preferences. This analysis does not take account of the fact that in London religious insurgency in the eighteenth century the great majority of demonstrators seem to have been settled London denizens. However, the growth of cities like London was achieved predominately by rural immigration, and this had the effect of reducing some of the sharp cultural and religious differences that had obtained in the late Middle Ages between city and country.[8]

A resurgence of the countryside – even apparent in the very demographic growth of towns – is apparent in Europe in the sixteenth century. The protest of the Pilgrimage of Grace against 'the heresies of Luther, Wyclif, Husse, Melangton, Elicampadus, Burcerus, Confessa Germaniae, Apologia Melanctnis, the Works of Tyndall . . .' is a protest of the inarticulate: even in its confusions and mis-spellings this reflects an obstinate cultural antipathy of country people to an urban religious civilisation. Such deep-seated resentment may well have conditioned the kind of compromise religious settlement, leaning strongly towards Catholic retentions, which a predominately rural country like England adopted in the sixteenth century. Similarly the ineradicable folk Catholicism of French peasants in the sixteenth century was one of the factors determining France's final readoption of Catholicism at the end of the century – as it may have been a factor in ensuring the return of Belgium to Catholicism.[9] When Catholicism was readopted in the areas recovered by the Church in sixteenth-century and seventeenth-century Europe it was resumed under the new forms of the Counter-Reformation. The Counter-Reformation meant more efficient official propaganda and it meant better official control. In Italy a mediaeval and early-sixteenth-century tradition of popular religious dissent and criticism was extinguished. This was achieved first through better canvassing on behalf of the official Church. The Counter-Reformation Church had at its disposal philanthropy, well-orchestrated fêtes, well-designed churches which functioned partly as preaching halls, and a whole, skilfully manipulated aesthetic infrastructure with which to reimpress its authority on the popular consciousness. The reinculcation of orthodox Catholicism in the Italian – and Belgian – populations in the course of the sixteenth and seventeenth centuries was achieved partly by a process of persuasion: the case for Catholicism was restated, the Church recruited powerful personalities like the Jesuit fathers, the Borromeo cardinals of Milan, and urban heroes like Philip Neri. But intensive re-Catholicisation was also achieved by more forceful and bureaucratic measures; by careful clerical scrutiny of religious confraternities and the suppression of unapproved societies like the Milanese *Humiliati*, by strict control of book production, by the use of the Holy Office, by the deployment of Spanish military and political power, and by the commitment of territorial dynasties like those of Savoy and Tuscany to the Counter-Reformation. Politics necessarily assisted the process. In an age of monarchism the liberties and cultural identities of cities were systematically eroded: in the Florence of the Medici Grand Dukes a Savonarolan was as rare as a republican, and only in an old-fashioned republic like Venice was the suspicion of the Inquisition, which was encountered in many late-mediaeval communes, still to be found in Catholic Europe. Through persuasion and coercion areas of Europe – Bohemia, Italy, Belgium, Poland – whose Catholic orthodoxy had been in the

fifteenth and sixteenth centuries open to varying degrees of doubt –
were re-Catholicised in depth in the seventeenth and eighteenth centuries. The victory was a victory of countryside over town, of prince
over republic, and of Church over dissent. In fact the possibility of the
survival of religious dissent in this atmosphere was exceedingly
remote: in Belgium we see a quiescent, or even fervent popular peasant Catholicism, in Sicily and Spain no lack of popular collaborators
with the Inquisition. The confirmation of Catholic Europe in its
orthodox Catholicism may have been more intense than it was durable
but it meant that criticism and dissent were no longer, as they had been
in the late Middle Ages, popular manifestations arising out of an
autonomous urban culture.[10]

Turning again to northern Europe, we may see in the case of England an intense rural reaction to religious enthusiasm and apparent
religious novelty in the hostile response of mobs to the early Methodists. But in England, too, the victories of official patriotic propaganda
and the rise of xenophobia resulted in a climate of popular opinion
unfavourable to religious dissent in the eighteenth century: because of
the existence in English Nonconformity of a discernible foreign element, Protestant alternatives to Anglicanism could be viewed as alien.
In addition, after 1660 the term Dissent in England became a catch-all
term for a socially variegated group extending from wealthy Whig
Presbyterian bankers to petit-bourgeois provincial sectarians like the
Quakers. Some of the popular antipathy to 'Dissent' in Hanoverian
England was antipathy to a social force that was portrayed as alien,
moneyed, insidiously powerful and, conceivably, irreligious. But it is
evident that the 'Dissent' that was the focus of the animus of the
Sacheverell and Priestly riots in Georgian England was little akin to
the religious dissent that had enjoyed considerable popular protection
and support – for example, in Marian England. In the eighteenth
century established churches over much of Europe won, however,
briefly some popular ascendancy, and did so at the expense of an old
religious dissenting tradition. Radical sects of the pre-Reformation,
like the Waldensians; of the Reformation, like the Mennonites; and of
the seventeenth century, like the Quakers, held on to their member-
ships and to their entrenched ideas, but they did so in increasing social
isolation, and without the anchorage in a demotic and urban culture
that radical movements had enjoyed in the transitional period of
European history of protest, Reformation and radicalism during the
fourteenth, fifteenth, sixteenth and seventeenth centuries. The erosion
of popular dissenting Christianity left Europe with highly official,
clerical forms of religion, closely tied to the *anciens régimes*. Radical
religious movements had functioned as rearguard protests against the

aggrandisement of monarchical states in the early modern period. The establishment of Renaissance personal monarchy, riding in harness with territorial churches, whether of the Reformation or of the Counter-Reformation, was a defeat for civic autonomy, popular urban culture and the religious articulation of that culture, religious dissent and its realisation in free socio-religious associations of the laity. The ascendancy – until the end of the eighteenth century in western Europe – of territorial monarchical states offered to England, France and the German Reich useful opportunities for stability after the turbulence of civil wars in the Reformation and post-Reformation period. The stability of the *anciens régimes* rested on a degree of re-ruralisation in Europe: the monarchies, aristocracies and established churches of this period reposed on rural bases, popular city culture and urban government were subjected to close monarchical and ecclesiastical controls and, of course, religious radicalism was subject over most of Europe to intense pressure. Gradually religious radicalism lost much of its popular constituency; in the eighteenth century it appeared that over most of Europe the religions of the masses were exactly those of the élites who governed them. This resulted in a failure of Christianity to articulate social and political dissent, as it had, for example, in the cities of the late Middle Ages and sixteenth century. For as long as a degree of social and economic stability was maintained in Europe, the monolithic nature of *ancien régime* religion did not adversely affect the popular currency of Christianity. But when rapid economic change began to affect the continent in the nineteenth century, the inability of Christianity, because of the extinction of the popular radical religious tradition, to express mass social grievances led to an avalanche of de-Christianisation in all countries affected by industrialisation.

Religious dissent, however, managed to survive both the *ancien régime* and the industrial revolution. The 'Christian' monarchies of the *ancien régime*, those of England and France, for example, were tied – even shackled – to conservative national churches which expressed the stability of rural societies. Such societies were organic and traditional, monolithic and, it was hoped, unanimous. Patriotism was burgeoning, though it was still linked to the symbols of the dynasty and of warfare. A national society was generally construed as a unanimous family. The eighteenth-century state itself still was relatively underemployed: it regulated foreign commerce, conducted diplomacy, waged war, punished crime and maintained existing social and religious relations. Needless to say, the states of the *ancien régime* had wider scope, were more dynamic and impersonal than their mediaeval predecessors, and it may be argued that the origins of a modern omnicompetent state, such as that of France, lay in the immediate pre-Revolutionary period.

None the less, though an advance on the primitive mediaeval state, the intermediate early modern polity was vastly less active than its nineteenth- and twentieth-century successor. The eighteenth-century state employed few servants (and those from limited categories of subjects), disposed of little income and kept out of large areas of national life. However, in France in the revolutionary period and in England in the early nineteenth century the modern state came into its own. The emergence of this impersonal engine was heralded by Utilitarian thinkers in England, and was endorsed by the rise of Romantic, and in England, Evangelical social compassion. More immediately, this kind of state was born out of the exigencies of early nineteenth-century warfare, and out of the problems of urbanisation and industrialisation. Unlike its *ancien régime* predecessors, this modern apparatus was neither rural nor religious in orientation. The demand for a 'career open to the talents' was a manifestation of the state's strength and impersonality. It was reflected in the possibility, which arose pre-eminently in England, of employing religious dissenters as state servants and legislators. Plurality was ratified by the new state, a religiously neutral institution such as some radicals had looked forward to as early as the sixteenth century. But, whereas religious radicalism had – unsuccessfully – challenged the erection of the intermediate new states of the sixteenth century, in the nineteenth century religious dissenters co-operated enthusiastically in the supplanting of the old leviathan by the new. In this sense the surviving forms of European religious dissent played a part in the creation of the 'democratic-totalitarian' states of the modern world: states which are pluralistic, tolerant and totally divorced from religious sanctions or restraints. In many cases, and increasingly in the twentieth century, modern states have implemented extensive economic and industrial legislation designed to protect citizens from the operation of market forces. In fact, this economic role is the most important manifestation of the sovereignty and competence of the modern state. The efficacy of much of this social legislation – from Bismarckian Germany to the present day – has taken the edge off social protest. In any case, social protest in modern industrial societies is entirely 'realistic' in tone – lacking the religious, and especially the millenarian, form that social protest took in early modern Europe. But whether or not social legislation is sufficiently protective in the modern world, social protest must seek a secular expression: the possibility of a religious articulation of protest is discounted by the de-Christianisation of Europeans. De-Christianisation in this case means the results of the successes of the European territorial churches in the eighteenth century in instilling their values and cults on mass populations. This victory involved the extinction of popular Christian radicalism – or the extinction rather of a people's Christianity in Europe.

Documents and Commentary

The documents in this appendix illustrate many features of the life, thought, ethics and political attitudes of radical Christians. Some points to note are: the rejection of external authority, especially the authority of the learned; diffidence towards the state, exemplified in refusal of oaths; and repudiation of established national churches, reflected in the Quakers' opposition to tithes. Another interesting theme in these documents is the recurrent citations of St Paul: the Apostle of the Gentiles may be regarded as a strong influence on the dissenting tradition – notably in his ideas on spirit and freedom. Scriptural references crop up constantly in these documents, but along with them there is also a preoccupation with individual reflection, judgement and illumination. With regard to social questions, concern with poor relief and with social redistribution frequently emerges. The documents also show that the characteristics of Christian dissent survived into the eighteenth century.

Most of the excerpts in this appendix are from the Quaker archives at Lancaster, the principal centre of Quakerism in north-west England. Taken together, these Quaker papers express the religious thought of humble, not well educated, and sometimes even illiterate, men and women. The language, which is sometimes ungrammatical and idiosyncratic, is almost always vivid. I have brought spelling and punctuation up to date for two reasons: first, because in some cases the original forms make it extremely difficult to understand the material; and secondly, to avoid a false impression of quaintness. The Quaker documents have been chosen to illustrate characteristics of radical sects in general. These documents are at Lancaster Friends' Meeting House ('LFMH').

Mediaeval heretics anticipated many assertions of the Protestant Reformation. The Lollard whose examination appears below denied that there was legislative power in the church, apart from the static requirements of Scripture. Opposed to feast-days, he rejected images, pilgrimages and most fast days; in this sense we can say that he anticipated the Reformation in its denial of sanctity in secular things. In repudiating oaths and tithes and in insisting that clerics had authority only in so far as they are virtuous, Florence takes classic radical positions; in proposing that tithes be distributed amongst the poor, he moves to a more socially radical viewpoint.

From George Townsend (ed.), *The Acts and Monuments of John Foxe* (8 vols, London, 1844), Vol. III, p. 584.

John Florence, a turner in Shelton, in the diocese of Norwich, was attached for that he held and taught these heresies (as they called them) here under written, contrary to the determination of the Church of Rome;

Imprimis, That the Pope and cardinals have no power to make or constitute any laws.

Item, That there is no day to be kept holy but only the Sunday, which God hath allowed.

Item That men ought to fast no other time, but the *Quatuor Temporum*.

Item That images are not to be worshipped, neither that people ought to set up any lights before them in the churches; neither to go on pilgrimages, neither to offer for the dead, nor with women that are purified.

Item That curates should not take tithes of their parishioners, but that such tithes should be divided among the poor parishioners.

Item That all such as swear by their life or power shall be damned, except they repent.

On Wednesday, August 2nd AD 1424, the said John Florence personally appeared before William Bernham, Chancellor to William Bishop of Norwich, where he, proceeding against him, objected the first article, touching the power of the Pope and cardinals; to which article the said John Florence answered in this manner, 'If the Pope lived uprightly as Peter lived he hath power to make laws. Otherwise I believe he hath no power'. But being afterwards threatened by the judge he acknowledged that he had erred and submitted himself to the correction of the Church and was abjured; taking on oath that from that time forward he should not hold, teach, preach, or willingly defend any error or heresy contrary to the determination of the Church of Rome; neither maintain help, nor aid any such that shall teach or hold any such errors or heresies, either privily or apertly, and for his offence in this behalf done he was enjoined this penance following: Three Sundays in a solemn procession, in the cathedral church of Norwich, he should be discip-

lined before all the people. The like also should be done about his
parish church of Shelton . . .'.

Late mediaeval heretics based their objections to Catholicism
primarily on the Scriptures. They contrasted the simplicity and laicism
which they saw in the New Testament with the complexity and clericalism of the Church. In the passage below John Tyball manifests the
typical Lollard's strict fidelity to Scripture. Tyball objected to all
manifestations of religion not found in the New Testament – venera-
tion of Mary, pilgrimages, images, sacramental Confession, and so on.
In true dissenting fashion, Tyball emphasised the value of the congregation, for example in the confession of sins. He exalted poor relief and
denigrated sacerdotalism. It is also interesting to note that, his scripturalism apart, Tyball stressed private judgement and the slow matura-
tion of his own ideas. The Tyball case shows that authentic Lollardy,
with its deliberately exaggerated irreverence, was still very much alive
under Henry VIII. It is difficult to believe that this vital tradition was
absorbed by the highly conservative Henrician Reformation.

From John Strype, *Ecclesiastical Memorials, relating Chiefly to
Religion, and the Reformation of it, and the Emergencies of the
Church of England under King Henry VIII, King Edward VI and
Queen Mary I* (3 vols, Oxford, 1822), Vol. I, pt II, pp. 50–1.

The Confession of John Tyball, a Lollard; charged with heresy.
Examined he saith that about seven or eight years past, he had
certain books of the four Evangelists in English, of one holy John,
and certain Epistles of Peter and Paul; which he burned the same
day at night (as he saith) that Sir Richard Fox was attached. And so
in continuance of time, by reading of the said books, and especially
by a chapter of Paul, which he wrote to the Corinthians . . . he fell
into those errors and heresies. That for some time he had thought
that the Blessed Sacrament of the Altar is not the very body of
Christ, but bread and wine, and done for a remembrance of Christ's
passion. And he thought and believed that a priest had no power to
consecrate the body of Christ.

Also he confesseth that he hath said, affirmed and believed that
every priest and bishop ought to have a wife upon the chapter of
Paul, where he saith these words: 'every bishop ought to be husband
of one wife, and to bring forth children'.

Also he saith that he hath said, affirmed and believed that it was
as good for man to confess himself alone to God, or else to any other
layman, as to a priest – upon the saying of Saint James, where he
saith: 'Show your sins one to another'. Which error he shewed and

taught Robert Faire of Steeple Bumstead about a twelvemonth past.

Also he saith that he hath taught that priesthood was not necessary. For he thought that every layman might minister the sacraments of the Church as well as any priest.

Also he confesseth that pilgrimages to images were not profitable; and that men should not worship or kneel to images in the church, nor set up candles or lights before them, for they be but stocks and stones.

Also he saith that he hath for some time doubted whether the pope or bishop had power to grant pardon. For some time he thought that they had power, and for some time he thought the contrary, because they had so much money for it. And, he said, he thought that it were better that their mitres, crosses, rings and other precious stones should be given to poor and needy people than so to wear them – according to the saying of Paul where he saith, 'wear ye no gold, silver nor pearls, nor precious stones'.

Also he saith that saints as Peter, Paul and others, be in heaven; but as for other souls of good men which departeth this world, he thinketh that they go not to heaven before the general resurrection; but be in some place of joy and pleasure, except they be helped to heaven by good prayer.

The independence of mind shewn by Tyball, especially in the last article, was even more marked in the case of Thomas Boges or Bowgas of Colchester, who was examined in the same year as Tyball (Strype, Vol. I, p. 57). Boges illustrates clearly the individualism of many heretics. He is opposed to all ceremonial and to formal churchmanship. His vehement iconoclastic language anticipates the physical attacks on holy objects which were perpetrated under Edward VI.

That a man should have no need to go on pilgrimage to Saint Thomas of Canterbury, or to Our Lady of Grace.
Also that there is no other church of God but man's conscience.
Also that I had as lief be buried in my own house as in the church.
Also that I would that Our Lady of Grace were in my bakehouse.
Also that it was demanded of me whether it was evil or well done to set a taper before the Sepulchre, I answered and said, It was nothing but to set a candle before the Devil, for vainglory of the World, as I and many other fools doth. Also that if I had the crucifix, the Image of Our Lady, and other saints and crosses set by the way, in a ship, I would drown every one in the sea.

The emphasis in mediaeval devotionalism on the humanity of Jesus could develop, under heretical auspices, into a virtual denial of His divinity. The fourteenth-century German heretic whose opinions are given below represents an advanced form of the spiritualisation and internalisation of religion. Sacraments, learning, external observances, the Scripture itself, all are set aside in favour of the illumination that comes to the adept – who is both liberated from the moral law and, perhaps, ranked with Jesus. This statement of belief is dated 1356 and is taken from M. Fleury, *Histoire Ecclésiastique* (36 vols, Paris, 1720–38), Vol. 20, p.173.

At Speyer the inquisitors took one named Berthold who taught the following errors. Jesus Christ in His Passion felt Himself so much abandoned by His father that He doubted greatly whether His soul must be saved or damned. In this same state the excess of sorrow made Him curse the holy virgin His mother; He cursed also the earth which had received His blood. Man can in this life arrive at such perfection that he will have no further need to pray or fast, and that nothing would any longer be sinful for him. Oral prayer is useless for salvation, it is enough to pray by the spirit. An ignorant layman without knowledge of books, but illumined by God, can profit himself and others better than the most learned priest – whether or not he be a doctor. The devout man taking his ordinary food can acquire as much grace as if he received the sacrament of the body and blood of Christ.

In contrast with heretics of the Free Spirit, like the one investigated at Speyer, Anabaptists were generally deferential to the Scripture and took its mandates literally – too literally for their opponents. Summaries of dissident doctrine made by the orthodox are usually unreliable, nor least for what they leave out. Speyer is the scene for the following excerption of Anabaptist beliefs. The Reichstag which met in the Rhineland city in 1529 saw a division between the estates on the confessional question – but a broad measure of agreement on the danger of Anabaptism. As the following passage, from Vol. 27 of Fleury's *Histoire Ecclésiastique*, shows, the Reichstag stressed the undesirability of the Anabaptists' exclusiveness, and of their repudiation of their civil and military responsibilities.

The first belief was that it was not permitted to a Christian to carry arms and to recognise the magistrates; this was based on these words of Jesus Christ: *The kings of the Gentiles exercise lordship over them; . . . But ye shall not be so* [Luke 22: 25]. The second was that it was never lawful to swear, not even when the magistrates obliged one to raise one's hand. The third was that God did not call faithful Christians either to dispense justice or to watch over the public peace. The fourth was that whoever refused to become an Anabaptist would be put on the left side and amongst the goats in the Last Judgement. The fifth was that the flesh of Moses was only to be found in the sect of the Anabaptists, and that there was none but the predestined. The sixth was that those sent to preach the Gospel were only to be found in their society. The seventh was that those who opposed the progress of Anabaptist doctrine would have to be considered reprobates.

Erasmus has been viewed as an apostle of tolerance – but there were limits to his broadmindedness, especially when the stability of the state and of property were endangered. On sacramental questions Erasmus believed in maintaining custom unless there were pressing reasons for change. In fact, the Dutch humanist's only concession – in the passage below – to sacramental radicalism was over the choice which parents could make of the timing of their children's christenings.

From J.A. Froude, *Life and Letters of Erasmus* (London, Longman, 1894), p. 345.
In Baptism let the old rule be kept. Parents may perhaps be left to decide whether it shall be administered in infancy or delayed to maturity. Anabaptists must not be tolerated. The Apostles bade the people obey the magistrates, though the magistrates were heathens. Anabaptists will not obey even Christian princes. Community of goods is a chimera. Charity is a duty, but property must be upheld. As to the Eucharist, let the old opinion stand . . .

The unfavourable view which the Speyer Reichstag and Erasmus took of the Anabaptists seemed justified in the light of the aggressive language and exclusive behaviour of the Münster Anabaptists. Bernhard Rothmann was a left-wing Lutheran pastor who converted to Anabaptism in 1534. His synopsis of Anabaptism can be found in Alexandre Weill, *Histoire de la Guerre des Anabaptistes* (Paris, Dentu, 1874), pp. 139–40. Rothmann represents his movement in a mood of extreme bitterness – far removed from the evangelistic mildness of Michael Sattler and Menno Simmons, but similar to the unrestrained polemic of Thomas Müntzer. Years of persecution put severe strains on the Anabaptists' vision of themselves as *die Stillen im Lande* – peaceful people in the midst of the world. The Münster revolution, triggered off by freak circumstances, was also a delayed reaction to repression. The Old Testament tone of Rothmann's words – even to the extent of advocating a Saturday Sabbath – is no accident: Anabaptists saw themselves, like the Israel of old, as encircled by hostile and idolatrous pagans. Making no distinction between Catholics and Lutherans, the Münster Anabaptists looked forward to the dissolution of secular government, of property and of 'mixed' marriages.

The baptism of infants is an abomination before God.
No Christian may frequent the churches of the infidels.
The consecrated host on the altar is the great Baal.
Saturday, not Sunday, is the Lord's Day.
For fourteen centuries there has not been one single true Christian in the whole world.
Catholics and Lutherans are impious pagans.
One should not obey the authority of pagans.
One owes obedience only to the authority of true regenerate Christians.
All marriages of unregenerate Christians are merely concubinage.
All Christians regenerated by Christ are equal. Their goods must be common.
All the old ceremonies, of the Lutherans as well as of the Catholics, are devilish inventions of Antichrist, who is called: Pope!

In contrast with Rothmann's bitter attack on the religions of 'the world', Menno Simmons in the following passage is concerned with the internal life of a religious society, oblivious to the world outside. The true church is made up of the converted, the reborn. Its members are pacifists – Simmons was anxious to clear the re-baptisers of the slur of association with the Münster episode – and they are unconcerned with politics. The sectarians are entirely scriptural in their doctrines, but their worship is centred on the Eucharist rather than on Scripture readings. Discipline is a major activity of the church; discipline is based on an assumption of human sinfulness, and when sin is incorrigible the ban is employed as the ultimate measure of discipline.

From Menno Simmons, *The Beautiful and Fundamental Doctrine of the Word of God* (1537 or 1538), in R. Barclay, *The Inner Life of the Religious Societies of the Commonwealth* (London, Hodder & Stoughton, 1876), p. 80.
These regenerate persons constitute the true Christian church, who worship Christ as their only and true king, who fight not with swords and carnal weapons but only with the spiritual Word of God and the Holy Spirit. They seek no kingdom but that of Grace. They conduct themselves as citizens of heaven. Their doctrine is the Word of the Lord and everything not taught therein they reject. They exercise, after the example and institution of Christ, the sacred supper in

commemoration of the death and benefits of Christ. Their church discipline is extended to all who are impenitent sinners without distinction and they withdraw from perverse apostates according to the Word of God. They lament every day their daily sins and carnal infirmities and by this course are always profiting. They have no other justification than that which is by faith of Christ and which is of God by faith. They leave the things that are behind and press towards the mark of their high calling . . .

Fellowship was a cherished aspect of the life of religious sects. However, the intellectual independence of each believer and the very intimacy and propinquity of congregational religious life sometimes stood in the way of the attainment of total agreement. Quakers were aware of the perils of doctrinal discord and of the censoriousness into which discipline could sometimes deteriorate.

LFMH, 2Axxvii, no. 4. Yearly Meeting advice to the Quarterly Meetings, 1752.
We therefore most tenderly exhort and intreat you to be particularly watchful against whatsoever hath a tendency to strife and division, and in an especial manner to guard against the private spreading of evil reports one of another, a practice most pernicious, and with your utmost care and vigilance to be discouraged and withstood. And in order to prevent the evil consequences of such a practice, we tenderly and with earnestness advise all Friends who are concerned to travel in the work of the ministry, as well as others, that they not only shut their ears against all private information of persons and things tending to the defamation of particular persons and families and to stir up disputes and contentions in Meetings of discipline, but also to rebuke and reprove the persons or persons who shall attempt to prejudice their minds with any private information of that nature, which are often false and attended with baneful consequences to the reputation of such persons or families who are so unkindly and unjustly dealt by, and may tend to lead such ministers and others who shall give ear to the same in a wrong line of judgement.

In typical radical religious groups women had rights of participation. As the following printed seventeenth-century Quaker passage shows, women were able to reflect on the general condition of the Society (at a time of some relaxation in persecution) and were also able to moralise on family life. In fact, the maintenance of marriage and the family was a major goal of radical religious ethics. In the document below there is an appreciation of the affective and voluntary aspects of marriage, which derives in part from the Protestant Reformation.

LFMH, 2Aii, no. 13.
*A testimony for the Lord and his Truth. Given forth by the Women Friends at their yearly Meeting at York; being a tender salutation of love to the Friends and sisters in their several Monthly Meetings in this County and elsewhere.*1668 printed.
God . . . in His infinite Mercy and Love has given us a day of ease and liberty as to the outward, and hath broken the bonds of many captives and hath set the oppressed free and opened the prison doors in a good measure . . . we should neither take nor give liberty to that part in any, which may give the Lord occasion to suffer our bonds to be renewed . . .

And now to you young women, whom our souls love and whom the Lord delighteth to do good unto and hath visited with tastes of his Love, be you ordered by Him in all things that in your modest and chaste behaviour, your comely and decent dress, in your apparel and in all other things you may be good examples to others . . . and be not too careful for preferment or riches in this world but be careful to know the Lord to be your portion . . .

And Friends, be not concerned in reference to marriage, out of God's fear, but first wait to know your Maker to become your husband and the bridegroom of your souls . . . O Friends, this state is happy, and blessed are they that attain it and live in it; the Lord is not unmindful of them, but in His own time if he see it good for them, can provide meet-helps for them; then will your marriage be honourable, being orderly accomplished with the assent of parents and the unity of Friends and an honour to God and comfort to your own souls; then husbands and children are a blessing in the hands of the Lord.

Women played a prominent part in the organisation as well as the intellectual life of radical religious groups. The following passages are from an undated eighteenth-century defence of women's full participation in the national organisation of the Society of Friends. Women, it was felt by the writer, had a special part to play in maintaining the strict moral discipline of the Society. None the less, although it was being argued – evidently against some opposition – that women had contribution to make, by the eighteenth century that contribution was viewed as the relatively subordinate one of 'help-meets' to men.

LFMH, 2Axxxvi, no. 25, n.d. but eighteenth century.
It's easy to foresee there will be, as has always been the case, many objecters against this work [of setting up a national Women's Meet-

ing], but inasmuch as the women have been allowed and believed to be under the same qualifications for the ministry as the men; and at the first setting up of the church discipline was advised and encouraged to have and keep the Meetings in order, to the governing not only of their families and their respective Meetings where they reside, but also Monthly and Quarterly, that they might be help-meets in the whole; ... and for the want of such Meetings, whereby the care and advice of the honestly concerned may be duly extended, undue liberty of many kinds have more room to gain ground upon them and they thereby exposed to their great loss in marriages and other ways.

Now we desire it may be duly considered how far a national Meeting for the women, attended by two or more from every county ... of solid, well-concerned women to attend such Meeting or Meetings, held at the same time and place when and where the men's is, whereby they might be assisted and advised by them upon occasions, how far it might contribute to retrieve the present loss and assist the whole ... We hope our men Friends will not reject it, but give us due assistance therein. We would further observe to them that it is not any part of our intention hereby to assume or take upon ourselves any authority or power that is not already intended ...

Though pacifists, Quakers were not always pacific. In this collection of documents we encounter Henry Knowles, of Thurnham in Lancashire, in a number of situations – seeking a place for his son, getting drunk and repenting, and here standing up to a tithe collector. Typical of a member of a fundamentalist group, Knowles had a keen conscience, vivid but homely powers of expression and some difficulty in always subordinating turbulent human instincts to the civilising influence of purist Christian ethics.

LFMH, 2Bxv, no. 50, n.d. but early eighteenth century.
About the eleventh day of the seventh month, I being loading my corn, the wife of John Gardner, tithe farmer in Thurnham, her husband being loading tithe from another part of the town, she came to the field to me and demanded of me to set out tithe, and I denying to do so, she offered to set it out herself; I told her I did believe she ought to demand no tithe and that I ought not nor would pay any, and therefore, although she did set it out, I would load it, it being my own corn; whereupon she sent for her husband, who coming said, 'it seems you will not set out no tithe; pray how much corn had you?' I told him he had no good authority to question me for that, nor I should not tell him. So he rushed into the field and,

not knowing as I suppose rightly how much I had, took five hattocks or shocks, worth three shillings and six pence, out of sixty-three, for which I did follow him to the barn and reproved him. There was by myself my wife and son, and as to steeplehouse lays I pay none, nor I believe none pays for me. Henry Knowles.

The repudiation by religious radicals of 'the world' included a rejection of the popular folk customs and rituals of early modern European life. In the wider society elaborate ceremony was used in all social encounters and at the moments of passage in human life – birth, adulthood, marriage, death. Religious radicals anticipated modern civilisation in the way they sought to reduce the ceremonial aspects of life. In the following passage Quakers denounce funeral rituals and the formal courtesies of social life.

LFMH, 2Axxvii, no. 8. Minutes 2, 3 and 4 of early Meeting minutes to Quarterly Meetings, 1717.
21y This Meeting, being informed that Friends in some places have gone into the vain and empty customs of erecting ornaments over the dead bodies of Friends by stones, inscriptions and tombstones, and being very desirous that Friends should keep to demonstrable plainness and simplicity in this as well as other respects, it is therefore the advice of this Meeting that all such monuments as are already in being over dead bodies of Friends should be removed as much as may be with discretion and convenience, and that none be anywhere made or set up by or over the dead bodies of Friends or others in Friends' burying places for time to come.
31y And according to the primitive innocency and simplicity of Friends, it is the advice of this Meeting that no Friends imitate the world in any distinction of habit or otherwise as marks or tokens of mourning for the dead.
41y That care be taken in the education of their youth and otherwise that they avoid all unbecoming gestures, cringings, bowings and ceremonies in salutation contrary to our ancient plainness and simplicity.

Christian radicals idealised a regular and serious life of sobriety, industry and orderly behaviour. Their values made them useful employees, all the more so as their standards of conduct were not yet generally adopted in early modern society. In the following passage a seventeenth-century Quaker expresses an agonised sense of guilt about his falling away from the restrained ethics which were, in the last analysis, self-imposed.

LFMH, 2Bxv, no. 1, 17 7 1683.

Whereas I Thomas Haresnape of Aughton in the County of Lancashire, tailor, having for a season frequented the Meetings of the people of God called Quakers, and having also likewise made profession of being led and guided by the light of Christ Jesus which enlighteneth every man that cometh into the world . . . yet for want of faithfulness to it did lend an ear to the subtle temptations of my soul's enemy and hearkened to the persuasions of some young men (formerly my companions) and thereby was drawn from my lawful employments to go to see a horse-race which was at Crosby the second day of the fifth month last past, and as I came homewards from thence I went in the company of the said young men into an alehouse – on Thomas Meadow's in Ince Town – and there was drawn to quarrelling and fighting, which I knew was contrary to the profession I did make and to the practice of the aforesaid people of God, who are taught by the said light of Christ, which is the grace of God, to keep unto soberness, peace and love; and now I do freely acknowledge the evil of my doings in this matter, not offering to plead ignorance of any excuse, for as I went all the way of my idle journey I knew I was going amiss, and I was sometimes almost prevailed upon by the light and strivings of the spirit of Christ to have returned home back again; but not freely giving up thereunto, I was drawn to commit the said shameful actions, for which I have had, justly, shame and inward condemnation by the reproof of the light which then I rebelled against, for which my offence I have great sorrow in my heart and could not obtain quietness in myself before I gave up to publish this my repentance for it, which hath been in my heart ever since the time I did it, and now hereafter I hope ever to be preserved from doing the like.

One of the most common complaints of Christian radicals against the established churches was that their discipline was inadequate. True discipline, it was argued, implied the use of reprimand and, ultimately, the ban, to correct disorderly behaviour. Like the discipline of other radical groups, Quaker discipline was communal, voluntary and intended, primarily, to reclaim the errant individual. Sometimes, it may be thought, discipline was employed where today sympathy would be looked for. The document below is one of the disownments, by which Quakers operated their church discipline.

LFMH., 2Bii, no. 1, 3.5.1695.

Whereas Robert Tatham of Highfield within the parish of Halton hath for many years come amongst us and borne the profession of a Quaker, and being left a widower with several children, took to him to keep his house a woman, which some Friends did advise him to be careful how he behaved himself towards her; but he, not minding their counsel nor the leadings or guidance of God's good spirit in the inward part (which is able to preserve from all evil) as it is obeyed and yielded unto; so he let his mind out after her and married her with a priest, which is contrary to the example of the holy men of God recorded in the scriptures of Truth, and contrary to good order practised amongst us – for marriage is an ordinance of God – so that he has gone from the counsel of God by His spirit in his own heart and rejected the counsel and advice of Friends that were sent to him. We can do no less for the clearing of the blessed Truth of our profession thereof but deny the said Robert Tatham to be one of us, until he, through true repentance, come to see and condemn his disorderly practices therein which he has run into and thereby has brought a great grief upon the spirit of God's people, for which God's righteous judgement is against him and he shall bear his own burden. Subscribed on the behalf of our Monthly Meeting at Lancaster, the 7th day of the 3rd Month, called May, a.d. 1695 p. Hen. Coward.

'Take it to the church' is the Gospel precept with regard to disputes between members of a congregation – a precept that religious radicals sought to apply carefully, in the process elaborating their own 'legal' structures and lessening their dependence on outside agencies of the state. The letter below is from a number of 'weighty Friends' to a Quaker who held a fellow-Quaker in the bonds of debt. This letter illustrates how humane sectarian methods were, compared with the contemporaneous legal treatment of poverty and debt.

LFMH, 1Bi (a), no. 11, 13 1 1742.
Jacob Goffe,
Loving Friend,
We understand that John Lancaster is thy debtor and at present thy prisoner for the same. He belonging to our Monthly Meeting, we have account from Friends of the particulars of his circumstances relating to his debts and credits, and find that he is insolvent (notwithstanding his account to the contrary), so according to their advice, he has assigned over his whole estate, both real and personal, to two Friends, for the use of his creditors, share and share alike, so that it appears to us that he is willing to do all that is in his power for the advantage of his creditors. We thought it our duty to acquaint thee herewith and apply to thee for his enlargement, for his lying there is very chargeable and occasions the delay of gathering in his effects, in order to satisfy his creditors, as far as they will extend,

which none can do as well as himself. Consider his poor family, having a wife and six small children, who live upon his creditors until his effects can be disposed of, all which still lessening his substance and render his condition worse and worse; therefore we entreat thee to have compassion on him in his present afflicting circumstances and order him his liberty.

We doubt not but thou knows others in cases of this nature and we shall be glad thou comply thereto to prevent further trouble and loss. Thou may depend that no care will be wanting of making the most of his effects and fully distributed among his creditors, so concluding with our love to thee, thy loving Friends,
> William Skirrow
> William Stout
> John Dilworth.

Sexual morality was a major preoccupation of the disciplinary activities of radical groups. Non-marital sex in early modern Europe involved the stigmas and insecurities of illegitimacy and unmarried motherhood. The strict sexual standards of most radical Christian groups offered some protection to their women members from sexual exploitation. The moral discipline involved appears harsh to us, but, as the following eighteenth-century Quaker disciplinary case shows, it was designed to reclaim rather than expel the 'sinner'.

LFMH, 2Bii, no. 14, 4 12 1739.
Whereas Elizabeth Rawlinson, junior, late of Hornby, hath been educated and made profession of the Christian religion as it is held forth by us the people called Quakers and has been tenderly advised publicly and privately by her relations and friends to a steady and circumspect perseverance therein. Yet, notwithstanding which, it's now evident that she has been very disorderly in her company-keeping and conversation, by her being delivered of a child without any pretence of being married; and lest any should think that we in any wise wink or connive at such a scandalous action amongst us, we do hereby disown her to be in unity with us until she come to sincere repentance and publicly condemn herself for the abovesaid crime.

Chastity was one of the traits that set puritan religious radicals apart from the loose-living world around them. It was all too easy for members of radical groups to fall in with prevalent mores – in the matter of sex as well as in such matters as drinking and dress. When a lapse took place sectarian discipline was applied with full severity, and seemingly innocent parties felt the sting of censure. This comes out in the following passage, but in the next document to it we see how an insistence on the need for mercy ran against the current of severity.

LFMH, 2Axxix, no. 9, 12 10 1756.
A Copy of the Denial of Benjamin Abbatt and his Wife.
Whereas Ann the wife of Benjamin Abbatt of Sendley Green near Wigan, a member of our Society, having been educated among the people called Quakers (and sometime since married amongst them), but since having so far disregarded the principles of truth she made profession of that about the 30th of the 10th month, she being at Wigan Fair (along with her husband and others) at the sign of the Buck in the Vine, where two credible persons saw her in an upper chamber along with a soldier in a very indecent and unbecoming posture, upon a bed, with the door bolted.

And whereas Benjamin, her husband, hath from time to time endeavoured to hide her wickedness therein, contrary to the clearest evidence against her, and, by refusing to let her confess the same to her parents and friends, and ask their forgiveness, when she was willing so to have done, but did his utmost to improve upon Friends by endeavouring, with lies and falsehoods, to make them believe that it was not so when it really was; which wicked actions of theirs, so contradictory to the known principles of our profession, call on us to give forth testimony against them and their evil practices.

Therefore, for the clearing of truth and our Society, we give forth this testimony of denial against them and do hereby declare that we disown being in unity and fellowship with them until such time as they come to sincere and unfeigned repentance and amendment of life, which for their welfare and wellbeing we desire.

Following on this 'disownment', the Quakers of Hardshaw Monthly Meeting registered a strong protest against the treatment of a wronged husband and innocent children. Church discipline had to be severe, but it had also to be just.

LFMH, 2Axxix, no. 10, 21 6 1757.
To Friends at their next ensuing Quarterly Meeting to be held in Lancaster 21st of the 6th month 1757.
. . . Sometime after that, the said monthly meeting of Fylde, by their paper of denial did exclude from membership the said Benjamin and his wife and thereby renounced all regard for them and their innocent children, in no way involved in either supposed or real crimes of the parents, at a time when a charitable disposition was highly needful to their distressed condition, who were in want of almost all the necessaries of life and who must have greatly suffered, if not have wholly perished in such time of general calamity, but for

our assistance and that of some well-disposed neighbours.

We need not mention to you, as being well known, the steps Benjamin took to reinstate himself with the Society after this denial; your own records will stand as a lasting memorial done to a person neither regularly dealt with, nor guilty of a crime meriting so severe an animadversion . . .

Excessive drinking was one of the most serious problems in early modern Europe. The moderate puritan asceticism of Reformed Christianity was adopted in its entirety by radical groups. The temperance code, sustained by church discipline, helped shelter radical Christians from the endemic drunkenness of pre-industrial European life. In the disownment of Robert Skirrow 'excommunication' is used as a severe form of rebuke – as a means to amend the culprit's behaviour.

LFMH, 2Bii, no. 2, 2 8 1699.
Whereas Robert Skirrow of Scotforth hath from his infancy frequented the assemblies of the people called Quakers and joined (in some degree) in society with them who make profession of the truth of God inwardly revealed through the operation of His spirit, which shows unto man what is good and what is evil, and, as obedience thereunto is given through faith in Christ Jesus, power also to resist the enemy of his soul's peace. But notwithstanding his profession aforesaid, he yielding to the temptations of his soul's enemy and to follow the vanities of this present world, and slighting the reproof of God's spirit in his own heart, hath been drawn forth to drink strong liquors and to frequent alehouses more than was necessary, to the disordering of himself and the spending of his precious time, so as to foresake his peace with the Lord, as he hath acknowledged; for which said vain course of living he hath been frequently reproved and tenderly advised by several of us the people called Quakers to repent of and forsake his said practices, whose advice he seemed to be affected with, promising for the future to be more careful, confessing that he was self-condemned for his disorderly living; yet, notwithstanding his said confession, and seeming repentance, he hath not only continued in the aforesaid excess but also, contrary to our practice and the practice of righteous people in former ages, as is recorded in the Scriptures of truth, is married to a woman by a priest; so that, for the removing any scandal that may be cast upon us or the truth we make profession of, from his said action we thought it our duty to give forth this, to certify all to whose hands it may come that we do disown his said actions and him in them until such time as he comes to unfeigned repentance for his rebellion against the manifestations of the spirit of God in his own conscience

and gainsaying our advice many times given him for his eternal good.

After a first wave of conversion, many radical Christian groups emerged as congregations made up of a number of families. The family played an important part in moral nurture and in the upholding of puritan standards of behaviour. In return, the church group lent its support to the authority of the family, as we see in this eighteenth-century Quaker case.

LFMH, 2Bii, no. 11, 4 1 1734.
It being the practice of us the people called Quakers to have the marriage of such as are of our communion to be public and with the knowledge and consent of parents as their natural right, and according to the practice of primitive times, as recorded in the holy Scriptures. But we are at present concerned to take notice that Sarah Lawson, daughter of Robert Lawson of Lancaster, who hath been educated and made profession of religion with us, has lately married a young man not of the same religious profession, and in a private manner, without the knowledge or consent of her father and brothers, which proceeding and marriage we can do not less than testify against and her, in her contempt of us and our order in proceeding in marriages.

Amongst the social services provided by church membership in radical groups was the possibility of reception and welcome in a place of settlement. Immigrants could be received into the society of a church group, and there provided with social assistance and moral oversight. The following passages show how Quakers tried to ensure that when some of their number migrated they were not left to their own devices. The network of the Society of Friends, through the device of 'removal certificates', ensured that discipline, care, fellowship and solicitude for the individual were not relaxed by reason of emigration.

LFMH, 2Axxvi, no. 5. A removal certificate from Lancaster Monthly meeting to Dublin Monthly Meeting, with, on the reverse, the certification of the Friend in question on his return from Dublin to Lancaster; 6 4 1715 and 11 9 1715.
To Friends in Dublin, These.
Dear Friends, After the salutations of endeared love to you, we hereby acquaint you that the bearer hereof (John Lancaster), who for a considerable time hast been a member of our Monthly Meeting, being desirous to sojourn among you for a time, and acquainting us therewith, we thought fit to signify to you that we own him to

be in unity with us, and that his conversation is answerable to the truth he makes profession of, which we hope will render him acceptable unto you, and as such we recommend him to your Christian care, desiring his growth and prosperity in the unchangeable truth; and in it remain your Friends and brethren.

To Friends of Lancaster Monthly Meeting.

Dear Friends,

With unfeigned love we tenderly salute you, hereby acquainting you that the within-named John Lancaster, having signified to us his intention of returning back to England, these may signify to you on his behalf that during his stay here he hath been of an orderly conversation, admitted a member of our Men's Meeting, and upon enquiry we do not find but that he is clear of all women in these parts on account of marriage.

In an age of increasing transatlantic travel and emigration, religious societies like the Quakers were able to offer a network of social and moral care to their members, especially their youth who were uprooting themselves from the protective environment of family, Meeting, village and small town. The following passage shows how this network operated, and shows too how Quakers, like other religious radicals, put human welfare before the pursuit of wealth.

LFMH, 2Ai, no. 8, 5 11 1699.

Dear Friends and Brethren,

In discharge of that Christian care and great duty of love which the Lord hath laid upon us as a peculiar people chosen of Him, we are concerned for the holy truth's sake to acquaint you, that our Friends and brethren in America, from the yearly meeting at Philadelphia in Pennsylvania, in this 7th month last past, sent the following account viz.

That whereas divers young men are sent over hither with some cargoes of goods, being the sons or servants of Friends, who not being committed to the care of some particular Friends, do often take extravagant courses, spending their money and debauching themselves, by reason of which a reproach is brought upon the truth and the Friends of it, especially in this place, for the prevention of which for the future, we give this advertisement.

Wherefore our tender advice and earnest desire is that kindly care be taken in your respective Monthly Meetings for all such young men as are convinced of the truth, or profess the same, who may have occasion to go beyond the seas into any foreign parts of the world, that they may first come to the Monthly Meeting to which they belong, for certificates of their conversations and behaviour, that Friends also may then have opportunity faithfully to exhort them, as in truth and righteousness they may see cause.

That they may be recommended to the oversight and care of some faithful Friends in those foreign parts where they go, and Friends are inhabitants, and they desire to advise and deal with such that shall take any evil course or act in any way contrary to their profession, at the Meetings in those parts.

There is also another occasion and sorrow fallen upon Friends and that is through great numbers of Friends crowding together on shipboard in order to transport themselves into foreign parts, which it's believed hath occasioned great sickness and mortality to many of them in their voyages, which we earnestly desire all Friends concerned may be very careful to avoid, for time to come, and that such that are merchants, masters of ships, owners and undertakers, may prevent as much as in them lies the endangering the healths and lives of passengers, by not suffering your ships to be so crowded but that they may be well and conveniently accommodated.

Radical Christian groups often provided extensive welfare services for church members. With the Quakers, apprenticeships for the young figures prominently among these social provisions, but, as Henry Knowles was aware, apprenticeships within the church-group had a religious and moral as well as a vocational function, and helped insulate the children of the sect from the corrupting influences of the 'non-Christian' world.

LFMH, 2Bi(a), no. 4. Henry Knowles of Thurnham, Lancs., to William Stout, Meeting clerk, at Lancaster, 21 11 1714.
Beloved Friend,
Having this time a sense upon my mind of the disadvantage and harm that hath befallen me by being brought up and having my conversation amongst the people of the world, by whose example, together with the corruption of nature which youth is often inclined unto, I have run into those things which hath brought trouble and sorrow and God's displeasure upon me, and, by the working of the enemy of man's eternal happiness, evil things and wild ungodly practices I learned amongst them hath been ready to cleave unto me. And now it being my duty to ensure that my children have not reason to complain of the like inconvenience, therefore do I communicate my desire unto thee at this time. My Friend, it is the desire of my soul unto the Lord that my children when I am gone may be as monuments of His inexpressible mercy, and this is what I desire of thee: that thou would be mindful to make enquiry for some place or business for this boy I have at home with me, amongst Friends. He

hath a great desire to get a trade – either joiner, wright, cooper or shoemaker – and I am willing to do what I am able to procure him a trade. I have respect unto Friends' kindness in what they have already done for me, and if I be not able to procure this boy a trade, I desire however that he may be placed amongst Friends. I could get him a trade or place, but my desire is to have him amongst Friends, where he may be taught the fear and true knowledge of God. So with my dear love unto thee, I bid thee farewell, thy really loving Friend Hen. Knowles.

For post-Reformation radicals, as for Calvinists, poor relief meant not only alleviating poverty but also attempting to stem it at its source, and even to abolish poverty itself, amongst the members of the church-group, through education and the creation of work. In the passage below seventeenth-century Quakers are considering the establishment of a workhouse for children; in particular they discuss ways to overcome the natural affections of indigent parents, and advance arguments in favour of taking children away from home. The 'queries' are redolent of calculated and unsentimental philanthropy; but the proposal to which they refer was not adopted by Quakers.

LFMH, 2Cxiv, no. 1, n.d. but late seventeenth century.
Query the 1st
Whether a place for education be really necessary and advantageous for poor Friends' children from 6 years old to 10 or 14?
Query 2nd. What number of suchlike children the county may afford and what arguments may be used to the parents to part with suchlike children?
3. What industry these children will be capable of, besides learning and good education.
4. What stock may be needful to their own industry to maintain these children, tutor and servants?
5. What place may be proper to settle such a family in, and what security must be given for such an undertaking?
6. What persons requisite for observers or trustees for such a concern, and to whom and how often to give up their accounts?

From the beginning Christianity has set up a sharp contrast between law and freedom. St Paul contrasted Christian freedom with Jewish law. This superiority of freedom over law was reasserted by Luther, and became a characteristic tenet of radicals of the Reformation period, as it had been with their mediaeval predecessors. Few groups took the doctrine of freedom to mean that any forms of conduct were permissible to them. None the less, the literal doctrine of Christian freedom made Christian radicals social subversives. The passage below establishes Christian freedom in a classic historical framework, which interprets law, government and the very Bible itself as developments since the golden age. Man, Mason argues, is inherently innocent – a kind of noble savage. This passage seems to illustrate the influence on early Quakers of the ideas of Gerrard Winstanley.

From Martin Mason, *Innocency Cleared; the Liberties and Privileges of God's People for Assembling Together in His Fear to wait upon Him* . . ., [printed] 1660, pp. 1–2
Come, let us reason together in meekness and moderation, O ye children of men that are now in authority, and tell me what it was that induced men to live in the fear of the Lord, and peaceably one with another before the reins of political government, or the rod of that authority had its institution, or the Bible had a beginning, if it was not a principle of God, or a measure of Himself, in every mortal which inwardly led him to be obedient to his maker?

The children of men in that golden age of the world, living the life of true innocency and true holiness, needed not then an outward law to restrain them from vice or vanity; were (by the inward law of God written in their hearts and by their love and obedience thereunto) a law unto themselves.

Lust was mortified and was not suffered to live in them; and therefore could not lord it over them: covetousness had not crept into their hearts, each man lived comfortably upon the creation and was contented with his portion, no man fought them to lord it over one another, every man fought over the good of his fellow-creature as his own; while this inward voice or law of God was regarded by them, all lording tyranny was a stranger to them . . .

The problem of relations with governments has taxed all radical religious movements. A common formula was to give such allegiance to secular governments as was consistent with Christian principles. Secular governments were held to be deserving of authority within their proper spheres of operation, or to be properly concerned with the sinful. As these formulae implied conditional and non-absolute forms of loyalty, they were not usually satisfactory to early modern governments. In the passage below we see Quakers trying, without complete success, to explain to the English government that, though they gave the government their complete allegiance, they could not give that allegiance in the form the government wanted. To a hostile observer the way they reserved to themselves conscientious scruples would appear as equivocation and disloyalty. The Quakers on this occasion – one of the peril for the regime – seemed to be saying, not that they would support the government, but that they would not overturn it. The Association was an oath pledging subjects to the support of William III's Protestant throne at a time when it was menaced by Jacobite conspiracy.

LFMH, 2Bxxv, no. 2, 23 2 1696.
The Ancient Testimony and Principle of the People called Quakers. Renewed with respect to the King and Government, and touching the present Association. We the said people do solemnly and sincerely declare that it hath been our judgement and principle from the first day we are called to profess the light of Christ Jesus manifested in our consciences unto this day, that the setting up and putting down kings and governments is God's peculiar prerogative for causes best known to Himself; and that it is not our work or business to have any hand or contrivance therein, nor to be busybodies in matters above our station, much less to plot and contrive the ruin or overturn of any of them, but to pray for the King and for the safety of our nation and good of all men, that we may live a peaceable and quiet life, in all godliness and honesty under the government which God is pleased to set over us.

And according to this our ancient and innocent principle we often have given forth our testimony, and now do, against all plotting, conspiracies and contriving insurrections against the King or the government, and against all treacherous, barbarous and murderous designs whatsoever, as works of the Devil and darkness; and we sincerely bless God and are heartily thankful to the King and government for the liberty and privilege we enjoy under them by law, esteeming it our duty to be true and faithful to them.

And whereas the said people are required to sign the said Association, we sincerely declare that our refusing to do so is not out of any disaffection to the King or government, nor in opposition to his being declared rightful and lawful King of these realms, but purely because we cannot for conscience sake fight, kill or revenge either for ourselves or any man else . . .

In general religious radicals of the Reformation period manifested a cautious attitude to secular governments. Even when governments relaxed persecution against them, they had to beware of taking full advantage of relief, lest they outrage hostile public opinion. In England under James II (1685–8) the king sought to waive the laws so as to offer indulgence to religious dissenters. Though the royal measures were widely regarded as unconstitutional, many Quakers saw in them an opportunity to worship and proselytise freely. None the less, so as not to give affront to Anglican opinion, they had to use their liberty with the greatest discretion. The document below is the postscript from a letter of James Park to the Quakers of the Northern Counties. It belongs to the period of James II's drastic attempts to ease the position of non-Anglicans.

LFMH, 2Bxxv, no. 14, 1687 or 1688.
And, dear Friends, sensibly prize this great mercy and kindness from God, that the King out of his favour hath extended liberty for us, to meet together, to serve and worship God, and for such an openness as there by now appears in most places in the nation for people to hear God's privy Truth declared, whereby the Truth of God may spread and come to be made known in the earth. This liberty ought to be used in great humility and lowliness of mind, and none to be puffed up with it, to abuse it or walk any way unworthy of it, lest the Lord should be provoked again to deprive us of that liberty which at present we do enjoy.

For early modern religious radicals persecution would mean anything from the stake, and death in prison, to the daily torments of local bullies. Even when, as with English Dissenters after 1689, the worst privations were over, legal oppressions could still play havoc with individual and family life. The following printed Quaker passage from the early eighteenth century shows how little difference statutory relief made to the conditions under which committed Dissenters lived.

The Suffering-Case of Several of the People Commonly Called Quakers on Suits Mostly Commenced for Tythes in the Court of Exchequer, since the Acts made for the more easy recovery of tythes, in the 7th and 8th of King William III. London 1709.
Nathaniel Astwood of Blow Norton having been prosecuted in the Court of Exchequer, about four years, at the suit of Nathaniel Best, Tythe-farmer under Nathaniel Vincent, Rector of the said Parish, for the non-payment of four years tythes, at £6 per annum demanded; (although the former tenants paid but £3 per annum) which surely for conscience sake he could not pay; and for that cause only, hath been a prisoner at Norwich, and at the Fleet, above a year, away from his six motherless children; having not only had his goods seized, by force of a sequestration, issued out of the Court of Exchequer, on the 28th of September 1708, to the value of £129.4.6d. (as appears by the appraisement and affidavits of two sufficient men), though appraised by the plaintiff's own servant and another man at but £70.5.4d; but also had his real estate seized of £14 per annum, and [Best] threatened the said Nathaniel Astwood's children, that he would not leave their father worth one groat. And

being earnestly desired to leave them a bed to lie on, he refused it, and said they must suffer with their father, and had not a compassionate neighbour lent them a bed, they must have lain on the floor.

From its very inception England's 1689 Toleration Act was impeded, in the facilities it gave to Dissenters to worship, by clerical and Tory interests. The Act afforded little real toleration, but even so it was resented by the advocates of a one-church state. Against uncompromising Dissenters like the Quakers, hoary myths were raised again – such as the curious idea that Quakers were Catholics in disguise. Some Quakers believed optimistically that the laws operated in their favour, but it appeared that their enemies could direct the laws of England against them.

LFMH, 2Ai, no. 6, 17 12 1690.
To William Stout of Lancaster, Shopkeeper.
Dear Friends and Brethren,
These are to acquaint you that a few priests in the County of Norfolk, instigated by our implacable adversary, Francis Bugg, having influenced some Justices and Grand Jury at the late Quarter Sessions of the said county to petition the Commons in Parliament against the people called Quakers, which, they have sent up; and likewise in the corporation of Edmondbury [sc. Bury St Edmunds] in Suffolk, the Alderman and some others, his assistants there, have sent another petition of the like import, both tending to bring Friends into question and to raise a new persecution against us. The one pretending many Romish emissaries among us, and the other most formidable heresies etc. And the said Norfolk priests before the late conference with them [have] threatened Friends in other counties with the like procedure against them as they intend in that county. It is therefore desired by this Meeting that some known faithful Friends (with what privacy they can) attend the several Quarter Sessions and Assizes in each respective county and corporation where Friends reside, to see if any such endeavouring be used as those before mentioned, for any complaints or petitions to the government against Friends; and if there be, to know who are the first movers thereto, and to use their interest to inform and persuade some of the Grand Jury and Justices, or some of the most moderate of them, to prevent such endeavourings and attempts, which are looked upon by many in authority as a confronting and opposing the Act of Toleration, it being for uniting the King's Protestant subjects in interest and affection.
Whereas these petitions and endeavours above-said are seen to

be of a contrary tendency and therefore in divers places rejected, . . . Friends are further desired to write to your representatives in Parliament to discourage the said petitions; and the letters you send to them, inclose to your correspondents here unsealed, that Friends may view them before delivered. So with our dear loves unto you we remain your Friends and brethren.

Signed on behalf of the Meeting for Suffering in London, the 17th of the 12th month 1690 by
Benjamin Bealing.

If Christian dissenters were to undergo persecution, it was vital for them to be aware of the historical and religious significance of their sufferings. In the passage below, a Lancashire Quaker links tithes to the history of ecclesiastical corruption and of the Reformation. By means of such historical analysis radical religionists were able to condemn the magisterial churches of the Protestant Reformation as being fundamentally unreformed. Note the vitriolic terms used for the worship and government of the Church of England.

LFMH, 2Bxv, no. 3, 8 10 1751.
For as much as since that time of my first convincement [i.e. conversion] and sincere belief of the principles and doctrines of truth professed, held forth and preached by the people called Quakers with whom I now walk in religious society, I have not in any wise been tried either by suffering in body or estate for refusing to pay tythes, steeple-house lays, church dues or church rates commonly so called; yet notwithstanding having had a pretty clear discovery of those things and the nature and first rise of them and being fully and evidently persuaded in my own mind that the same are and altogether have been since the dispensation of the Gospel demanded, set up and instituted by worldly Popish priests and hireling ministers, only tend to the maintenance and upholding and carrying on of a carnal, fruitless, idolatrous, superstitious, dark worship and ministry, quite contrary to that divine and spiritual worship established by Christ himself, His apostles and ministers. As an opposer, therefore, and disowner of such laws as these church rates etc. and suchlike unreasonable demands, I give this as my testimony against them and the payment of them, believing them to be altogether unChristian and unlawful and do not doubt but when it doth befall me to be made a sharer in the sufferings of Friends on account of the non-payment thereof, I shall be enabled through divine assistance to cheerfully and patiently to undergo the same. Given under my hand this eighth day of the tenth month Anno 1731
Thomas Tarbock.

Thus, when persecuted, religious radicals often showed a sense of the meaning of their sufferings and of the place of those sufferings in history. In the following passage a seventeenth-century Quaker connects his objections against tithes both to Scripture history and to the history of Protestant martyrs in the Reformation and pre-Reformation, as set out in Foxe's *Book of Martyrs*. This Quaker boldly imputes to Jesus an anachronistic condemnation of tithes; to some extent 'Christ' is a pseudonym for the individual's own conscience. Thorpe was in fact a fifteenth-century Lollard, not a Tudor Protestant.

LFMH, 2Bxv, no. 3, 1679.
The Lord Jesus Christ came to put an end to the first priesthood that took tithes, so the priesthood is changed and the law is changed that gave them tithes, so that it's plain to all those whose eyes the Lord has opened that Christ has put an end to all those things, as the Apostle to the Hebrews doth fully demonstrate, so that I dare not pay any such things, lest I should sin against God and so wrong my own soul, for I am certainly persuaded that both those that willingly pay tithes and those that receive them do in effect deny Christ come in the flesh, who was to put an end to all such things. And this my testimony is the same with several of the martyrs in Queen Mary's days, as William Thorpe for one, who has burned for the testimony of a good conscience; besides, the practice and example of Christ and His apostles, as their doctrine doth clearly demonstrate, was against such things . . .

In the interactions between European states and the religious radicals, the radicals were faced with conflicting alternatives. Either they could work for a civil and legal amelioration of their group condition and work to lessen the impact of persecution upon themselves; or they could maintain a hostile and alienated stance towards 'non-Christian' laws and institutions, and accept persecution willingly as a form of Christian witness. The latter course usually characterised religious dissent, and it is vividly expressed in the following mid-eighteenth-century document, an excerpt from a letter in which the Quaker Jonathan Hill comments on some of his impressions of northern Friends. Hill's quietism is entirely scriptural.

LFMH, 2Bxxv, no. 8, 8 4 1741.
And there is one thing I have to remind you of, which is this: when I was at your Quarterly Meeting at Lancaster, you was appointing men over each Particular Meeting to oversee the same, lest if any couple should marry or the like and the priest should prosecute them (if I remember aright) they might at the county's charge be

righted by law, it being illegal, as you call it. But Friends, are you weary of bearing the cross of Christ, that you run to the arm of flesh for succour? Are you weary with resting under the power of the Almighty that you run to the power of wicked men for refuge? Is this acting in the meekness and gentleness of Christ, who when He was reviled reviled not again? When He suffered he threatened not, but committed His cause to the hand of Him that judgeth righteously. How doth it agree with the words of Christ which sayeth, 'I say unto you that you resist not evil, but if anyone sue thee at the law and take away thy coat, let him have thy cloak also'? Likewise Paul speaks against this practice of going to law before unbelievers, saying, 'why do you not rather suffer wrongs? why do you not rather suffer yourselves to be defrauded?' According to Christ and the Apostle it appears to be more Christian-like to suffer patiently than to resist. But there is one place in Scripture which upon a just comparison looks much the same way, and this it is; when the Philistines was hard upon Saul king of Israel, and he was distressed, he went from the Lord to the witch of Endor. It appears to me to be the same thing, to flee from the power of God to the power of men. Friends, flee not the cross of Christ, and if any suffer as a Christian let him not be ashamed, but rather let him glorify God, which has counted him worthy to suffer for His name and truth's sake. And fear not man, whose breath is in his nostrils, for wherein is he to be accounted of? But rather fear God, and stand in His power, that the power of darkness may have no place in you. How you'll take this I know not, whether in the love of God, as I write it to you, or whether you'll be ready to judge me for it I am uncertain. But for the clearing of myself before God have I written this epistle and to His spirit do I direct every one of you, that you may be led unto all truth, for God is not the author of confusion, but of peace. To Him, therefore, be given all honour and power and thanksgiving and praise, for ever and for evermore.

Jonathan Hill.

Radical religionists frequently saw themselves as the persecuted victims of worldly powers. Persecution was witness – witness to the radicals' fidelity to the Christlike and Apostolic tradition of suffering. Along with the wish to seek suffering, there sometimes arose a wish to avoid it, and to seek political and legal methods of relief from civil persecution. Both these tendencies were apparent in Quakerism. Jonathan Hill advised Quakers to welcome oppression. In the following passage, in a contrary tendency, we see Benjamin Bealing suggesting measures by which persecution might be alleviated.

LFMH, 2Bxxv, no. 1.   London, 19 8 1695.
Benjamin Bealing
Dear Friends,
Where any would be members of Parliament and desire your votes
'tis advisable that where you are free to vote at all you do it for such
as are prudent and for liberty of conscience towards God, and will
vote for our relief in case of oaths. And to that end it would be well
to go to them yourselves; or where you are not acquainted to take
such along with you before the time of the election who have
interest in them. And if they will redress our grievances when they
shall sit in Parliament then you may engage on their behalf, for now
is the time to engage them in our interest when we are most capable
of advancing theirs, and be sure offend not such as were our friends
last sitting nor others if it may be; and where two would be elected
and neither can be gained on our behalf, then be silent and vote not
at all, and let Friends be circumspect and unanimous for the matter
of the moment and mind that you attend your members a little
before they come up, and remind them of our sufferings and expose
not to everybody; which with my love in the blessed truth is from
your loving Friend
        B.B
Communicate this to Friends in Boroughs and Corporations.

Radical religious groups were intimately caught up in the life of
towns. While they found urban areas fertile grounds for mission, they
also objected to the moral irregularities of town life – the moral
collapse that often happened to individuals faced with the anonymity
and indifference of urban existence. At the time when Thomas Rudd
visited it, Liverpool was a fast-growing commercial centre. Like many
other religious radicals, Rudd may have felt that trade and wealth led
inevitably to sin. Rudd's main assault, though, was on the Anglican
worship, which had strong roots in the Lancashire port. In common
with many other religious radicals he showed no attitude of tolerance
to other Christian forms of worship. He represents a religious radicalism ever ready to confront the world, to seek to overcome it, to conduct
a mission towards it, and to accept the reward of persecution from his
encounter. The Liverpool borough authorities, including the staunch
Whig JP, treated him as a harmful crank.

LFMH, 2Bxxv, no. 6, 1699.
The Suffering Case of Thomas Rudd, now prisoner in the County
Gaol of Lancaster, offered to the Judge Surton for release.
The said Thomas Rudd being a man that feared the Lord and much
grieved with the profaneness and immorality that is so frequently

met with in most places, especially in the cities and great towns in this and other countries [sc. counties], which did bring a concern upon him publicly to warn people to fear and dread the Great God of Heaven and Earth, in many of the cities and great towns in England, Scotland and Ireland, and about a year ago, he being in the town of Liverpool, was concerned to warn the inhabitants in the streets to repent and fear God, that His judgements might not fall upon them, for sin and iniquity; which Christian exhortation did offend Thomas Sweeting, the then Mayor of Liverpool, and some other magistrates in that town, that they endeavoured to construct [sc. construe] him so doing as a breach of peace, and did thereupon commit him by a warrant to the house of correction at Preston, taking from him his horse, saddle and bridle, and sold them to defray the charge of sending him to Preston aforesaid where he remained prisoner about a month, after which he was released by order of the said magistrates.

For the said Thomas Rudd, considering the unChristian dealing of the said magistrates with him and also the rude behaviour of the inhabitants of Liverpool and especially of some of the Justices of the Peace and servants, who in the time of his godly exhortation to them did very much abuse him by burning his clothes with hot oils and tearing them off his body and throwing dirt out of the channel at him; he could not be clear till he went again to the said town to warn them, and also to the public place of worship, where observing them to say in their public prayers to God; 'We are the sheep of thy pasture and the lamps of thy fold etc.,' and also when they began to sing psalms to the glory and praise of God, he did at a vacant time (not interrupting their worship) in much fear and dread publicly query of them how they could call themselves sheep of God's pasture or lambs of His fold, or sing to the praise and glory of God while they did persecute him for warning them in their streets to fear the great God of Heaven and Earth; for which said query the aforesaid Thomas Sweeting committed him to the town prison at Liverpool, where he was confined prisoner about a month, after which said time of imprisonment Cuthbert Sharples, now Mayor of Liverpool and Thomas Johnson of the said town, Justice for the Peace, did grant a warrant to remove the said Thomas to the County Gaol of Lancaster where he now is prisoner upon account aforesaid.

Intense civil persecution elicited from radical religious groups a heightening of chiliastic expectations. Such expectations afforded great comfort, in that they stipulated a radical turning of the tables, a reversal of power in which the persecuted would have the upper hand. After the Restoration in 1660 English Quakers underwent a series of spasms of intensified persecution. Such a spasm took place in the Tory-Anglican reaction of the last years of Charles II's reign. In the developing industrial town of Leeds power was concentrated in the hands of a knot of interrelated Anglican magistrates, who applied the penal laws severely. In the passage below, from a printed pamphlet, a Quaker woman warns the West Riding town of the wrath to come. The genre was established by the admonition delivered by George Fox against the 'bloody town of Lichfield', but this convention was itself based on the warnings of Old Testament prophets to various miscreant cities.

From Isabel Wails, *A Warning to the Inhabitants of Leeds*, 1685, p. 1.

The Lord in making haste to recompense every one of you according to your doings; for He is risen to be a swift witness against the ungodly: and I plainly tell you all, who these lines may come before to be read or heard, if you sow to the flesh, of the flesh you shall reap corruption, but if ye sow to the spirit ye shall reap of the spirit life everlasting . . . God is highly displeased at your doings; for His anger is kindled and the vials of His wrath are ready to be poured upon you, who have wilfully transgressed against Him: and except ye repent, and let true judgement come over the head of the transgressor, you cannot escape, but you must drink of the cup of His indignation, which is held forth for them that will not take His counsel, nor hearken unto Him when He calls.

Notes

CHAPTER 1

1 George Grosjean, *Le Sentiment national dans la Guerre de Cent Ans* (Paris: Bossard, 1928), pp. 228–30. A fifteenth-century writer described the English as 'a race of people accursed ... ravishing wolves, proud, pompous, deceitful hypocrites'.

2 Václav Novotný, *Hus v Kostnici a Česká Šlechta. Poznamky a Dokumenty* (Prague: SPS, 1915), pp. 61–4; Count Lützow, *The Hussite Wars* (London: Dent, 1914).

3 Roland H. Bainton, *Here I Stand. A Life of Martin Luther* (London: Abingdon, 1951), p. 121. Bainton quotes Luther's significant remark at the Leipzig disputation: 'Let me talk German. I am being misunderstood by the people' (p. 116).

4 24 Hen. 8 c.12; for Parker's *De Antiquitate Britannicae Ecclesiae*, see V.J.K. Brook, *A Life of Archbishop Parker* (Oxford: Clarendon, 1962), pp. 322–5.

5 See, for example, Cromwell's speech to the Nominated Parliament in 1653, in W. C. Abbott, *The Writings and Speeches of Oliver Cromwell*, 2nd edn (New York: Russell & Russell, 1970), Vol. III, pp. 52–66.

6 G. H. Williams, 'The two social strands in Italian Anabaptism ca. 1526–ca. 1565', in L. P. Buck and J. W. Zophy (eds), *The Social History of the Reformation* (Columbus: Ohio State University Press, 1972), pp. 156–207.

7 See, for example, Keith L. Sprunger, *The Learned Doctor William Ames. Dutch Backgrounds of English and American Puritanism* (Champaign-Urbana, Ill.: Illinois University Press, 1972). Sprunger recalls a passage from William Perkins which illustrates the puritan concept of the Christian's isolated pilgrimage through the world at large: 'How can the world loue them that hate it, and haue little acquaintance with it, and are on earth as pilgrimes, wayting eury day for happie passage ... to their owne home, euen to the heauenly citie of Ierusalem.'

8 C. Hill, 'The English Revolution and the brotherhood of man', in *Puritanism and Revolution* (St Albans: Panther, 1968), pp. 126–53; W. C. Braithwaite, *The Beginnings of Quakerism* (London: Macmillan, 1912), ch. XVI.

9 Irmgard Höss, 'The Lutheran Church of the Reformation: problems of its formation and organization in the middle and north German territories', in Buck and Zophy (eds), op. cit., pp. 317–39.

10 Martin Luther, *Three Treatises* (Philadelphia: Muhlenburg, 1943), pp. 10–12.

11 Robert M. Kingdom, 'The control of morals in Calvin's Geneva', in Buck and Zophy (eds), op. cit., pp. 3–16; Gottfried Seebass, 'The Reformation in Nürnberg', in ibid., pp. 17–40; Gerhard Hirschmann, 'The second Nürnberg church visitation, 1560–1561', in ibid., pp. 355–80.

12 H. C. Porter, *Puritanism in Tudor England* (London: Macmillan, 1970), pp. 89, 91–2.

13 Daniel Neal, *The History of the Puritans; or Protestant Nonconformists; from the Reformation in 1517, to the Revolution in 1688*, 5 vols (London: Baynes, 1822), Vol. I, pp. 70–1.

14 Though see Alan Cole, 'The Quakers and the English Revolution', *Past and Present*, vol. 10 (1956), pp. 39–54.

15 J. Beresford (ed.), *The Diary of a Country Parson*, 5 vols (Oxford: Clarendon, 1968), Vol. I, p. 12; LFMH, 2Ai, no. 64; 2Cix, no. 84.

16 Quoted by David Potter, *People of Plenty* (Chicago: Chicago University Press, 1966), p. 15.

17 Denys Hay (ed.), *The Anglica Historia of Polydore Vergil a.d. 1485–1537*, Camden Series, vol. 84, 1950.

18 Pompeo Molimenti, *Venice* (London: Murray, 1907), pt. I, ii, p. 149.

19 Quoted in Janet Nelson, 'Society, theodicy and the origins of medieval heresy', *Studies in Church History*, Vol. 9 (1972), p. 69.

20 R. W. Southern, 'Aspects of the European tradition of historical writing', *TRHS*, 5th ser., vol. 20 (1970), pp. 173–96.

21 G. Strauss, *Manifestations of Discontent in Germany on the Eve of the Reformation* (Bloomington, Ind.: Indiana University Press, 1971), pp. 3–34.

22 Marjorie Reeves, *The Influence of Prophecy in the Later Middle Ages. A Study in Joachimism* (Oxford: Clarendon, 1969), pp. 301–2.

23 For example, *Calendar of State Papers, Spanish*, XI, p. 161.

24 *The Diary of Dr. Thomas Cartwright, Bishop of Chester, August 1686–October 1687*, Camden Soc., 1st ser., vol. 22 (1843), p. 74; D. H. Wilson, *King James VI and I* (London: Johnathan Cape, 1956), pp. 172–3; *DNB*, Vol. I, p. 471.

25 See, for example, John Chandos, *In God's Name. Examples of Preaching in England 1534–1662* (London: Hutchinson, 1971).

26 See C. S. Lewis, *A Preface to Paradise Lost* (Oxford: Clarendon, 1960), p. 18.

27 Paul S. Seaver, *The Puritan Lectureships. The Politics of Religious Dissent* (Palo Alto, Calif.: Stanford University Press 1970). Seaver reminds us, with a quotation from Elizabeth I, of the conflicting interests of the princely state and of reformist Christianity: 'that it was good for the church to have few preachers' (p. 17).

28 Claire Cross, ' "He-goats before the flocks": a note on the part played by women in the founding of some civil war churches', *Studies in Church History*, Vol. 8 (1972), p. 197.

29 *Calendar of State Papers, Foreign*, 1553–8, p. 153.

30 John Bunyan, *The Holy War made by Shaddai upon Diabolus for the Regaining of the Metropolis of the World*, ed. J. Brown (Cambridge: Cambridge University Press, 1905), *passim*.

31 For example, *The Advice to the Men of Shaftesbury or a Letter to a Friend Concerning the Horrid Popish Plot* (London, 1681), warned against 'an Amsterdam Religion, and Arbitrary Government in the hands of many'.

32 Valerie Pearl, *London and the Outbreak of the Puritan Revolution* (Oxford: Clarendon, 1961); on the other hand, a great city could assume a quite different, though still biblical, symbolism – that of Babylon: see W. Lamont and S. Oldfield (eds), *Politics, Religion and Literature in the Seventeenth Century* (Oxford: Clarendon, 1975), p. 60, and Hugh Latimer's 'Sermon of the Plough' in Chandos, op. cit., pp. 12–13.

33 Michel Mollat and Philippe Wolff, *The Popular Revolutions of the Late Middle Ages* (London: Allen & Unwin, 1973), p. 155.

34 Howard Kaminsky, *A History of the Hussite Revolution* (Berkeley: California University Press, 1967), pp. 294–5.

35 *DNB*, Vol. 7, pp. 180–1; A. F. Pollard, *Wolsey* (London: Longman, 1929), p. 35.

36 Hirschmann, in Buck and Zophy (eds), op. cit., p. 364; see also M. T. Clanchy, 'Remembering the past and the good old law', *History*, vol. 55 (1970), pp. 165–76.

37 Roy Strong, *Splendour at Court. Renaissance Spectacle and Illusion* (London: Weidenfeld & Nicolson, 1973), pp. 24–5.

38 *Pompa Triumphalis Introitus Ferdinandi Austriaci Hispaniarum Infantis etc. in Urbem Antwerpiam 1635* (Antwerp, 1642, reprinted by Blom Inc., New York, 1971).

39 P. W. Thomas, 'Two cultures? Court and country under Charles I', in Conrad

Russell (ed.), *The Origins of the English Civil War* (London: Macmillan, 1973), pp. 177–8; S. R. Gardiner (ed.), *Documents relating to the Proceedings against William Prynne in 1634 and 1637*, Camden Soc., 2nd ser., vol. 18 (1877), pp. 9 ff.

40 O. W. Furley, 'The pope-burning processions of the late seventeenth century', *History*, vol. 44 (1959–60), pp. 16–23.

41 P. Geyl, *The Revolt of the Netherlands* (London: Williams & Norgate, 1932), p. 45; Geyl shows how the Dutch-language civilisation upheld in these chambers of rhetoric was threatened by the francophone culture of the dynasty.

42 For the 'Sermon of St. John the Baptist' (1566), see F. Grossman, *Breugel. The Paintings* (London: Phaidon, 1966), pp. 122–4.

43 Alexander Murray, *'Piety and Impiety in 13th-century Italy'*, *Studies in Church History*, vol. 8 (1972), pp. 83–106.

44 For Savonarola and the Renaissance, see Eugenio Garin, *La Cultura del Rinascimento* (Bari: Laterza, 1973), p. 125.

45 For example, Felicity Heal, 'The Family of Love and the diocese of Ely', *Studies in Church History*, Vol. 9 (1972), pp. 213–23.

46 R. T. Vann, *The Social Development of English Quakerism* (Cambridge, Mass.: Harvard University Press, 1969), p. 193.

47 See the symposium 'Cities, courts and artists', *Past and Present*, vol. 19, pp. 19–25.

48 John Tonkin, *The Church and the Secular Order in Reformation Thought* (New York: Columbia University Press, 1971), pp. 5–11.

CHAPTER 2

1 Max Weber, *The Protestant Ethic and the Spirit of Capitalism*, trans. T. Parsons (London: Allen & Unwin, 1930); R. H. Tawney, *Religion and the Rise of Capitalism* (London: Murray, 1926).

2 M. Spinka (ed.), *The Letters of John Hus* (Manchester: Manchester University Press, 1972), pp. 14–15.

3 V. Romano (ed.), *Girolamo Savonarola. Prediche sopra i Salmi*, 2 vols (Rome: Belardetti, 1969), Vol. II, pp. 171, 251–3.

4 M. J. Kitch, *Capitalism and the Reformation* (London: Longman, 1969), pp. 37–8; G. S. Holmes, 'The Sacheverell riots', *Past and Present*, vol. 72 (1976), pp. 63–4.

5 *The Works of Sir William Temple, Bart.*, 4 vols (London, 1770), Vol. I, pp. 179, 187–8.

6 H. R. Trevor-Roper, *Religion, the Reformation and Social Change* (London: Macmillan, 1972), pp. 24 ff.; A. Biéler, *La Pensée economique de Calvin* (Geneva: Georg, 1961), p. 391; B. Gagnebin, *À la rencontre de Jean Calvin* (Geneva, Georg, 1964), p. 52; Kitch, op. cit., p. 23.

7 C. J. Dyck, 'Anabaptism and the social order', in J. C. Brauer (ed.), *The Impact of the Church upon its Culture*, 2 vols (Chicago: Chicago University Press, 1968), Vol. II, pp. 207, 209; J. Horsch, *Mennonites in Europe* (Scottdale, Pa: Mennonite Publishing House, 1942), pp. 367–8, 260, 227–30, 251–5; F. H. Littell, *The Origins of Sectarian Protestantism* (London: Macmillan, 1964), pp. 124–5; J. A. Hostetler, *Hutterite Society* (Baltimore: Johns Hopkins University Press, 1974), pp. 30–4.

8 Temple, *Works*, Vol. I, p. 179.

9 M. Spufford, 'The social status of some seventeenth-century rural dissenters', *Studies in Church History*, Vol. 8 (1972), pp. 203–11; J. Davis, 'Lollard survivals and the textile industry in the south-east of England', *Studies in Church History*, Vol. 3 (1966), pp. 191–202; F. Bate, *The Declaration of Indulgence 1672* (London: Constable, 1908), pp. 94, 97–8; W. M. Wigfield, 'Recusancy and Nonconformity in

Bedfordshire', *Publications of the Bedfordshire Historical Record Society*, vol. 20 (1938), pp. 177, 180.

10 John Bunyan, *The Holy War*, pp. 397–8.

11 George Fox, *A Warning to all the Merchants in LONDON, and such as buy and sell, with an Advisement to them to lay aside their superfluity, and with it nourish the poor* (London, 1658); G. Nuttall, 'Overcoming the world; the early Quaker programme', *Studies in Church History*, Vol. 10 (1973), pp. 145–64; LFMH, 2Ai, nos. 61, 62, 2Aii, no. 57; *Selection of Advices from Yearly Meeting, 1675–1703*, p. 80; *Lancaster Monthly Meeting Minute Book (LMMMB), 1675–1718*, p. 196; 2Bii, no. 4.

12 *LMMMB, 1675–1718*, p. 231; *Lancaster Particular Meeting Minute Book (LPMMB), 1698–1740*, p. 158; 2Axxvii, nos. 50, 64–5; *Lancaster Quarterly Meeting Minute Book (LQMMB), 1669–1711*, 6 5 1693, 4 2 1700; A. Raistrick, *Quakers in Science and Industry* (Newton Abbot: David & Charles, 1968), pp. 339–46, and *passim*; *Memoir of the Life of Elizabeth Fry, . . . edited by two of her daughters*, 2 vols (London: Gilpin, 1847), Vol. I, pp. 38–9; A. Hare, *The Gurneys of Earlham*, 2 vols (London, Allen, 1847), Vol. I, p. 26.

13 O. C. Watkins, *The Puritan Experience* (London: Routledge & Kegan Paul, 1972), pp. 18–24; cf. B. Groethuysen, *The Bourgeois. Catholicism vs. Capitalism in Eighteenth-Century France* (London: Barrie, 1968), pp. 170–225; Samuelsson, quoted in Kitch, op. cit., p. 173; LFMH, *LQMMB, 1669–1711*, 7 8 1697.

14 P. Brock, *Twentieth-Century Pacificism* (New York: Van Nostrand, 1970), p. 256; e.g. J. Moorman, *A History of the Franciscan Order* (Oxford: Clarendon, 1968), pp. 307–38.

15 Savonarola, *Prediche*, Vol. II, p. 171.

16 A. Meusel, *Thomas Müntzer and seine Zeit* (Berlin: Aufban, 1952), p. 187.

17 W. C. Braithwaite, *The Second Period of Quakerism* (Cambridge: Cambridge University Press, 1961), p. 36; LFMH, *Lancashire Quarterly Meeting Sufferings, 1701–1717*, 1 6 1701; V. Brook, *Whitgift and the English Church* (Edinburgh: Edinburgh University Press, 1957), p. 134; for another example of Nonconformist legalism, see 'A Narrative of the Imprisonment and the Usage of Col. Hutchinson', in *The Harleian Miscellany* (1744–6), Vo. III, pp. 33–4; Penn, quoted in A. Lloyd, *Quaker Social History 1669–1738* (London: Longman, 1950), p. 80.

18 C. Hill, *Puritanism and Revolution* (St Albans: Panther, 1968), pp. 78, 146; see also B. Capp, *The Fifth Monarchy Men* (London: Faber, 1972), pp. 151–3, 167.

19 LFMH, *LMMMB, 1675–1718*, pp. 4–5 (1675).

20 W. C. Braithwaite, *The Beginnings of Quakerism* (London: Macmillan, 1912), pp. 420–30; extracts from the ms. *Journal of John Kelsall of North Wales (1683–1743)* (in the possession of John Kelsall of Quernmore, Lancs.), p. 79.

21 W. Haller, *Tracts on Liberty in the Puritan Revolution* (New York: Octagon, 1965), Vol. I, p. 113; C. Hill, *Change and Continuity in Seventeenth-Century England* (London: Weidenfeld & Nicolson, 1975), p. 229.

22 C. Hill, *The World Turned Upside Down* (London: Temple Smith, 1972), pp. 271–2.

23 Jacob Boehme, *Six Theosophic Points and other writings*, trans. J. Earle (East Lansing, Michigan: Michigan University Press, 1958), p. 179.

24 *Theologia Germanica*, trans. S. Winkworth (London: Macmillan 1893), p. 193; Boehme, op. cit., pp. 194, 200; *The Journal of the Rev. John Wesley in 4 volumes* (London: Everyman, n.d.), Vol. II, p. 9; J.R. Jacob, 'Restoration Reformation and the origins of the Royal Society', *History of Science*, vol. 13 (1975), p. 158; Braithwaite, *Second Period of Quakerism*, p. 528.

25 John Lilburne, *Come Out of Her My People*, 1639 (University of Exeter, The Rota, 1971), p. 24.

26 From a work attributed to Knollys, *A Glimpse of Sion's Glory* (1641) in S. Prall, *The Puritan Revolution* (London: Routledge & Kegan Paul, 1968), p. 87.

27 From *The True Levellers' Standard Advanced* (1649) in C. Hill (ed.), *Winstanley. The Law of Freedom and other writings* (Harmondsworth: Pelican, 1973), pp. 77–8.

CHAPTER 3

1 M. Aston, 'Lollardy and the Reformation', *History*, vol. 49 (1964), pp. 156–7.
2 G. Leff, *Heresy in the Later Middle Ages*, 2 vols (Manchester: Manchester University Press, 1967), Vol. I, pp. 17–18, 31–2, 282–3; B. R. Bolton, 'Mulieres sanctae', *Studies in Church History* Vol. 10 (1973), pp. 77–95; J. M. Clark and V. J. Skinner (eds), *Meister Eckhart. Selected Treatises and Sermons* (London: Faber, 1958), pp. 31 ff., G. G. Coulton, *Studies in Medieval Thought* (London: Nelson, 1944), p. 164.
3 K. B. McFarlane, *Lancastrian Kings and Lollard Knights* (Oxford: Clarendon, 1972), pp. 210 ff.
4 S. Ozment, *The Reformation in the Cities* (New Haven: Yale University Press, 1975), p. 30.
5 K. W. Bolle, 'Structures of Renaissance mysticism', in R. Kinsman (ed.), *The Darker Vision of the Renaissance* (Berkeley: California University Press, 1974), pp. 121–6, 135–6.
6 Ozment, op. cit., pp. 38–42; e.g. 'The Reformation of the Emperor Sigismund', in G. Strauss (ed.), *Manifestations of Discontent in Germany on the Eve of the Reformation* (Bloomington, Ind.: Indiana University Press, 1971), pp. 14–15; J. B. Russell, *Dissent and Reform in the Early Middle Ages* (Berkeley: California University Press, 1965), pp. 127–9.
7 B. Bolton, 'Innocent III's treatment of the "Humiliati" ', *Studies in Church History*, Vol. 8 (1972), pp. 73–82; Leff, op. cit., Vol. II, p. 449; R. Lerner, *The Heresy of the Free Spirit* (Berkeley: California University Press, 1972), p. 51.
8 J. Bossy, 'The Counter-Reformation and the people of Catholic Europe', *Past and Present*, vol. 47 (1970), pp. 58–60.
9 For example Matthew 18: 15–17, and Acts 2: 42–47.
10 Ozment, op. cit., p. 85.
11 I. Kingston-Siggins, *Luther* (Edinburgh: Oliver & Boyd, 1972), pp. 119–20.
12 ibid., p. 82; A.G. Dickens, *The German Nation and Martin Luther* (London: Arnold, 1974), p. 119.
13 E. G. Rupp, *Patterns of Reformation* (London: Epworth, 1969), pp. 113–14, 207; R. Davies, *The Problem of Authority in the Continental Reformers* (London: Epworth, 1946), pp. 82–7; R. Walton, *Zwingli's Theocracy* (Toronto: Toronto University Press, 1967), p. 55.
14 I. Corinthians 12.
15 N. Z. Davis, *Culture and Society in Early Modern France* (London: Duckworth, 1975), p. 11; T. F. Merrill, (ed.), *William Perkins 1558–1602* (The Hague: De Graaf, 1966), pp. 102–26.
16 C. P. Clasen, *Anabaptism. A Social History, 1525–1618* (London: Cornell University Press, 1972), pp. 51–62, 324–34, 74–7, 349–58, 293–5.
17 B. R. White, *The English Separatist Tradition* (Oxford: Clarendon, 1971), *passim*.
18 D. Abbatt, *Quaker Annals of Preston and the Fylde* (London: Headley Brothers, 1931); LFMH, *LWMMMB, 1676–1749*, August 1677; *LMMMB, 1675–1718*, pp. 71, 204; *LQMMB, 1669–1711*, 6 11 1686, 7 8 1708; 2Axxxi, nos. 37–40, 45; 2Ci, nos. 38, 56, etc.; *LPMMB, 1698–1740*, p. 154; J. D. Marshall (ed.), *The Autobiography of William Stout of Lancaster* (Manchester: Manchester University Press, 1967), *passim*.
19 Ozment, op. cit., p. 60; LFMH, *LMMMB, 1675–1718*, pp. 257, 542–3, 255–6.
20 G. F. Nuttall, *Visible Saints* (Oxford: Blackwell, 1957), ch. II; LFMH, 2Bviii, x, xi.

21 LFMH, 2Ai, no. 62; *Selection of Advices from Yearly Meeting, 1675–1703*, p. 86; *LQMMB, 1669–1711*, 3 5 1684; *LPMMB, 1698–1740*, p. 105.
22 J. A. F. Thomson, *The Later Lollards, 1414–1520* (Oxford: Clarendon, 1965), pp. 45, 241–2.
23 *LW*, Vol. 54, pp. 424–5; Vol. 35, pp. 395–7; Vol. 36, p. 118.
24 G.H. Williams, *The Radical Reformation* (Philadelphia: Westminster Press, 1962), pp. 42–3; *LW*, Vol. 35, p. 31.
25 Kingston-Siggins, op. cit., p. 90.
26 ibid., p. 98.
27 M. Reeves, *The Influence of Prophecy in the Later Middle Ages* (Oxford: Clarendon, 1969), pp. 16, 138.
28 S. Ozment, *Mysticism and Dissent* (New Haven: Yale University Press, 1973), pp. 159–61; W. C. Braithwaite, *The Beginnings of Quakerism* (London: Macmillan, 1912), pp. 23, 289–93, 252; H. C. Porter, 'The nose of wax: Scripture and the spirit from Erasmus to Milton' *TRHS*, 5th series, vol. 14, pp. 155–74; C. Hill, *The World Turned Upside Down* (London: Temple Smith, 1972), pp. 116, 184 and *passim*.

CHAPTER 4

1 D. Knowles, *The Religious Orders in England*, 2 vols (Cambridge: Cambridge University Press, 1948), Vol. I, p. 159; G. Leff, *Heresy in the Later Middle Ages*, 2 vols (Manchester: Manchester University Press, 1967), Vol. II, p. 480.
2 P. Hughes, *A History of the Church*, 3 vols (London: Sheed & Ward 1947), Vol. III, pp. 482–3.
3 A. Hilgenfeld, *Die Ketzergeschichte des Urchristentums* (Leipzig: Fues's Verlag, 1884), p. 411, based on Irenaeus, *Adversus Haereses*: see also, for example, A. Dulles, *A History of Apologetics* (London: Hutchinson, 1971), pp. 18–19.
4 G. Franz, *Der Dreissigjahrige Krieg und das Deutsche Volk* (Stuttgart: Fischer, 1961), p. 82.
5 H. H. Bowen, *The Low Countries in Early Modern Times* (London: Harper & Row, 1972), pp. 73–4.
6 I. Schöffer, 'Protestantism in flux during the Revolt of the Netherlands', in J. S. Bromley and E. H. Kossman (eds), *Britain and the Netherlands*, Vol. II (Groningen: Wolters, 1964), p. 69; G. Parker, *The Dutch Revolt* (London: Allen Lane, 1976), pp. 58–60, 201–4.
7 For a brief introduction to these categories see B. Wilson, *Religious Sects* (London: Weidenfeld & Nicolson, 1970), pp. 22–5.
8 P. Geyl, *The Netherlands in the Seventeenth Century* (London: Benn, 1964), pp. 214, 221; further examples of popular bigotry, and of legal intolerance, in the Dutch Republic are provided in R. Murris, *La Hollande et les hollandais au xviie et au xviiie siècles, vus par les français* (Paris: Champion, 1925), pp. 220, 224.
9 *English Historical Documents*, Vol. VIII, ed. A. Browning (London; Eyre & Spottiswoode, 1953), pp. 400–3.
10 W. J. Townsend *et al.*, *A New History of Methodism*, 2 vols (London: Hodder, 1909), Vol. I, pp. 323–9; P. S. Belasco, *Authority in Church and State* (London: Allen & Unwin, 1928), p. 226.
11 G. S. Holmes, *The Trial of Dr. Sacheverell* (London: Eyre Methuen, 1973), *passim*; G.V. Bennett, *The Tory Crisis in Church and State* (Oxford: Clarendon, 1975), pp. 110–18 and *passim*.
12 H. Davis (ed.), *Jonathan Swift, The Examiner and other pieces written in 1710–11* (Oxford: Blackwell, 1966), p. 144.

13 G.V. Bennett, *White Kennett, 1660–1728, Bishop of Peterborough* (London: SPCK, 1957), p. 152.

14 E. Timberland, *The History and Proceedings of the House of Lords from the Restoration in 1660* . . ., 8 vols (London, 1742), Vol. III, pp. 209, 215.

15 ibid., pp. 210, 214, 215.

16 LFMH, *LMMMB, 1675–1718* pp. 4, 5; J. Sykes, *The Quakers. A New Look at their Place in Society* (London: Allen & Wingate, 1958), pp. 176–8; Sykes's views belong in the tradition of Victorian liberal Quaker optimism about the place of the Society in English life; compare W. Beck and T. Ball, *The London Friends' Meeting* . . . (London: Kitto, 1869), pp. 66–7: the Quakers after the Toleration 'were not recognized as amongst the gatherings of Christian people . . . the Established Church had at last come to acknowledge that the Quaker had proved his cause . . . and had no ulterior motive dangerous to the peace of the realm'.

17 R. B. Barlow, *Citizenship and Conscience. A Study of the Theory and Practice of Religious Toleration in England during the Eighteenth Century* (Philadelphia: Pennsylvania University Press, 1962), p. 74.

18 The Dissenters, wrote Burnet, 'must remember that the Church of England is the only establishment that our religion has by law, so it is the main body of the nation, and all the sects are but small and struggling parties; if the legal settlement of the Church is dissolved, the lesser bodies will be at mercy' – in Belasco, op. cit., p. 226.

19 N. Sykes, *From Sheldon to Secker* (Cambridge: Cambridge University Press, 1959), p. 75.

20 LFMH, *Lancashire Women's Quarterly Meeting Minute Book* (*LWQMMB*), *1675–1777*, 2nd Month, 1705; *Yearly Meeting Epistles*, 1691; *LQMMB, 1669–1711*, 11 7 1701, 14 7 1701, 10 9 1701, 1 10 1702, 17 7 1701, 22 6 1701, 13 and 16 7 1701, 17 7 1701; C. Haigh, *Reformation and Resistance in Tudor Lancashire* (Cambridge: Cambridge University Press, 1975), p. 23.

21 Barlow, op. cit., p. 75; LFMH, *Lancashire Quarterly Meeting Sufferings, 1701–1717*, 10 9 1701 and *passim*; for another view, based partly on a Midlands county, see E. J. Evans, 'Our faithful testimony', *Journal of the Friends' Historical Society*, vol. 52 (1968–71), p. 121.

22 LFMH, *LWQMMB, 1675–1777*, 1702, 1707; *LMMMB, 1675–1718*, pp. 566, 17, 21, 230, 563, 228, 544, 201.

23 D. Coomer, *English Dissent under the Early Hanoverians* (London: Epworth, 1946), p. 16.

24 LFMH, *LWQMMB, 1675–1777*, 5th Month 1692, 2nd Month 1695, 5th Month 1695, 5th Month 1718; *Lancaster Testimonies of Disownment from 1695*, no. 1.

25 LFMH, *LMMMB, 1675–1718*, p. 222; cf. C. J. Dyke, 'Anabaptism and the social order', in J. C. Brauer (ed.), *The Impact of the Church upon its Culture* (Chicago: Chicago University Press, 1968), pp. 214–21; Timberland, op. cit., Vol. III, p. 210.

26 LFMH, *LQMMB, 1669–1711*. pp. 309, 312.

27 LFMH, *LMMMB, 1675–1718*, p. 293; *LQMMB, 1669–1711*, 5 8 1693.

28 ibid., 7 8 1708, 4 2 1706; *LWQMMB, 1675–1777*, 2nd Month, 1721; Barlow, op. cit., pp. 91–2; *DNB*, Vol. 20, p. 445; J. C. Nimmo (ed.), *Burke's Writings and Speeches*, 12 vols (Cambridge: Cambridge University Press, 1972), Vol. IV, p. 168; J.D. Walsh, 'Methodism and the mob in the 18th century', *Studies in Church History*, vol. 8 (1972), pp. 213–29; U. Henriques, *Religious Toleration in England* (London: Routledge & Kegan Paul, 1961), p. 54.

29 D. F. Aberle, 'A note on relative deprivation theory as applied to millenarian and other cult movements', in S. L. Thrupp (ed.), *Millenial Dreams in Action* (The Hague: Mouton, 1962); LFMH, *LWQMMB, 1675–1777*, 2nd Month 1712, 5th Month 1713, 2nd Month 1729.

30 Barlow, op. cit., pp. 205–6; J. Orcibal, *Louis XIV et les Protestants* (Paris: Vrin,

1951), p. 156; D. J. Roorda, 'The ruling classes in Holland in the seventeenth century', in Bromley and Kossman (eds), op. cit., Vol. II, pp. 121–2; W. Addison, *Religious Equality in Modern England* (London: SPCK, 1944), pp. 16–17; E. Williams, *The Ancien Régime* (London: Bodley Head, 1970), p. 33.

CHAPTER 5

1 W. H. C. Frend, *The Donatist Church* (Oxford: Clarendon, 1952), ch. XIII and *passim*; H. J. Warner, *The Albigensian Heresy* (New York: Russell reprint, 2 vols in 1, 1967), Vol. I, ch. IV; B. Reay, 'The Muggletonians: a study in seventeenth-century English sectarianism', *Journal of Religious History*, vol. 9 (1976); P. Collinson, *The Elizabethan Puritan Movement* (London: Jonathan Cape, 1967), pt 4.

2 H. Maisonneuve, *Études sur les origines de l'Inquisition* (Paris: Vrin, 1942), p. 56; A.S. Turberville, *Mediaeval Heresy and the Inquisition* (London: Allen & Unwin, 1920), ch. IV; G. Walter, *The Growing Storm* (London: Paternoster, 1961), p. 153.

3 H. Grundmann, 'Héresies savants et héresies populaires au moyen age', in Jacques le Goff (ed.), *Héresies et sociéties dans l'Europe pré-industrielle* (Paris: Mouton, 1968), pp. 209–27; A. R. Myers (ed.), *English Historical Documents*, Vol. IV (London: Eyre & Spottiswoode, 1969), p. 852.

4 J. C. Stalnaker, 'Anabaptism, Martin Bucer, and the shaping of the Hessian Protestant Church', *Journal of Modern History*, vol. 48 (1976), pp. 602–43.

5 B. J. Kidd, *Documents Illustrative of the Continental Reformation* (Oxford: Clarendon, 1911), pp. 455–8; the 'Donatist' pamphlets were written by the parish minister George Gyfford: *A short Treatise against the Donatists of England, whom we call Brownists . . .* (London, 1590); *A short Reply vnto the last printed bookes of Henry Burrow* [sc. Barrow] *and John Greenwood, the chief ringleaders of the Donatists in England* (London, 1591); and *A plaine Declaration that our Brownists be full Donatists, by comparing them together out of the writings of Augustin . . .* (London, 1590). See also, for example, Richard Bancroft's attack in 1589 on 'Arians, Donatists, Papists, Libertines, Anabaptists . . .', in S. B. Babbage, *Puritanism and Richard Bancroft* (London: SPCK, 1962), p. 27. Bullinger's attitude to Anabaptism is revealed in his *An Holsom Antidotus or counter-poysen, agaynst the pestyllent heresye and secte of the Anabaptistes newly translated out of lati[n] into Englysh . . .* (London, 1548: reprinted, New York: Da Capo, 1973).

6 The Schleitheim Articles can be found in L.W. Spitz, *The Protestant Reformation* (Englewood Cliffs: Prentice Hall, 1966), pp. 89–96; Robert Barclay, *An Apology for the True Christian Divinity*, 10th edn (London, 1841), p. 283; C.H. Hereford Percy and E. Simpson (eds.), *Ben Jonson*, 11 vols (Oxford: Clarendon), Vol. VI, 2nd edn. 1954, pp. 82–5, 133–6, etc.; Friends' House (London) Library, *Monthly Meeting Minutes of Swarthmore Meeting*, Vol. I, 12 January 1671/2 (I owe this reference to Mr Nicholas Morgan); Helen Crosfield, *Margaret Fox of Swarthmoor Hall* (London: Headley Bros, 1913) pp. 198–9.

7 Thomas Edwards, *Gangraena: or a catalogue*, in 3 parts (London, 1646).

8 E. A. Wrigley, 'A simple model of London's importance in changing English society and economy 1650–1750', in D. A. Baugh (ed.), *Aristocratic Government and Society in Eighteenth-Century England* (New York: Watts, 1975), p. 63; Wrigley concentrates on the impact of the population flow on the country at large, but it doubtless also affected the metropolis itself.

9 M. H. and R. Dodds, *The Pilgrimage of Grace 1536–1537 and the Exeter Conspiracy 1538*, 2 vols (London: Cass, new impression, 1971), p. 346.

10 Pietro Verri, *Storia di Milano, 2 vols (Florence: Sansoni, 1963), Vol. II, pp. 341 ff.;*

G. Gerard-Meersseman, 'La Riforma della Confraternite laicali in Italia prima del Concilio di Trento', in Maccarme et al. (eds), Problemi di Vita Religiosa in Italia nel Cinquecento (Padua: Antenore, 1960), pp. 17–30; E. Cochrane, Florence in the Forgotten Centuries 1537–1800 (Chicago: University of Chicago Press, 1973), pp. 132–9.

Suggestions for further reading

The notes to each chapter contain many references to books and articles which can be followed up without difficulty. The purpose of these additional notes is to provide a context of information for the various chapters. I have deliberately selected only a few works for each chapter.

INTRODUCTION

Good illustrations of the violence and hostility present in early modern European societies can be found in N. Z. Davis's essay 'The rites of violence' in her collection *Culture and Society in Early Modern France* (London: Duckworth, 1975), pp. 152–87, and in Lawrence Stone, *The Family, Sex and Marriage* (London: Weidenfeld & Nicolson, 1977), pp. 93–105. In *The Revolution of the Saints* (London: Weidenfeld & Nicolson, 1966) Michael Walzer suggests how the Reformation may have affected the evolution of modern personality traits; see also E. P. Thompson, 'Time, work-discipline and industrial capitalism', *Past and Present*, vol. 36–8 (1967).

CHAPTER 1

There is a great profusion of good textbooks on 'middle period' European history. I have selected J. B. Wolf's *Early Modern Europe 1500–1789* Glenview, Ill.: Scott & Foresman, 1972 and J. D. Hardy's *Prologue to Modernity: Early Modern Europe* (New York: Wiley, 1974); these are useful and concise surveys. The three central centuries covered in this book are dealt with most admirably in the following surveys: Margaret Aston, *The Fifteenth Century: The Prospect of Europe* (London: Thames & Hudson, 1968); H. G. Koenigsberger and G. L. Mosse, *Europe in the Sixteenth Century* (London: Longman, 1968); and D. Pennington, *Seventeenth-Century Europe* (Longman, 1970). More specific material on the nation and the state can be found in *Renaissance, Reformation and Absolutism*, edited by Norman Cantor and Michael Werthman (New York: Crowell, 1972); this is a collection of classic historical essays, including H. Rosenberg's 'Absolute monarchy and its legacy'. I have been much influenced by J. H. Shennan's long-range study, *The Origins of the Modern European State 1450–1725* (London: Hutchinson, 1974). The interaction between national history and national awareness is brilliantly illuminated in the collection edited by Orest Ranum, *National Consciousness, History, and Political Culture in Early-Modern Europe* (Baltimore: John Hopkins University Press, 1975). G. E. Swanson's *Religion and Regime. A Sociological Account of the Reformation* (Ann Arbor: University of Michigan Press, 1967) is an erudite, taxing and, possibly, over-ambitious book – but well worth trying.

CHAPTER 2

For the background of economic history, a thorough and intelligible survey is provided by H. Kellenbenz's *The Rise of the European Economy* (London: Weidenfeld & Nicolson, 1976). Fernand Braudel's *Capitalism and Material Life 1400–1800* (London: Weidenfeld & Nicolson, 1973) is characteristically penetrating. Kurt Samuelsson provides an exceptionally clear treatment of the debate over Protestantism and capitalism in *Religion and Economic Action. A Critique of Max Weber* (trans. E. G. French, New York: Harper Torch, 1957). The three-volume work by Ernst Troeltsch, *The Social Teaching of the Christian Churches* (trans. Oliver Wyon, London: Allen & Unwin, 1931) remains a classic of the Weberian method; Volume 2 covers the Reformation and the post-Reformation.

CHAPTER 3

A. G. Dickens, *Reformation and Society in Sixteenth-Century Europe* (London: Thames & Hudson, 1966) provides a most readable introduction. From the many lives of Luther I have chosen Gerhard Ritter, *Luther. His Life and Work* (London: Collins, 1963) and the collection edited by H.G. Koenigsberger, *Luther. A Profile* (London: Macmillan, 1973). Two books on Reformation radicalism, both written from a sympathetic standpoint, are L. Verduin's vigorously written study *The Reformers and their Stepchildren* (Exeter: Paternoster, 1964) and R. Bainton's fascinating collection of his own essays, *Studies on the Reformation* (London: Hodder & Stoughton, 1964).

CHAPTER 4

Joseph Lecler's magisterial *Toleration and the Reformation* (2 vols, trans. T. L. Westow, London: Longman, 1960) stands alongside the four-volume study by W. K. Jordan, *The Development of Religious Toleration in England* (London: Allen & Unwin, 1932, and Cambridge, Mass.: Harvard University Press, 1938). N. Sykes, *From Sheldon to Secker. Aspects of English Church History 1660–1768* (Cambridge: Cambridge University Press, 1959) offers profound insights into the post-Restoration and Georgian Establishment.

CONCLUSION

A most stimulating work by R. I. Moore on the earlier mediaeval period. *The Birth of Popular Heresy* (London: Arnold, 1975) combines documents and commentary. For the Inquisition G. G. Coulton's classic study has the revealing title *Inquisition and Liberty* (London: Heinemann, 1938). Two surveys of the Counter-Reformation stand out above the rest: A. G. Dickens, *The Counter-Reformation* (London, Thames & Hudson, 1968), and H. O. Evennett's *The Spirit of the Counter-Reformation* (ed. J. Bossy, Cambridge: Cambridge University Press, 1968).

Bibliography

This bibliographical guide has been devised for the use of sixth-formers, university students and other non-specialist readers. Most of the works listed are readily obtainable English and American books and articles such as will be found in most good English-language libraries. A few works in French, Dutch, German and Italian have also been included.

This bibliography is by no means intended to be exhaustive and some readers may be surprised at the omission of well-known works. One principle of selection has been the relative modernity of the books listed: *most* come from the postwar period, though obviously a number of classics included in the bibliography carry earlier dates. As for the articles included, the cut-off point for the selection of these is usually around 1950, for no better reason than that to include all relevant articles in the complete run of many journals would result in a grossly swollen bibliography. Most of the journals cited are easily available British and American serials. The American journal *Church History* is published by the American Society for the Study of Religion (Scottdale, Pennsylvania). The Australian *Journal of Religious History* is published by the University of Sidney (Sidney, New South Wales, Australia). Two important serials to which I have not given enough space are the *Mennonite Quarterly Review* (Goshen, Indiana) and *The Journal of the Friends' Historical Society* (Friends' House, London).

Throughout the bibliography I have used standard rules of citation, but I have tried to avoid abbreviations and conventions which confuse the ordinary reader. The place of publication of a book is not given if it is London; when an American publication has a London office the place of publication is, similarly, sometimes not given.

The method of arranging the bibliography has been thematic rather than chronological. The thematic categories are artificial and tend to overlap one another. Readers will also notice that some works mentioned in the notes to chapters also, naturally, reappear in this bibliographical chapter.

The bibliography may show up some further areas of European religious history into which research might profitably by undertaken. Subjects that come to mind are the Beghard movement and the Waldensians: there seems to be a need for a modern study, in English, of each of these phenomena. As for a new area of study – that of women in radical religious movements – this field is quickly being opened up and it is very much to be hoped that a book will be written on this subject.

Bryan Wilson's *Religious Sects: A Sociological Study* (Weidenfeld & Nicolson, 1970) provides a readable popular introduction to the subject of religious sects in society. For the Christian religion in general, Ninian Smart's *The Phenomenon of Christianity* (Collins, 1979) is useful and has brief summaries on the

Reformation and the radical reformation. A review of heresy, written from a distinctly Roman Catholic viewpoint, is R. A. Knox's *Enthusiasm. A Chapter in the History of Religion* (Oxford: Clarendon, 1950). Another Roman Catholic classic is August Franzen's *A Concise History of the Church*, revised and edited by J. P. Dolan and published by Burns and Oates in 1969.

The very early history of Christian heresy is dealt with in a number of works, from which I select S. L. Greenslade's *Schism in the Early Church* (SCM Press, 1953) and W. H. C. Frend's *The Donatist Church: A Movement of Protest in Roman North Africa* (Oxford: Clarendon, 1952). Frend's work is a classic study of the relationship between, on the one hand, religious dissent and on the other, economic, social, political, regional and ethnic disaffection. Amongst the discussions of Frend's book are P. R. L. Brown's 'Religious dissent in the Later Roman Empire: the case of North Africa' (*Past and Present*, vol. 46, 1961–2), and R. A. Markus's 'Christianity and dissent in Roman North Africa: changing perspectives in recent work' (*Studies in Church History*, Vol. 9, ed. Derek Baker, Cambridge: Cambridge University Press, 1972).

When we come to look at the Middle Ages, we find that lay piety, ecclesiastical criticism and reformism were generated to a large extent in the towns and arose as part of the reawakening of urban life in the central Middle Ages. H. E. J. Cowdrey writes, in 'The papacy, the Patarenes and the church of Milan' (*Transactions of the Royal Historical Society*, 5th series, vol. 18, 1968), about the strident criticism by the Patarenes of the Milanese church. It was, of course, the official Church that brought Christianity to the laity of communes like Milan, and C. N. L. Brooke studies the christianisation of the towns in 'The missionary at home: the Church in the towns, 1000–1250' (*Studies in Church History*, Vol. 6, ed. G. J. Cuming, Cambridge: Cambridge University Press, 1970). It could be said that features of Catholic revivalism were peculiarly suited to town life, and Barbara H. Rosenwein and Lester K. Little discuss the integration of mendicancy with urban life and culture in 'Social meaning in the monastic and mendicant spiritualities', *Past and Present*, vol. 63 (1974). Similarly, Brenda M. Bolton in 'Old wealth and new poverty in the twelfth century' (*Studies in Church History*, Vol. 11, ed. Derek Baker, Oxford: Blackwell, 1977) argues that the *vita apostolica*, centred on poverty, was a response to urban conditions of 'dislocation, overcrowding and uncertainty'. The fortunes of the poverty ideal can be studied in John Moorman's *A History of the Franciscan Order from its Origins to the Year 1517* (Oxford: Clarendon, 1968). Lest we exaggerate the missionary success of the Franciscans and others in the towns, we have a picture of belief – and disbelief – in Italian towns in Alexander Murray's 'Piety and impiety in thirteenth-century Italy' (*Studies in Church History*, Vol. 8, ed. G. J. Cuming and Derek Baker, Cambridge: Cambridge University Press, 1972). Cities provided seedbeds for faith, incredulity and heresy. 'The origins of medieval heresy' is the title of R. I. Moore's article in *History*, vol. 55 (1970), and in it he traces the way in which the official Hildebrandine reform campaign – rather than 'outside' influences – engendered heresy from the twelfth century onwards. Again, in 'Some heretical attitudes to the renewal of the Church' (*Studies in Church History*, Vol. 14, ed. Derek Baker, Oxford: Blackwell, 1977), Moore argues that heresy took off from a launching pad of assumptions (especially about holiness) which were shared with the 'orthodox'. How thin was the dividing line between orthodox lay piety and lay pious heresy can be seen by studying the Lombard Humiliati. Brenda Bolton, in 'Innocent III's treatment of the "Humiliati" ' (*Studies in Church History*, Vol. 8, ed. G. J. Cuming and Derek Baker, Cambridge: Cambridge University Press, 1972) shows how this lay evangelical movement grew up in response to the problems and opportunities of urban life and how Pope Innocent – if not the whole Innocentine Church – had sufficient vision to assimilate the movement. Glimpses into the life of the Humiliati – their stress on the family and work, their relations with the papacy, their employment of preaching and their social membership – are given by Dr Bolton in 'Sources for the early history of the Humiliati' (*Studies in Church History*, Vol. 11, ed. Derek Baker, Oxford: Blackwell, 1975); 'belonging to the humiliati', writes Dr Bolton, in a phrase that could apply to any urban piety group, 'therefore may have meant belonging to a fraternity which safeguarded them from the ill-effects of . . . [the] social climate'. Ecclesiastical officialdom could recognise the healthy instincts leading to the formation of societies like the Humiliati, or it could spurn such formations; the pull between negative and positive official attitudes to lay piety is examined by Brenda Bolton in 'Tradition of temerity: papal attitudes to deviants, 1159–1216', *Studies in Church History*, Vol. 9, ed. Derek Baker (Cambridge: Cambridge University Press, 1972). It is true, as Dr Bolton points out, that heresy was generated in part by official negativism: it is also true that it was set off by complex psycho-social factors, which Janet L. Nelson examines in 'Society, theodicy and the origins of heresy: towards a re-assessment of the medieval evidence', *Studies in Church History*, Vol. 9, ed. Derek Baker (Cambridge: Cambridge University Press, 1972). The roots of heresy are also examined by C. N. L. Brooke in 'Heresy and religious sentiment: 1000–1250' (*Bulletin of the Institute of Historical Research*, vol. 41, 1968); here Dr Brooke reveals the complexity and diversity of European religious attitudes in the centuries he covers. Early medieval heresy, its forms and categories, are the subject of J. B. Russell's *Dissent and Reform in the Early Middle Ages* (Los Angeles: California University Press, 1965). The social sources of popular heresy in the eleventh and twelfth centuries are traced in R. I. Moore's *The Origins of European Dissent* (New York: St Martin's Press, 1977). Moore's contribution to the series Documents of Medieval History: *The Birth of Popular Heresy* (Arnold, 1975) follows the rise of mediaeval heresy – with special emphasis on urbanisation and official reformism – from the eleventh century to the Cathars and Waldensians. Another useful collection of documents with commentary is *Heresies of the High Middle Ages* by Walter L. Wakefield and Austin P. Evans (New York: Columbia University Press, 1969), a book which ranges over the twelfth, thirteenth and early fourteenth centuries, and which focuses on the Cathars and Waldensians. For the Waldensians we have two Italian accounts: Ernesto Comba's *Breve Storia dei Valdesi* (Turin: Libreria Editrice Claudiana, 1923) is an heroic account of the movement, not overlooking the rise of a military ethos in the 'pacifist' movement after the Reformation; Enea Balmas's edition of Gerolamo Miolo, *Historia breve e vera de gl'affari de i Valdesi delle Valli* (Turin: Claudiana, 1971) gives a late sixteenth-century history and description of the Waldensians by one of their pastors. For the Cathars, there is a number of works. In *The Medieval Manichee* (Cambridge: Cambridge University Press, 1947) Sir Steven Runciman discerned a Bogomil influence on mediaeval heresy. Catharism and Waldensianism are the subject of Christine Thouzellier's *Catharisme et Valdeisme en Languedoc à la fin du XIIe et au début du XIIIe siècle* (Leuven: Editions Nauwelaerts, 1969). A fascinating illustration of how we know about mediaeval heresy through orthodox sources is provided by Christine Thouzellier's *Un Traité cathare inédit du début du XIIIe siècle d'après le Liber Contra Manicheos de Durand de Huesca* (Leuven: Editions Nauwelaerts, 1961). Meridionale heresy is put under the microscope in Emmanuel Le Roy Ladurie's *Montaillou: Cathars and Catholics in a French Village, 1294–1324* (translated by Barbara Bray, Scolar Press, 1978). An established work on the Cathars and their suppression is H. J. Warner's *The Albigensian Heresy*, reissued, 1967, as two volumes in one by Russell & Russell of New York. Cathars, Waldensians and the official response to them fill the pages of Walter L. Wakefield's *Heresy, Crusade and Inquisition in Southern France, 1100–1250* (Allen & Unwin, 1974). Heresy and its repressive antidote were also dealt with by A. S. Turberville in *Mediaeval Heresy and the Inquisition* (Allen & Unwin, 1920) and in Henry Charles Lea's late-Victorian classic, *A History of the Inquisition in the Middle Ages*, partially reprinted, with an introduction by Professor Ullman, as *The Inquisition of the Middle Ages: Its Organisation and Operation* (Eyre & Spottiswoode, 1963). Two French works on the Inquisition are J. Guiraud, *Histoire de l'Inquisition au Moyen Age* (Paris: Picard, 1935–8) and Henri Maisonneuve, *Études sur les origines de l'Inquisition* (Paris: Vrin, 1942).

Heresy in the high and later Middle Ages is investigated by Malcolm Lambert in *Medieval Heresy: Popular Movements from Bogomil to Hus* (Arnold, 1977). The classic encyclopaedia on heresy over the better part of a millennium is Jacques le Goff's collection, *Hérésies et sociétés dans l'Europe pré-industrielle 11e–18e siècles* (Paris/The Hague: Mouton, 1968). Gordon Leff's *Heresy in the Later Middle Ages: The Relation of heterodoxy to Dissent c.1250–c.1450* (2 vols, Manchester: Manchester University Press, 1967) shows how the Church was responsible for creating heresy – by failing to live up to moral standards, by defining and alienating heresy. Professor Leff anticipated this thesis in his article 'Heresy and the decline of the medieval Church' (*Past and Present*, vol. 19, 1961): the rigidity of the Church, he wrote, its opposition to 'any form of non-ecclesiastical development' forced pious lay people 'to look outside the church for spiritual fulfilment'. The relationship between piety, the institutional Church, lay associations and heresy can be examined through a study of the Beghards – see, for example, E. W. Mcdonnell, *The Beguines and Beghards in Medieval Culture* (New York: Octagon, 1969); for a specific heresy traceable to Beghardism, Robert E. Lerner's study of *The Heresy of the Free Spirit in the Late Middle Ages* (Berkeley: University of California Press, 1972) offers a sustained defence of the Free Spirit against the charge of practical libertinism; nor was the Free Spirit, says Lerner, a movement, but rather an extensive manifestation of lay mysticism.

Many readers would doubtless welcome an introduction to mysticism. I suggest: Rufus M. Jones, *Studies in Mystical Religion* (Macmillan, 1909); Frank Happold, *Mysticism. A Study and an Anthology* (Harmondsworth:

Penguin, 1963); and David Knowles, *What is Mysticism?* (Burns & Oates, 1967). Ray C. Petry's edition of *Late Medieval Mysticism* (SCM, Library of Christian Classics, 1957) includes selections from Ruysbroek, Hugh of St Victor and Bonaventura. A condensed study of the rise and spread of the Rhineland–Low Countries mysticism is provided by Jean Ancelet-Hustache's *Master Eckhart and the Rhineland Mystics* (translated by Hilda Graeff, Longman, 1957). The essential orthodoxy of mysticism is underlined by Kees W. Bolle in his article on Renaissance mysticism in the collection edited by R. S. Kinsman, *The Darker Vision of the Renaissance* (Berkeley: University of California Press, 1974). The English mystical tradition is examined by Eric Colledge in *The Medieval Mystics of England* (Murray, 1962); two studies of Julian of Norwich give us a close insight into that tradition: Paul Molinari, SJ, *Julian of Norwich: The Teaching of a 14th Century English Mystic* (Longman, 1958); and Sr Anna Maria Reynolds, *A Shewing of God's Love: The Shorter Version of 'Sixteen Revelations of Divine Love' by Julian of Norwich* (Longman, 1958). The impact of mysticism, and especially the all-pervading influence of *Theologia Deutsch*, on radical variants of the sixteenth-century Reformation, is examined in Steven E. Ozment's *Mysticism and Dissent: Religious Ideology and Social Protest in the Sixteenth Century* (Yale University Press, 1973). Again, the influence of the *Theologia* is revealed – along with the persistence of mediaeval devotionalism, family religion and the cult of the divine humanity – by Gordon Rupp in 'Protestant spirituality in the first age of the Reformation', *Studies in Church History*, Vol. 8, ed. G. J. Cuming and Derek Baker (Cambridge: Cambridge University Press, 1972). Devout reading was a foundation of lay religion, though it was often made available by clerics. Thus Michael G. Sargent discusses 'The transmission by the English Carthusians of some late medieval spiritual writings', *Journal of Ecclesiastical History*, vol. 27 (1976). Some idea of the availability in England of devotional literature can be gained from Peter Revell's edition of *Fifteenth Century English Prayers and Meditations: A Descriptive List of Manuscripts in the British Library* (New York: Garland, 1975). Roger Lovatt in 'The *Imitation of Christ* in late medieval England' (*Transactions of the Royal Historical Society*, 5th series, vol. 18, 1968) points out a contrast between the less vitalising traditional native works and the classics of continental devotionalism. No such discrepancy existed in the case of the archetypal lay dévot, Thomas More, whose *Utopia*, says Dermot Fenlon, in 'England and Europe: *Utopia* and its aftermath' (*Transactions of the Royal Historical Society*, 5th series, vol. 25, 1975), arose out of an extensive urge to translate 'interior prayer into external activity in the families, towns and courts of Europe'. The whole movement of the *Devotio Moderna* is examined, with characteristic sympathy, by Albert Hyma in his book *The Christian Renaissance* (2nd edn, Hamden, Conn.: Archon, 1965). Gerard Groote, who helped to introduce the pious Netherlands bourgeoisie to patristic and New Testament Christianity, is the subject of E. F. Jacob's 'Gerard Groote and the beginnings of the "New Devotion" in the Low Countries', *Journal of Ecclesiastical History*, vol. 3 (1952).

The sacrament of Penance played a vital part in the fostering of lay spirituality and also created the classic private encounter between clerics and their pious clients. The development of confessional techniques can be studied through Pierre Michaud-Quantin's *Somme de casuistiques et manuels de confession au Moyen Age (XII–XVI siècles)* (Leuven: Éditions Nauwelaerts, 1962); see also T. N. Tentler, *Sin and Confession on the Eve of the Reformation* (Princeton University Press, 1977). The refinement of the techniques of Confession, as part of the internalising and psychologising of religion (processes considerably assisted by the *Devotio Moderna*), is the theme of John Bossy's fascinating article 'The social history of confession in the age of the Reformation' (*Transactions of the Royal Historical Society*, 5th series, vol. 25, 1975).

Confession on the private level, preaching to the congregation – both were ways of awakening the religious mind. There are two classic studies of the mediaeval English sermon by G. R. Owst: *Preaching in Medieval England* (Cambridge: Cambridge University Press, 1926) and *Literature and Pulpit in Medieval England* (Cambridge: Cambridge University Press, 1933). High mediaeval English sermons, dominated by imagery, Scripture and moralising, focused on social justice, devotion to the Crucified, contrition and hellfire, Mary and the reform of the clergy: see Jenifer Sweet's 'Some thirteenth-century sermons and their authors', *Journal of Ecclesiastical History*, vol. 4 (1953). By the fifteenth century a typical preacher was articulating pessimism and reverence for Christian kingship; see Roy M. Haines, 'Church society and politics in the early fifteenth century as viewed from an English pulpit' (*Studies in Church History*, Vol. 12, ed. Derek Baker, Oxford: Blackwell, 1975). The emancipation of the laity in England and its search for piety and religious association is examined in Emma Mason's 'The role of the English parishioner, 1100–1500', *Journal of Ecclesiastical History*, vol. 27 (1976). On European popular religion there is Étienne Delaruelle's *La Pieté populaire au Moyen Âge*, with an introduction by Raoul Manselli and André Vauchez (Turin: Bottega d'Erasmo, 1975). Examining an area of vigorous religious life, J. Toussaert has written *Le Sentiment religieux en Flandre à la fin due Moyen Âge* (Paris: Librairie Plon, 1968). A judicious summary of the rise of the lay piety is included in Wallace F. Ferguson's article in *American Historical Review*, vol. 59 (1953): 'The Church in a changing world: a contribution to the interpretation of the Renaissance'. One really exciting collection, with sections on late mediaeval theology and confessional method, lay piety and education, art, preaching and Erasmus, is *The Pursuit of Holiness in Late Medieval and Renaissance Religion. Papers from the University of Michigan Conference* (Leiden: Brill, 1974). This collection is the subject of a review article by John Bossy, 'Holiness and society', in *Past and Present*, vol. 75 (1977), in which Professor Bossy focuses on religion and pious associations, and on the religious quality of societies.

Piety may become heresy when fertilised by dissident theology, as the instance of Wyclif and the English Lollards shows. A manuscript source for Wyclif, the early Lollards (and for the Hussites, and many other aspects of mediaeval reformism and dissent) is the *Fasciculi Zizaniorum*, discussed by James Crompton in *Journal of Ecclesiastical History*, vol. 12 (1961). For Wyclif himself, his life and thought, the Peasants' Revolt, the struggle raging aroung the heresiarch, and Lollardy up to the end of the fourteenth century, we have Herbert B. Workman's 1926 work, *John Wyclif: A Study of the*

English Medieval Church (2 vols in 1, Hamden, Conn.: Archon, reprinted 1966). K. B. McFarlane's *John Wyclif and the Beginnings of English Nonconformity* (English Universities Press, 1952) is a condensed study of Wyclif's thought, career, disciples and followers down to 1413. In *Lancastrian Kings and Lollard Knights* (Oxford: Clarendon, 1972), McFarlane examined the piety of a group of puritanically inclined and highly devout knightly laymen. Wyclif's preoccupation with reform of and through institutions is the subject of William Farr's *John Wyclif as Legal Reformer* (Leiden: Brill, 1974). Wyclif's basic assumptions about rule are analysed in Michael Wilkes, 'Predestination, property and power: Wyclif's theory of dominion and grace' (*Studies in Church History*, Vol. 2, ed. G. J. Cuming, Nelson, 1965). Wilks follows Wyclif's conversion to anti-papalism in 'The early Oxford Wyclif: papalist or nominalist' (*Studies in Church History*, Vol. 5, ed. G. J. Cuming, Leiden: Brill, 1969). The Oxford teacher's recourse to English history and tradition (in the context of his solascripturalism) is the subject of Edith C. Tatnall's 'John Wyclif and *Ecclesia Anglicana*', *Journal of Ecclesiastical History*, vol. 20 (1969). As a philosopher Wyclif was a realist and as a trinitarian an orthodox teacher, as is made plain in A. duPont Breck, *Johannis Wyclif: Tractatus de Trinitate* (Boulder, Col.: University of Colorado Press, 1962).

Like Luther after him, Wyclif fathered radicalism largely through his sponsorship of the Scriptures. The relationship between tradition and Scripture in his thought is dealt with by Michael Hurley, SJ, in *Scriptura Sola: Wyclif and his Critics* (New York: Fordham University Press, 1960). The long-established standard work on the Lollard scriptural source is Margaret Deanesly's *The Lollard Bible* (Cambridge: Cambridge University Press, reprinted 1966). We need a reminder that the Wyclifites were not the only people concerned with Scripture translation, and it is provided by Michael Wilks in 'Misleading manuscripts: Wyclif and the non-Wyclifite Bible', *Studies in Church History*, Vol. 11, ed. Derek Baker (Oxford: Blackwell, 1975). In fact the heresity of Bible translation seems to have been established only in the fifteenth century – see Ann Hudson, 'The debate on Bible translation, Oxford 1401', *English Historical Review*, vol. 90 (1975). Ann Hudson has also produced the excellent *Selections from English Wyclifite Writings* (Cambridge: Cambridge University Press, 1978), a collection with learned and helpful introduction and notes, whose utility for some students may be diminished by the uncompromising textual retention of Middle English. The Lollards were insatiable with regard to their Bible and their books, and the way in which the heretical community supplied its own market is revealed by Margaret Aston in 'Lollards and literacy', *History*, vol. 62 (1977). Ann Hudson shows, in 'Some aspects of Lollard book production' (*Studies in Church History*, Vol. 9, ed. Derek Baker, Cambridge: Cambridge University Press, 1972), the extent to which the Lollard book industry was involved with the copying and circulating of sermons. Authentic Wyclifite thought was passed on to grass-roots Lollards, as is indicated by Ann Hudson in 'A Lollard compilation on the dissemination of Wyclifite thought', *Journal of Theological Studies*, new series, vol. 23 (1972). In an atmosphere of mounting suspicion and reaction, Lollards, or persons thought to be Lollards, lived on at the erstwhile academic headquarters of the movement – see F. D. Logan, 'Another cry of heresy at Oxford: the case of Dr.

John Holland, 1416', *Studies in Church History*, Vol. 5, ed. G. J. Cuming (Leiden: Brill, 1969). In the year before Holland's case the international Church had condemned Wyclif, an event studied by Edith Tatnall in 'The condemnation of John Wyclif at the Council of Constance', *Studies in Church History*, Vol. 7, ed. G. J. Cuming and Derek Baker (Cambridge: Cambridge University Press, 1971). Something of the attitude of domestic English Church to dissenters is revealed by M. Haines in ' "Wilde witte and wilfulness": John Swetstock's attack on those "poyswunmongeres", the Lollards', *Studies in Church History*, Vol. 8, ed. G. J. Cuming and Derek Baker (Cambridge: Cambridge University Press, 1972). As Margaret Aston points out, in 'Lollardy and sedition' (*Past and Present*, vol. 17, 1960), church and state regarded Lollardy as heresy-and-sedition. The Lollards themselves reacted to official disfavour with a fair amount of tactical nicodemism: see Ann Hudson's 'A Lollard Mass', *Journal of Theological Studies*, new series, vol. 23 (1972). Not that the Catholic counter-attack was entirely a matter of mindless repression; W. R. Jones studies part of the case for Catholicism in 'Lollards and images: the defence of religious art in later medieval England', *Journal of the History of Ideas*, vol. 34 (1973).

Two first-rate general textbooks on fifteenth-century England take in the Lollards: E. F. Jacob, *The Fifteenth Century, 1399–1485* (Oxford: Clarendon, 1961), and J. R. Lander, *Conflict and Stability in Fifteenth-Century England* (Hutchinson, 1969). The standard work on the fifteenth-century Lollards is J. A. F. Thomson's *The Later Lollards, 1414–1520* (Oxford University Press, 1965), a work which distils a mass of records so as to highlight central features of the heresy, such as scripturalism, reductionalism and rationalism. The development within Lollardy of a strident, self-reliant, violently anti-clerical religion is shown up in A. K. McHardy's article, 'Bishop Buckingham and the Lollards of Lincoln diocese', *Studies in Church History*, Vol. 9, ed. Derek Baker (Cambridge: Cambridge University Press, 1972). More comes to light about the Lollards – instances of female leadership, the prominence of wool and leather craftsmen, extensive missionary travel, and so on – in a regional study by John Fines: 'Heresy trials in the diocese of Coventry and Lichfield, 1511–12', *Journal of Ecclesiastical History*, vol. 14 (1963). The way in which the weaving trade was linked to Lollardy is examined in another regional study, by J. F. Davis: 'Lollard survivals and the textile industry in the south-east of England', *Studies in Church History*, Vol. 3, ed. G. J. Cuming (Leiden: Brill, 1966). For the North of England, A. G. Dickens's *Lollards and Protestants in the Diocese of York, 1509–1558* (Oxford University Press, for the University of Hull, 1959) reveals the continuity of popular dissenting thought from the pre-Reformation to the Reformation. Professor Dickens has also discussed the links between Lollardy and the popular English Reformation in his article 'Heresy and the origins of English Protestantism', in *Britain and the Netherlands*, Vol. 2, ed. J. S. Bromley and E. H. Kossman (Groningen: Wolters, 1964). *Lollardy and the Reformation in England* is the title of James Gairdner's massive four-volume study, published by Macmillans between 1908 and 1913 – an emphatically subjective work in the high Victorian–Edwardian tradition, full of reference to 'sincere fanaticism' and 'the vagaries of fanaticism'. Though it recycles Gairdner's title, Margaret Aston's article on 'Lollardy and the Reformation' (*History*, vol. 49, 1964) is a much more detached piece of work and studies the resurgence of Lollardy in Reformation England, the rehabilitation of Wyclif and the Lollards and the establishment of a Lollard-Protestant martyrology. In another essay, 'John Wycliffe's Reformation reputation' (*Past and Present*, vol. 30, 1965), Dr Aston examines the way in which Wyclif was reconstructed to fit English Reformation needs.

We can fit Wyclif into a late mediaeval Dissenting context, which includes Hus. A set of translations, with valuable introductions, of major late mediaeval works on such themes as pastoral ministry, conciliarism and inner religion, is Matthew Spinka's *Advocates of Reform: From Wyclif to Erasmus* (SCM Press, 1953). Wyclif and Hus feature together in Michael Wilks's study, 'Reformatio Regni: Wyclif and Hus as leaders of religious protest movements' (*Studies in Church History*, Vol. 9, ed. Derek Baker, Cambridge: Cambridge University Press, 1972) – an article which demonstrates the indispensability to the success of the Wyclifite and Hussite reformations of official leadership. Strong in Bohemia, Wyclif's influence extended to Poland, as we learn from Margaret Schlauch's 'A Polish vernacular eulogy of Wyclif', *Journal of Ecclesiastical History*, vol. 8 (1957). The English ecclesiastical establishment was all too aware of England's responsibility for east European dissent and this embarrassed awareness, along with the feeling that England in the 1420s was ripe for a heretical revival, lay behind the extraordinary excursion studied by G. A. Holmes in his article 'Cardinal Beaufort and the crusade against the Hussites', *English Historical Review*, vol. 88 (1973).

Bibliographical coverage for Hus and the Hussites is provided by Václav Mudroch in 'The age of John Hus in recent historical literature (1948–1961)', which appears in Miloslav Rechcigl (ed.), *Czechoslavakia Past and Present*, Vol. I (The Hague/Paris: Mouton, 1968). Another study of the present state of research, with comments on the enduring features of Hussitism, is Jaroslav Krejci's 'The meaning of Hussitism', *Journal of Religious History*, vol. 8 (1974–5). The social and political background to the Hussite Reformation is dealt with in two articles by R. R. Betts: 'The social revolution in Bohemia and Moravia in the late Middle Ages' (*Past and Present*, vol. 2, 1952), and 'Social and constitutional developments in Bohemia in the Hussite period', *Past and Present*, vol. 7 (1955). A recent work, J. M. Klassen's *The Nobility and the Making of the Hussite Revolution* (New York: Columbia University Press, 1978), deals with one of the most vital social ingredients in the Czech Reformation; several aspects of the Czech religious renewal – the University of Prague and the origins of the reform, English influences, Hus, and Jerome of Prague – are examined in R. R. Betts's *Essays in Czech History* (University of London, Athlone Press, 1969); see also S. H. Thomson's *Czechoslavakia in European History* (Princeton, NJ: Princeton University Press, 1943). Howard Kaminsky's magisterial *A History of the Hussite Revolution* (Berkeley: California University Press, 1967) traces the Czech Reformation, from early reformism in Matthew of Janov and Jakoubek of Stribro, through the rise of radicalism climaxing in Tabor, to the consolidation of conservatism. 'The Religion of Hussite Tabor' is the title of Kaminsky's piece in Miloslav Rechcigl's *The Czechoslovak Contribution to World Culture* (The Hague:

Mouton, 1964); in this article Kaminsky, focusing on the thought of 'Bishop' Nicholas of Pelhřimov, examines Tabor, not only as a sudden eschatological experiment, but also as a relatively stable, non-sectarian puritan social order. The Taborites also feature in Michel Mollat's and Phillipe Wolff's *The Popular Revolutions of the Late Middle Ages*, translated by A. L. Lytton-Sells (Allen & Unwin, 1973) A valuable local study of the Hussite Reformation is the article by Milič Čapek, 'The influence of the Czech Reformation in the district of Kladsko', which examines the initial identification of Czech national and reformist impulses, along with the later development of the state-sponsored *modus vivendi* between communities; this appears in Miloslav Rechcigl's *Czechoslovakia Past and Present*, Vol. II (The Hague: Mouton, 1968). A succinct account, with a Marxist orientation, of the Czech Reformation in Josef Maček's *The Hussite Movement in Bohemia* (Lawrence & Wishart, 1965).

The acknowledged expert on Hus is Matthew Spinka. His life of Hus – *John Hus: A Biography* (Oxford University Press, 1968) is a fully rounded study, filling in the European context and explaining the Czech theologian's place within it. Spinka's translation and edition of *The Letters of John Hus* (Manchester: Manchester University Press, 1972) followed on his edition and translation of material, from Hus's sermons, and from accounts of his trial and of the Council, which go to make up Spinka's *John Hus at the Council of Constance* (New York: Columbia University Press, 1965). The drama of Hus before the Council provides Professor Spinka with further opportunity, in 'Hus's trial at the Council of Constance' (*Czechoslovakia Past and Present*, ed. Miloslav Rechcigl, The Hague: Mouton, 1968), to draw attention to the Czech theologian's thought, career, scripturalism and anti-legalistic but still sometimes traditional ecclesiology. Traditionalism – especially the refusal to make practical distinctions between sheep and goats – checked the direction of Hus's predestinarian ecclesiology – a point made in Spinka's book *John Hus' Concept of the Church* (Oxford University Press, 1966). More information on Hus's theory of the church comes in S. Harrison, *Magistri Johannis Hus: Tractatus De Ecclesia* (Cambridge: Heffer, 1956).

Other Czech reformists also receive attention. Howard Kaminsky's 'On the sources of Matthew of Janov's doctrines' (*Czechoslovakia Past and Present*, Vol. II, ed. Rechcigl, The Hague: Mouton, 1968) sets Matthew against a Czech background which included John Milič and a European background which included Abbot Joachim. Paul de Vooght's *Jacobellus de Stříbro († 1429), premier théologien du hussitisme* (Leuven: University Library, 1972) is a study of the influential scripturalist, conciliarist and pioneer of practical utraquism. Politco-militarist Hussitism features in Franz von Lützow's 1914 work, published by Dent, *The Hussite Wars*, and in Frederick G. Heymann's *George of Bohemia, King of Heretics* (Oxford University Press, 1965); see also Otakar Odložilík's *The Hussite King: Bohemia in European Affairs, 1440–1471* (New Brunswick, NJ: Rutgers University Press, 1965).

There is a number of studies on the further reaches of radicalism within the Bohemian Reformation. The ambitious work by Theodora Büttner and Ernst Werner, *Circumcellionen und Adamiten: zwei Formen mittelaltlicher Haeresie* (Berlin: Akademie Verlag, 1959) sets out to compare the ultra-Donatist

Circumcellions of late Roman North Africa with the fifteenth-century Bohemian Adamites: two chronologically disparate movements, linked by social
protest issuing in chiliasm. The quietists in the Bohemian lands were the Unity
of Brethren; the intriguing question of the relationship, especially in Moravia,
between this isolationist, pacificist, puritan movement and later Anabaptism is
raised in Peter Brock's *The Political and Social Doctrines of the Unity of Czech
Brethren in the Fifteenth and Early Sixteenth Centuries* (The Hague: Mouton,
1957). The Brethren are considered in the light of tradition, radicalism and the
Reformation (and in the context of recent research) by M. S. Fousek in 'The
ethos of the Unitas Fratrum' (*Czechoslovakia Past and Present*, Vol. II, ed.
Rechcigl, The Hague: Mouton, 1968). Two tracts – on Christian pacifism and
separatism – by the mentor of the Unitas, the Christian anarcho-egalitarian
Peter Chelčický, have been translated by Howard Kaminsky as 'Treatises on
Christianity and the social order'; they appear in W. M. Bowsky's collection
Studies in Medieval and Renaissance History, Vol. I (Lincoln, Neb.: Nebraska
University Press, 1964). The survival of the Brethren into the Reformation
period gets attention in Miloš Štrupl's 'John Blahoslav, "Father and
Charioteer of the Lord's People in the *Unitas Fratrum*" ', which appears in
Rechcigl's second volume of *Czechoslovakia Past and Present* (The Hague:
Mouton, 1968).

In Sylvia Thrupp's collection *Millenial Dreams in Action: Essays in Comparative Study* (The Hague: Mouton, 1962) Howard Kaminsky writes on
Taborite millenialism; Donald Weinstein also contributes on Savonarola – and
the whole collection forms a wide-ranging symposium on the psychology and
sociology of millenialism. Further illumination on the fascinating relationship
between the golden age in the future and the golden age in the past comes in
George Boas's *Essays on Primitivism and Related Ideas in the Middle Ages*
(Baltimore, Md: John Hopkins University Press, 1966) and in Ernest Tuve-
son's *Millennium and Utopia* (Gloucester, Mass.: Peter Smith, 1972); for
social primitivism and the myth of the golden age, see also F. Graus, 'Social
Utopias of the Middle Ages', *Past and Present*, vol. 38 (1967). The past was
inseparable from the future in mediaeval prophetic writing, as is made plain by
R.W. Southern's published lecture on scriptural and non-scriptural sources for
mediaeval prophecy, 'Aspects of the European tradition of historical writing:
3: History as prophecy' (*Transactions of the Royal Historical Society*, 5th
series, vol. 22, 1972); of Joachim of Fiore Professor Southern writes, 'he was
no revolutionary in intention' – an observation confirmed by Antonio Crocco
who, in his *Gioacchino da Fiore: la piu' singolare ed affascinante figura del
medioevo christiano* (Naples: Edizioni Empireo, 1960), underlines Joachim's
thoroughly orthodox vision of the glorification of the Church in the future. The
standard work in English on the prophet Joachim is Marjorie Reeves's *The
Influence of Prophecy in the Later Middle Ages: A Study in Joachimism*
(Oxford: Clarendon, 1969); this long-range study – going into the seventeenth
century – examines the Joachimite prophetic cannon and its impact on Christian movements both conventional and heterodox. The extraordinary durabil-
ity and ubiquity of the Joachimite genre is also brought home in Dr Reeves's
'Some popular prophecies from the fourteenth to the seventeenth centuries
(Studies in Church History, Vol. 8, ed. G. J. Cuming and Derek Baker,

Cambridge: Cambridge University Press, 1972), and in the study by Marjorie Reeves and Beatrice Hirsch-Reich of The 'Figurae' of Joachim of Fiore (Oxford: Clarendon, 1972) – an examination of the intricate pictorial symbolism used to illustrate Joachim's works. As a welcome addition to our knowledge of Joachimism, we have Delno C. West's Joachim of Fiore in Christian Thought: Essays on the Influence of the Calabrian Prophet (2 vols, New York: Franklin, 1975). Franciscan Joachimism features in E. Randolph Daniel's The Franciscan Concept of Mission in the High Middle Ages (Lexington: Kentucky University Press, 1975), and Joachimist-influenced Spiritual Franciscan dissent is examined in the collection by John H. Mundy and others, Essays in Medieval Life and Thought (Cumberlege, 1955). The impact of Joachimistic prophecy in late mediaeval England becomes clear from M. W. Bloomfield's Piers Plowman as a Fourteenth-Century Apocalypse (New Brunswick, NJ: Rutgers University Press, 1962). In England such prophetic traditions survived – and revived – at least down to the civil wars, and beyond, with Charles I featuring as an unlikely second Charlemagne, in which guise he appears in Harry Rusche's article 'Prophecies and propaganda, 1641 to 1651', English Historical Review, vol. 84 (1969); earlier – in English Historical Review, vol. 80 (1965) – Rusche looked at political astrology in his article, 'Merlini Anglici'. The function of prophecy as a vehicle for urban proletarian social protest between the eleventh and the sixteenth centuries is illuminated in Norman Cohn's The Pursuit of the Millennium (Secker & Warburg, 1957). In 'Medieval prophecy and religious dissent' (Past and Present, vol. 72, 1976), Robert E. Lerner shows how all-pervading late mediaeval popular prophecy was, and how it worked as an anticipation of the Reformation; this is also the theme of Jacques Solé's review article 'Les origines de la Réforme: Protestantisme, eschatologie et Anabaptisme', Annales, vol. 28 (1973).

On the eve of the Reformation the most articulate exponent of the prophetic and Joachimist philosophies was Savonarola. His Italian background can be examined in Peter Laven's Renaissance Italy, 1464–1534 (Batsford, 1966) and his religious environment in Denys Hay's The Church in Italy in the Fifteenth Century (Cambridge: Cambridge University Press, 1977). As a preacher – his chosen medium – Savonarola can be studied in modern editions of his sermons – for example, Girolamo Savonarola Semplicità della vita christiana a cura di Raimondo M. Sorgia (Alba: Edizioni Paoline, 1976), and Girolamo Savonarola Prediche sopra i Salmi (Rome: Berladetti, 1969). Amongst the many accounts of Savonarola are Pasquale Villari, The Life and Times of Girolamo Savonarola (Allen & Unwin, 1896); Roberto Ridolfi, The Life of Girolamo Savonarola (Routledge & Kegan Paul, 1959); Michael de la Bedoyere's The Meddlesome Friar: The Story of the Conflict between Savonarola and Alexander VI (Collins, 1957); and Donald Weinstein's Savonarola and Florence: Prophecy and Patriotism in the Renaissance (Princeton, NJ: Princeton University Press, 1971); in this work Professor Weinstein traces the stages whereby Fra Girolamo adopted established Florentine expectations about the destiny of the city. The content of these expectations is the subject of Weinstein's 'The myth of Florence', in N. Rubenstein (ed.), Florentine Studies: Politics and Society in Renaissance Florence (Faber, 1968). More information on Florentinism comes from George Holmes in 'The emergence of an urban ideology at Florence c.1250–1450' (*Transactions of the Royal Historical Society*, 5th series, vol. 23, 1973) – an essay which deals with the profusion of Florentine lay religious organisations, the role of the clergy as popularisers of devotionalism and of scholastic ideas, lay education and culture, and communal republican historical visions. Even so, a republican ideal may have coexisted with an oligarchic reality: see P. J. Jones, 'Communes and despots: the city state in late medieval Italy' (*Transactions of the Royal Historical Society*, 5th series, vol. 15, 1965), and Gene A. Bruckner, *Renaissance Florence* (Wiley, 1969). As for the religion of the Florentines, the persistence of heresy, its wide class recruitment, its function as part of Savonarola's background, and the dominance of the Fraticelli – these are the themes of John L. Stephens's 'Heresy in medieval and Renaissance Florence' (*Past and Present*, vol. 54, 1972), to which Marvin Becker adds a comment in *Past and Present*, vol. 62 (1976), stressing the popular social tone of fourteenth-century Florentine heresy.

Looking at the development of Italian religious radicalism in the post-Savonarolan period, Oliver Logan's piece 'Grace and justification: some Italian views of the sixteenth and early seventeenth centuries' (*Journal of Ecclesiastical History*, vol. 20, 1969) examines the impact of 'evangelical' literature, for example upon pious bourgeois and artisans in Venice. The most popular and influential work was, of course, *The Benefit of Christ Crucified*, of which there is a modern edition by Salvatore Caponetto: *Benedetto da Mantova, Il Beneficio di Christo con le versioni del secolo XVI: documenti e testimonianze* (Chicago: Newbury Library, 1972). For the world of Italian evangelicalism, note Dermot Fenlon's *Heresy and Obedience in Tridentine Italy* (Cambridge: Cambridge University Press, 1972). The disintegration of the evangelical Italy which produced Ochino, Valdesianism and nicodemism is recorded in Philip McNair's *Peter Martyr in Italy: An Anatomy of Apostasy* (Oxford: Clarendon, 1967). Philip McNair has also written 'Ochino's Apology: three gods or three wives' (*History*, vol. 60, 1975) which deals with the personal tragedy of the gifted ex-Capuchin.

In writing about the sixteenth-century Reformation, historians now tend to stress its continuous rather than its revolutionary characteristics. The collection edited by Steven Ozment, *The Reformation in Medieval Perspective* (Chicago: Quadrangle Books, 1971), includes Gerhard Ritter on the devotional movement represented by Wessel Gansfort; Heiko Oberman on Luther and mysticism; H. C. Porter on the later Devotio Moderna; and Berndt Moeller on lay piety in its approved and orthodox forms. Heiko Oberman's *Forerunners of the Reformation: The Shape of Late Medieval Thought Illustrated by Key Documents* (Lutterworth Press, 1967) has excerpts from, for example, Gansfort, Biel, Staupitz, Hus, Lefèvre d'Étaples and Erasmus. Erasmus, the leading figure of the immediate pre-Reform, is the subject of a range of studies from which I select: R. L. DeMolen, *Erasmus* (Arnold, Documents of Modern History, 1973); Stefan Zweig's lively liberal polemic, *Erasmus* (translated by Eden and Cedar Paul, Cassell, 1934); Johan Huizinga's *Erasmus of Rotterdam* (Phaidon, 1952); the collection of studies on Erasmian thought, J. C. Margolin's *Recherches Érasmiennes* (Geneva: Droz, 1969); also on Erasmus's thought George Faludy's *Erasmus of Rotterdam*

(Eyre & Spottiswoode, 1970); and W. E. Campbell's comparative study, *Erasmus, Tyndale and More* (Eyre, 1949).

There is, of course, a large number of useful background books for students on the Reformation period. A. G. Dickens's *The Age of Humanism and Reformation: Europe in the Fourteenth, Fifteenth and Sixteenth Centuries* (Englewood Cliffs, NJ: Prentice Hall, 1972) is a kind of super-survey. Fernand Braudel's dazzling work, *The Mediterranean and the Mediterranean World in the Age of Philip II* (translated by Siân Reynolds, Collins, 1972), covers geography, economics, empires, societies and war, and deals with an extensive area over a lengthier period than its title suggests. H. G. Koenigsberger's and G. L. Mosse's *Europe in the Sixteenth Century* (Longman, 1968) provides probably the best textbook for the whole century. G. R. Elton's contribution to Collins's economically priced Fontana History of Europe, *Reformation Europe, 1517–1559* (first issued 1963) provides a concise and vivid summary; in the same series, J. H. Elliot's *Europe Divided, 1559–1598* (1968) gives due attention to politics, and especially to the Revolt of the Netherlands. The Reformation era is also well covered in Volume II of the *New Cambridge Modern History* (Cambridge: Cambridge University Press, 1958) edited by G.R. Elton; Volume III of the *Cambridge History*, edited by R. B. Wernham (Cambridge: Cambridge University Press, 1968) deals with the period of the Counter-Reformation. Another excellent and economical student book is A. G. Dickens's *Reformation and Society in Sixteenth Century Europe* (Thames & Hudson, 1966); it leaves out the Counter-Reformation, which is the subject of Professor Dickens's textbook *The Counter-Reformation* (1968) in the same Thames & Hudson illustrated paperback series. Hans Hillerbrand's *Christendom Divided: The Protestant Reformation* (Hutchinson, 1971) tends to play down theology in favour of piety and has a useful section on the radical reformation. Professor Hillerbrand has also produced the lively introduction. *The World of the Reformation* (Dent, 1975), and a collection of documents, *The Reformation in its own Words* (SCM Press, 1964). Students particularly appreciate Owen Chadwick's *The Reformation* in the Pelican History of the Church series (Harmondsworth, 1964). J. M. Todd's survey *Reformation* (Darton, Longman & Todd, 1972) includes a section on the mediaeval background. Émile G. Léonard's *A History of Protestantism*, Volume I, edited by H. H. Rowley (Nelson, 1965) also has material on the roots of the Reformation in mediaeval religion. R. H. Bainton's *Studies on the Reformation* (Hodder & Stoughton, 1964) deals with Luther and emphasises the liberalism and modernity of Reformation radicalism. The Protestant mainstream, the sectarian reformation and modern problems of state and church all feature in J. S. Whale's *The Protestant Tradition: An Essay in Interpretation* (Cambridge: Cambridge University Press, 1955).

Several works study the key role of Scripture in the Reformation: see, for example, George H. Tavard's *Holy Writ or Holy Church. The Crisis of the Protestant Reformation* (Burns & Oates, 1959), a Roman Catholic account of the tension between the Bible and ecclesiastical authority, including comments on Luther's freedom in the use of Scripture; see also John K. S. Reid's *The Authority of Scripture: A Study of Reformation and Post-Reformation Understanding of the Bible* (Methuen, 1957); in addition, H. C. Porter's vivacious article 'The nose of wax: Scripture and the spirit from Erasmus to Milton' (*Transactions of the Royal Historical Society*, 5th series, vol. 14, 1964) reveals the ingenuity with which Scripture was subjected to convenient interpretation.

T. F. Torrance's *Kingdom and Church: A Study in the Theology of the Reformation* (Oliver & Boyd, 1956) surveys the theology of Luther, Bucer and Calvin from the point of view of eschatology; in the *Journal of Ecclesiastical History*, volume 6 (1955) Professor Torrance also wrote of 'Kingdom and church in the thought of Martin Butzer'. That reflections on the position of the church in society were governed by eschatology is a theme of John Tonkin's *The Church and the Secular Order in Reformation Thought* (New York: Columbia University Press, 1971). J. W. Allen's fifty-year-old standard, *A History of Political Thought in the Sixteenth Century* (Methuen University Paperback, reprinted 1960) remains authoritative, as does Ernst Troeltsch's three-volume work, *The Social Teaching of the Christian Churches* (translated by Olive Wyon, Allen & Unwin, 1931), whose second volume covers the social and political thought of Lutherans, Calvinists, Separatists and sixteenth- and seventeenth-century radicals in general.

There is a great range of material on the Protestant Reformation in its German homeland – see Lawrence D. Stokes's *Medieval and Reformation Germany to 1648: A Select Bibliography* (Historical Association, 1972); (the Historical Association also produces an *Annual Bulletin of Historical Literature*, and this has sections on *inter alia* British and European history in the late Middle Ages, the sixteenth century and the seventeenth century.) Gerald Strauss's *Pre-Reformation Germany* (Macmillan, 1972) is a collection which includes Berndt Moeller on pre-Reformation religious life. Two studies concentrating on the Reformation as a German phenomenon are H. Holborn, *A History of Modern Germany, the Reformation* (Eyre & Spottiswoode, 1965) and Franz Lau and Ernst Bizer, *A History of the Reformation in Germany to 1555* (Black, 1969). Gerald Strauss's article, 'Success and failure in the German Reformation' (*Past and Present*, vol. 67, 1975) shows how types of disciplinarian pietism arose in the sixteenth century out of a realisation of the failure of the 'official' German Reformation to achieve the moral change that was looked for. The dawning of popular disappointment at the mainstream Reformation's failure to achieve a combination of Christian discipline and liberty is a theme in Steven E. Ozment's *The Reformation in the Cities: The Appeal of Protestantism to Sixteenth-Century Germany and Switzerland* (New Haven: Yale University Press, 1975). In the study of the Swiss-urban extension of the Reformation, and well-documented religious transformation of Zürich holds the centre of attention: see N. Birnbaum, 'The Zwinglian Reformation in Zürich (*Past and Present*, vol 15, 1958); G. R. Potter provides a full biography of the Zürich reformer in *Zwingli* (Cambridge: Cambridge University Press, 1976). For the Reformation in the German cities the standard work is Berndt Moeller's *Imperial Cities and the Reformation* (edited and translated by H. Midelfort and M. Edwards, Philadelphia: Fortress Press, 1972); in this collection there is material on the Reformation as a distinctly civic phenomenon and on the different responses of German cities, north and south, to the Reformation. Individual urban studies of the German Reformation include Gerald Strauss, 'Protestant dogma and city government: the case of Nuremberg' (*Past and Present*, vol. 36, 1967), which examines the interaction between religious Reformation and political management; Miriam Chrisman's *Strasbourg and the Reform: A Study in the Process of Change* (New Haven: Yale University Press, 1967) studies, *inter alia*, the religious administration of the council of religion and also the Strasburg Anabaptists; the needs of urban society in the Reformation period are considered by R. W. Scribner in 'Civic unity and the Reformation in Erfurt', *Past and Present*, vol. 66 (1975).

Has any other historical figure – Jesus perhaps? – received as much biographical attention as the central titan of the German Reformation? The majestic American edition of Luther's *Works*, under the general direction of Helmut Lehmann and Jaroslav Pelikan (St Louis, Missouri: Concordia), commenced in 1959, is still in progress. Judicious selections from Luther's writings and talk have been made by E. G. Rupp and Benjamin Drewry in *Martin Luther* (New York: St Martin's Press, 1970), and by I. D. Kingston Siggins in *Luther* (Oliver & Boyd, 1972). A. G. Dickens's *The German Nation and Martin Luther* (Arnold, 1974) places special emphasis on the mediation and circulation of Luther's ideas and on the urban Reformation. Professor Dickens's earlier *Martin Luther and the Reformation* (English Universities Press, 1967) is a brilliantly condensed study. H. A. Oberman's *Luther and the Dawn of the Modern Era* (Leiden: Brill, 1974) is a collection of papers which includes a study of Luther's nominalist, humanist and Augustinian sources. E. G. Rupp's *The Righteousness of God: Luther Studies* (Hodder & Stoughton, 1953) gives space to a summary of modern German and Scandinavian scholarship. A highly regarded biography is Gerhard Ritter's *Luther. His Life and Work* (translated by John Riches, Collins, 1963). There is a highly readable hagiography by R. H. Bainton, *Here I Stand* (Hodder & Stoughton, 1951). Note also Gerhard Ebeling's examination of the Reformer's thought in *Luther* (Collins, Fontana Paperback, 1970), and V. H. H. Green's *Luther and the Reformation* (Methuen University Paperbacks, 1969), and E. M. Carlson's *The Re-Interpretation of Luther* (Philadelphia: Westminster Press, 1948). Prominent amongst the modern reinterpretations is Erik Erikson's psychoanalytical bombshell, *Young Man Luther: A Study in Psychoanalysis and History* (Faber, 1959). Other studies of Luther include Richard Marius's explanatory biography, *Luther* (Philadelphia/New York: Lippincott Press, 1974); Richard Friedenthal's well-written and detailed *Luther* (translated by John Nowell, Weidenfeld & Nicolson, 1970). The growth of the Reformer's ideas is examined by Heinrich Roehmer in *Martin Luther: Road to Reformation* (Meridian Books, 1957). James Atkinson's *The Trial of Luther* (Batsford, 1971) is an account of Luther's contest with the papal Church, and Robert H. Fife has produced a massive study, *The Revolt of Martin Luther* (Oxford University Press, 1957). Edited by H. G. Koenigsberger, *Luther: A Profile* (Macmillan, 1973) is a selection of excerpts from a number of classic studies of Luther, giving us the theological, political, psychological, economic, philosophic and devotional versions of the founder of the Reformation. James Atkinson's *The Great Light: Luther and the Reformation* (Exeter: Paternoster Press, 1968) is a synthesis of modern Reformation studies, giving centrality to Luther.

Luther the scripturalist is the subject of A. Skevington Wood's *Captive to the*

Word: Martin Luther: Doctor of Sacred Scripture (Exeter: Paternoster Press, 1969). Luther's social and political thought features in F. E. Cranz's *An Essay on the Development of Luther's Thought on Justice, Law and Society* (Cambridge, Mass.: Harvard University Press, 1958). Luther's answer to the question, does Christian freedom issue in social freedom? occupies Robert N. Crossley in *Luther and the Peasants' War: Luther's Actions and Reactions* (Jericho, NY: Exposition Press, 1974). The roots of Luther's spirituality are examined by Bengt R. Hoffman in *Luther and the Mystics: A Re-examination of Luther's Spiritual Experiences and his Relationship to the Mystics* (Minneapolis: Augsburg Publishing, 1976). Luther shared the mystical heritage with many pious German Christians, some of whom were to emerge as radical reformers. Mark U. Edwards's book, *Luther and the False Brethren* (Stanford, Calif.: Stanford University Press, 1975) deals with Luther's left-wing antagonists, such as Agricola and Karlstadt – disruptive individuals who brought out the authoritarian and the traditionalist in Luther. Karlstadt put in an appearance – as a relative moderate – in a vivid moment in the history of the urban Reformation, studied by James S. Preus in *Carlstadt's 'Ordinaciones' and Luther's Liberty: a Study of the Wittenberg Movement, 1521–22* (Cambridge, Mass.: Harvard University Press, 1974); during the early Wittenberg Reformation a vital question of the Reformation was put with peculiar force: could a local community enact an autonomous religious transformation? For more on Karlstadt there is Ronald J. Sider's work, *Andreas Bodenstein von Karlstadt: The Development of this Thought, 1517–1525* (Leiden: Brill, 1974). Far more formidable and disturbing than Karlstadt was Thomas Müntzer. As with Gerrard Winstanley, the problem of the man is whether to take him as an authentic early modern chiliastic visionary or as a remarkable harbinger of modern socialism; his theories on government are studied in the context of Luther's political thought in Carl Hinrichs, *Luther und Müntzer: ihre Auseinandersetung über Obrigkeit und Widerstandsrecht* (Berlin: Walther de Gruyter, 1952). Note also three German works on Müntzer: M. M. Smirin, *Die Volks Reformation des Thomas Münzer und der Grosse Bauernkrieg* (Berlin: Dietz Verlag, 1956); Alfred Meusel, *Thomas Müntzer und seine Zeit* (Berlin: Aufbau-Verlag, 1952); and Ernst Bloch, *Thomas Münzer als Theologe der Revolution* (Frankfurt-am-Main: Suhrkamp Verlag, 1963). Müntzer and Karlstadt appear together in E. G. Rupp's vivid and illuminating *Patterns of Reformation* (Epworth, 1969).

The whole field of unorthodox piety in the Reformation period was surveyed with deep personal sympathy by Rufus Jones in *Spiritual Reformers of the Sixteenth and Seventeenth Centuries* (Macmillan, 1914). More recently, Steven E. Ozment has examined Reformation radicalism in *Mysticism and Dissent. Religious Ideology and Social Protest in the Sixteenth Century* (New Haven: Yale University Press, 1973); Müntzer, of course, makes his appearance in this book, as do Castellio, Denck, Franck and other towering individualists, and if Schwenkfeld does not have a separate section to himself in Professor Ozment's study, he receives monographic treatment from Paul L. Maier in *Caspar Schwenkfeld on the Person and Work of Christ: A Study of Schwenkfeldian Theology at its Core* (Assen: Royal Van Gorcum, 1959), a work which explains Schwenkfeld's christology, according to which the glorification, or deification, of Jesus made possible the glorification of the believer. Trinitarian orthodoxy came under heavy attack in the Reformation period, and nowhere more savagely than by Michael Servetus, whose story is told by R. H. Bainton in *Hunted Heretic: The Life and Death of Michael Servetus 1511–1553* (Beacon, 1960). See also Jerome Friedman's article, 'Michael Servetus: exegete of divine history', *Church History*, vol. 43 (1974).

The spectrum which includes the spiritualists and the Anabaptists is surveyed in the collection put together by G. H. Williams, *Spiritual and Anabaptist Writers: Documents Illustrative of the Radical Reformation*; this excellent selection appears as volume XXV of the Library of Christian Classics (SCM Press, 1957), a volume which also contains Angel M. Mergal's *Evangelical Catholicism as represented by Juan de Valdés*. G. H. Williams has produced the encyclopaedia of the left-wing Reformation, *The Radical Reformation* (Weidenfeld & Nicolson, 1962). An account of the views and practices of central German Anabaptists, along with an analysis of the faulty approach to them on the part of official Lutherans, is presented by John S. Oyer in *Lutheran Reformers against Anabaptists: Luther, Melanchthon and Menius and the Anabaptists of Central Germany* (The Hague: Nijhof, 1964). An Italian account of Anabaptism, Ugo Gataldi's *Storia dell' Anabattismo dalle origini a Münster* (Turin: Claudiana, 1972), gives particular attention to the themes of peace and war in Anabaptism. For central European Anabaptism, Claus-Peter Clasen's *Anabaptism: A Social History, 1525–1648: Switzerland, Austria, Moravia, South and Central Germany* (Ithaca, NY: Cornell University Press, 1972) attempts a statistical study and also provides a descriptive analysis of Anabaptism. In Carl S. Meyer's collection, *Sixteenth Century Essays and Studies, I, II* (St Louis, Missouri: Foundation for Reformation Research, 1970) Abraham Friesen writes on Marxist interpretations of Anabaptism. An enthusiastic view of the radicals is given by G. F. Hershberger in *The Recovery of the Anabaptist Vision* (Scottdale, Pa: Herald Press, 1957). The liberal emphasis on the way in which the Anabaptists prefigure modern religious pluralism is evident in Cornelius J. Dyck's essay 'Anabaptism and the social order', which appears in *The Impact of the Church upon its Culture. Reappraisals of the History of Christianity* (Essays in Divinity, vol. 2 edited by J. C. Brauer, Chicago: University of Chicago Press, 1968). An aspect of Anabaptist politics is examined by P. D. L. Avis in 'Moses and the magistrate: a study in the rise of Protestant legalism', *Journal of Ecclesiastical History*, vol. 26 (1975). Dr Avis shows how Reformation radicals, frequently labelled as libertarians, transformed themselves, with the aid of their own version of Mosaic law, into repressive theocrats – as they did, of course, at Münster. Also on Anabaptist politics, Walther Kirchner's article 'State and Anabaptists in the sixteenth century: an economic approach' (*Journal of Modern History* [University of Chicago], vol. 46, 1974) deals with the many sources of friction between the radicals and the authorities. The political attitudes of personalities and subdivisions of the radical reformation are also dealt with by James M. Stayer in *Anabaptists and the Sword* (Lawrence, Kan.: Coronado Press, 1972), and Anabaptist economics are examined in P. J. Klassen's *The Economics of Anabaptism* (The Hague: Mouton, 1964). A substantial study of Anabaptist (and Quaker) pacifism occupies part of Peter Brock's *Pacifism in*

Europe to 1914 (Princeton, NJ: Princeton University Press, 1972). Amongst studies of Anabaptist ecclesiology are: F. H. Littell's *The Origins of Sectarian Protestantism: A Study of the Anabaptist View of the Church* (Macmillan, 1964); Walther Klaasen's article 'The Anabaptist understanding of the separation of the church', *Church History*, vol. 46 (1977); and F. H. Littell's study of the influence of the New Testament community on Anabaptism, 'The Anabaptists and the Christian tradition', *Journal of Religion and Theology*, 1947.

Amongst studies of Anabaptism in various regions, the Moravian Hutterites and their development in the early sixteenth and early seventeenth centuries are studied in John A. Hostettler's *Hutterite Society* (Baltimore: John Hopkins University Press, 1974). Also useful on the Hutterites is a source-work heavily concerned with the life and ethics of fundamentalist Christians, the *Account of our Religion, Doctrine and Faith given by Peter Rideman to the Brothers whom men call Hutterites* (Rifton, NY: Plough Publishing, 1970). For the brethren in Italy we have an article by G. H. Williams in the collection of essays edited by L. P. Buck and J. W. Zophy, *The Social History of the Reformation* (Columbus: Ohio State University Press, 1972), while for Switzerland there is the well-established 1882 work of Henry S. Burrage, *A History of the Anabaptists in Switzerland*, which deals with the Zürich origins of the movement, its establishment, spread and sufferings (reprinted by Lennox Hill (Burt Franklin) of New York in 1973). There is a good deal of work on the radical reformation in the Low Countries. Johan Decavele's *De Dageraad van de Reformatie in Vlaanderen (1520–1565)* (Brussels: Paleis der Academiën, 1975) includes material on the Chambers of Rhetoric as disseminators of critical ideas. Alastair Duke's study, 'The face of popular religious dissent in the Low Countries, 1520–1530' (*Journal of Ecclesiastical History*, vol. 26, 1975), shows how, in the immediate pre-Anabaptist period, Netherlands dissent was an urban or industrial phenomenon, attractive to immigrants partly by reason of the religious meetings' solution to the problems of anonymity. The roots of Anabaptism in mediaeval Netherlands devotionalism and the role of Menno Simmonsz are two subjects in Cornelius Krahn's *Dutch Anabaptism: Origin, Spread, Life and Thought (1450–1600)* (The Hague: Nijhof, 1968). Menno Simmonsz along with Dirk Philips also appears in W. E. Keeney's study of Anabaptist ideas on Scripture, conversion, separation and the church, *The Development of Dutch Anabaptist Thought and Practice from 1539–1564* (Nieuwkoop: De Graaf, 1968). Cornelius J. Dyck traces the slow rise of traditionalism, from a scripturalist and primitivist base, in 'The place of tradition in Dutch Anabaptism', *Church History*, vol. 43 (1974). Some idea of the importance of the Netherlander Menno Simmonsz can be gained from Irvin B. Horst's *Bibliography of Menno Simmonsz, ca.1496–1561, Dutch Reformer* (Nieuwkoop: De Graff, 1962). John Horsch's *Mennonites in Europe* (Scottdale, Pa: Mennonite Publishing House, 1942), is an extensive survey which takes in pre-Reformation roots and Swiss and Rhineland growths, and emphasises the Mennonite virtues of peace and withdrawal. Robert Friedmann's *Mennonite Piety throughout the Centuries* (Goshen College, Ind.: Mennonite Historical Society, 1949) traces the influence of Anabaptism on Dutch pietism and the influence of pietism on Anabaptism; Friedmann believes that in the seventeenth and eighteenth centuries the rise of pietism in many sects moderated the earlier polarisation between the state and gospel Christianity. There is more on the rise of pietism in Martin H. Prozesky's article 'The emergence of Dutch pietism' (*Journal of Ecclesiastical History*, vol. 28, 1977), in which it becomes clear that disappointment with the shortcomings of the Reformation – especially with self-indulgence in society and hair-splitting among the theologians – led in the early seventeenth century to a movement in favour of personal austerity and an emotional religion based on the small group. Christian Hoburg epitomised this dissatisfaction with the Reformation mainstream and sought a personal, anti-institutional faith, emphasising pacifism: see Martin Schmidt's 'Christian Hoburg and seventeenth-century mysticism', *Journal of Ecclesiastical History*, vol. 18 (1967).

The subversive influence of the Netherlands spread far and wide. As Wallace Kirsop shows in 'The Family of Love in France' (*Journal of Religious History*, vol. 3, 1964–5), the threads of that intriguing group, in its manifestations as a secret, learned freemasonry, operating behind a Catholic mask, can be traced to the Antwerp establishment of the typographer-royal Christophe Plantin. The founder of the Family, Henry Niklaes, endowed the sect with his pliant nicodemism, and his doctrines of illuminism and the in-dwelling of God as love appealed both to sophisticated Antwerp humanists and to simple workers. The Family's spread into England, noted by Felicity Heal in 'The Family of Love in the diocese of Ely' (*Studies in Church History*, vol. 9, ed. Derek Baker, Cambridge: Cambridge University Press, 1972), was part of the massive importation of Netherlands ideas, including tolerationist and Separatist thought, which is described in John J. Murray's article 'The cultural impact of the Flemish Low Countries on sixteenth- and seventeenth-century England', *American Historical Review*, vol. 62 (1956–7). The general effect of continental baptismal dissent in early Tudor England is the subject of I. B. Horst's *The Radical Brethren: Anabaptism and the English Reformation to 1558* (Nieuwkoop: De Graaf, 1972). Perhaps, though, England did not need to import religious radicalism, having a late mediaeval native dissenting tradition. In another study of the slightly strange diocese of Ely, Margaret Spufford uncovers an intense popular religious dissent: 'The quest for the heretical laity in the visitation records of Ely in the late sixteenth and early seventeenth centuries' (*Studies in Church History*, vol. 9, ed. Derek Baker, Cambridge: Cambridge University Press, 1972).

For the English Reformation the modern bibliographical guide is Derek Baker's *The Bibliography of the Reform, 1450–1648: Relating to the United Kingdom and Ireland for the Years 1955–70* (Oxford: Blackwell, 1975). English popular beliefs in an age of religious change are the subject of Keith Thomas's magisterial *Religion and the Decline of Magic: Studies in Popular Beliefs in Sixteenth and Seventeenth Century England* (Weidenfeld & Nicolson, 1971). The best general account of the English Reformation is A. G. Dickens's *The English Reformation* (Collins, Fontana Paperback, 1964 *et seq.*). In *Pioneers of the Reformation in England* (Church Book Room Press, 1964), M. L. Loane studied some of the men who bridged the period between Lollardy and Protestantism: Barnes, Rogers, Bradford. Tyndale and others also figure prominently in William A. Clebsch's *England's Earliest Protestants, 1520–1535* (New Haven: Yale University Press, 1964), which examines continental religious influences in the years when Lollardy was on the verge of giving way to Protestantism. E. G. Rupp's *Studies in the Making of the English Protestant Tradition* (Cambridge: Cambridge University Press, 1947) has essays on Lollard survivals and Protestant origins, on continental influences and on Protestant martyrs. A relatively obscure individual, the religious entrepreneur, Joyce, is brought to light by C. C. Butterworth and A. G. Chester in *George Joyce, 1495–1553: A Chapter in the History of the English Bible and the English Reformation* (Oxford University Press, 1962). Champlin Burrage's *The Early English Dissenters in the Light of Recent Research (1550–1641)* was first published in 1912 and has been reissued (1967) by Russell & Russell of New York; the first volume is a historical account, the second a lengthy collection of varied and uncommon documents illustrating all aspects of English and Anglo-Dutch religious radicalism in the period. Continental Anabaptist influences (see also I. B. Horst, above) are discussed in D. M. Himbury's *British Baptists: A Short History* (Carey Kingsgate Press, 1962). Similarly Ernest A. Payne's *Free Churchmen, Unrepentant and Repentant, and Other Papers* (Carey Kingsgate Press, 1965) includes an essay on early contacts between English Baptists and Mennonites.

Claire Cross's excellent student paperback, *Church and People, 1450–1660: The Triumph of the Laity in the English Church* (Collins, Fontana, 1976) provides, using an extended chronology, an account of the English Reformation as a popular movement. A sound elementary introduction for sixth-formers is H. G. Alexander's *Religion in England, 1558–1662* (University of London Press, 1968). Claire Cross's article 'Popular piety and the records of the unestablished churches' (*Studies in Church History*, vol. 11, ed. Derek Baker, Oxford: Blackwell, 1975) looks into the sources for the history of Lollardy, Separatism and mid-seventeenth-century religious radicalism. Out of the heightened religious consciousness of the period arose the pious associations which F. W. B. Bullock studies, looking at England and Germany, in *Voluntary Religious Societies, 1520–1799* (St Leonards-on-Sea: Budd & Gillatt, 1963). Fundamentally the whole puritan movement was a matter of religious consciousness, piety, conduct and way of life; for this, see Christopher Hill, *Society and Puritanism in Pre-Revolutionary England* (Secker & Warburg, 1964). The acute puritan consciousness is highlighted in Owen C. Watkins's study of autobiographies, *The Puritan Experience* (Routledge & Kegan Paul, 1972); see also M. M. Knappen's edition of *Two Elizabethan Puritan Diaries* (Studies in Church History, Gloucester, Mass.: Smith, 1966); Alan McFarlane's *Diary of Ralph Josselin* (Oxford University Press, 1976) and the *Autobiography* of Richard Baxter, of which the most convenient edition is the 1931 Dent Everyman version republished in 1974. The thought of a famous guide for pious souls, William Perkins, can be studied in the edition of his *Works*, by Ian Breward (Ampleford: Sutton Courtenay Press, 1970). Ian Breward also discusses the significance of William Perkins – as an exponent of non-judicial penitential casuistry, as an unconscious prophet of Separatist ecclesiology and as a severe teacher of Christian economics – in *Journal of Religious History*, vol. 4 (1966–7). Jens G. Møller writes of the origins, before

Perkins, of the theology of the covenant, that agreement between believers and their God which formed the basis of congregational ethics and church-making: 'The beginnings of puritan covenant theology', *Journal of Ecclesiastical History*, vol. 14 (1963). The covenant was linked to conversion in the puritan cult of self-awareness; F. W. B. Bullock has made a compilation of personal accounts of the conversion experience, *Evangelical Conversion in Great Britian, 1516–1695* (St Leonards-on-Sea: Budd & Gillatt, 1966). Marc L. Schwarz reviews the richness of lay religious thought in early seventeenth-century England in 'Some thoughts on the development of a lay religious consciousness in pre-civil war England' (*Studies in Church History*, vol. 8, ed. G. J. Cuming and Derek Baker, Cambridge: Cambridge University Press, 1972). The religious emancipation of the laity was largely accomplished through the medium of clerical sermons, and J. W. Blench provides an analysis of the style and content of Tudor sermons in *Preaching in England in the Late Fifteenth and Sixteenth Centuries: A Study of English Sermons, 1450–1600* (Oxford: Blackwell, 1964). Millar Maclune's *The Paul's Cross Sermons, 1534–1642* (Toronto: Toronto University Press, 1958) conveys the uproarious, contentious atmosphere surrounding the delivery of these popular, urban, endowed mass sermons. Special attention is given to preaching in Horton Davies's *Worship and Theology in England, II: From Andrewes to Baxter and Fox, 1603–1690* (Princeton, NJ: Princeton University Press, 1975); see also Martin Seymour-Smith (ed.), *The English Sermon, I: 1550—1650*, and C. H. Sisson (ed.), *The English Sermon, II: 1650–1750* (Cheadle Hume: Carcanet Press, 1976). One of the preachers' themes in the subject of Ronald E. McFarland's article, 'The response to grace: seventeenth-century sermons and the idea of thanksgiving', *Church History*, vol. 44 (1975).

On the puritan movement the following surveys are recommended: H. C. Porter, *Puritanism in Tudor England* (Macmillan, 1970), an enlivening collection of documents and commentary; the scholarly classic, Patrick Collinson's *Elizabethan Puritan Movement* (Cape, 1967); Patrick McGrath's introduction for sixth-formers and university students, *Papists and Puritans under Elizabeth* (Blandford, 1967); and the earlier, American work, M. M. Knappen's *Tudor Puritanism: A Chapter in the History of Idealism* (Gloucester, Mass.: Smith, 1963). The violent pamphlet warfare that drew the dividing line between puritans and puritan Separatists is chronicled by D. J. McGinn in *John Penry and the Marprelate Controversy* (Rutgers, NJ: Rutgers University Press, 1966). The standard work on the first Separatists is B. R. White, *The English Separatist Tradition from the Marian Martyrs to the Pilgrim Fathers* (Oxford University Press, 1971). H. Gareth Owen, in 'A nursery of Elizabethan Nonconformity, 1567–72' (*Journal of Ecclesiastical History*, vol. 17, 1966), charts the origins of Separatism in a London parish in which foreign immigration and a tradition of urban constitutional independence were supportive factors. London at large is the focus for M. Tolmie's *The Triumph of the Saints. The Separate Churches of London 1616–1649* (Cambridge: Cambridge University Press, 1977), a work which examines the revival and explosion of English Separatism in the seventeenth century. Needless to say, in that period the Netherlands influence which we noted earlier was still strong, and can be studied in two works by Keith Sprunger, his book *The Learned Doctor William*

Ames. Dutch Backgrounds of English and American Puritanism (Urbana: Illinois University Press, 1972), and an article, 'English Puritans and Anabaptists in early seventeenth century Amsterdam', *Mennonite Quarterly Review*, vol. 46 (1972). Despite constant continental borrowings, English radical Protestantism was developing a peculiar intensity in which, perhaps, the Lollard legacy outweighed the Calvinist code. English Separatist thought can be studied first hand in the following corpus: Albert Peel and Leland Carlson (eds.), *The Writings of Robert Harrison and Robert Browne* (Allen & Unwin, 1953); Leland Carlson (ed.), *The Writings of John Greenwood, 1587–1590, together with the joint writings of Henry Barrow and John Greenwood, 1587–1590* (Allen & Unwin, 1962); Leland Carlson (ed.), *The Writings of Henry Barrow, 1587–1590* (Allen & Unwin, 1962); and finally Leland Carlson (ed.), *The Writings of Henry Barrow, 1590–1591* (Allen & Unwin, 1966). A glimpse into the worship of the Separatists is given in Horton Davies's *Worship and Theology in England, I: from Cranmer to Hooker, 1534–1603* (Princeton, NJ: Princeton University Press, 1970).

Tudor Separatism is the well-spring from which the stream of English radical churchmanship flows. When, in the eighteenth century, it was time to survey the course of the stream – to write a *Book of Martyrs* for an age of reason – the Dissenting minister Daniel Neal produced his *History of the Puritans . . . 1517 to . . . 1688*, of which I have used the five-volume 1822 edition, published by William Baynes. The long-range history of freechurchmanship is, in fact, almost an recognised genre. Michael Watt's ambitious and successful *The Dissenters. From the Reformation to the French Revolution* (Oxford: Clarendon, 1978) is the latest contribution. The collection edited by C. Robert Cole and Michael E. Moody, *The Dissenting Tradition: Essays for Leland H. Carlson* (Athens: Ohio University Press, 1975), includes Patrick Collinson on the gradual rise of a separating mentality in Elizabethan puritanism and also has C. H. George on Gerrard Winstanley. Erik Routley, in *English Religious Dissent* (Cambridge: Cambridge University Press, 1960), has produced a condensed introduction, encompassing pre-Reformation influences and the history of Dissent from the sixteenth to the twentieth century. R. Tudor Jones's *Congregationalism in England, 1662–1962* (Independent Press, 1962) follows the history of Independency after the Restoration and into the eighteenth century and deals with sacraments, preaching, mission and with the main centres of Congregational life, especially in Wales. For a documentary study of Independency-Congregationalism there is Williston Walker's *The Creeds and Platforms of Congregationalism* (Philadelphia: Pilgrim Press, 2nd edn, 1969), in which the earliest documents are from the English and Amsterdam origins of the movement. Henry Martyn Dexter's *The Congregationalism of the Last Three Hundred Years, As Seen in its Literature* (1879, reprinted by Gregg International Publishing, Westmead, Farnborough, Hampshire, 1970) is a vast compilation of Congregational history in England, Holland and America. Douglas Horton's translation of *The Answer to the Whole Set of Questions of . . . William Apollonius . . . Concerning Church Government . . .* (Oxford University Press, 1958) sets out the ecclesiology of the 'moderate' Independency of the 1640s, and A. G. Matthews's edition of *The Savoy Declaration of Faith and Order, 1659* (Independent Press, 1959) makes avail-

able the classic statement of the doctrines and government of the Congregational churches. A documentary corpus for the life of the minister John Owen,
who represents Independency in a period of prosperity, and in a later period of
eclipse, is edited by Peter Toon: *The Correspondence of John Owen
(1616–1683), with an Account of His Life and Work* (Clarke, 1970); Peter
Toon has also written, in *God's Statesman; The Life and Work of John Owen,
Pastor, Educator, Theologian* (Exeter: Paternoster Press, 1971), an account of
his hero who, after the disaster of the Restoration, really was forced into a
genuinely Congregational ministry. An archetypal Independent – and powerful advocate of toleration – was Hugh Peter (1598–1660), the subject of R. P.
Stearn's *The Strenuous Puritan* (Urban: University of Illinois Press, 1954).
The standard work on Independency in the decades of the English Revolution
is G. F. Nuttall's *Visible Saints: The Congregational Way, 1640–1660* (Oxford:
Blackwell, 1957) in which the main principles of Congregationalism are set
out. G. F. Nuttall also examined Welsh puritanism in his study of Walter
Cradock, Vavasor Powell and Morgan Llwyd, *The Welsh Saints* (Cardiff:
University of Wales Press, 1957).

How radical *were* the Independents? The question was asked in *Past and
Present*, vol. 47 (1970) in the form of a symposium, in which a number of
historians took as their starting-point Stephen Foster's article, 'The Presbyterian Independents exorcised', *Past and Present*, vol. 44 (1969). The whole
debate has a small history of its own; suffice it to say that Independency's
authentic ecclesiological radicalism surfaced after the collapse of the Republic.
The church-governmental ideas of mid-century Independent leaders are
examined by Tai Liu in 'In defence of dissent: the Independent divines on
church government', *Transactions of the Congregational History Society*, vol.
21 (1972). The role of the Independents in the Revolution is studied by
George Yule in *The Independents in the English Civil War* (Cambridge:
Cambridge University Press, 1958). The problems of what was for Independents an impossible mix of state support and Christian liberty are sketched by
Sarah Gibbard Cook in 'The Congregational Independents and the Cromwel-
lian constitutions', *Church History*, vol. 46 (1977).

The Baptist faith is grounded in the acceptance of that act of total separation
before which many mid-seventeenth-century Independents hesitated. B. R.
White, however, in 'The organisation of the Particular Baptists, 1644–1660'
(*Journal of Ecclesiastical History*, vol. 17, 1966), shows that, whatever sever-
ances took place from the world outside the sect, internally congregation
autonomy was combined with a London-oriented federalism. The attempt to
equip a group of separate and radical churches with the rudiments of a federal
organisation is further studied by G. F. Nuttall in 'The Baptist Western
Association, 1653–1658', *Journal of Ecclesiastical History*, vol. 11 (1960).
The sixteenth- and seventeenth-century Baptists of Wales feature in Mansell
Johns's *Welsh Baptist Studies* (Cardiff: South Wales Baptist College, 1976).
Not only Wales but even orthodox Scotland was affected by radicalism and
separatism in the seventeenth century. What was feared in the 1630s and
1640s, a Scots Separatism (see David Stevenson, 'The radical party in the
Kirk, 1637–45', *Journal of Ecclesiastical History*, vol. 25, 1974), actually took
place in the 1650s: see 'The emergence of schism in seventeenth-century

Scotland' by Gordon Donaldson, in *Studies in Church History*, vol. 9, ed. Derek Baker (Cambridge: Cambridge University Press, 1972).

As we saw, the history of the British left-wing churches since the Reformation, or since the seventeenth century, is a major genre – one that goes back, in fact, to the Reformation itself, when the characteristic Protestant preoccupations with history, with the history of the church and with history *as* the history of the church, were first and definitively laid down. John Foxe was the founding father of English Protestant historiography. A standard version of the *Acts and Monuments of the Church* is George Townsend's eight-volume edition (Seeley, Burnside & Seeley, 1843–9). A penetrating study of the Protestant view of the past is C. H. George's 'Puritanism as history and historiography', *Past and Present*, vol. 41 (1968); Foxe is the particular focus for John T. McNeill's 'John Foxe: historiographer, disciplinarian, tolerationist', *Church History*, vol. 43 (1974). The *Acts and Monuments* as an extended essay in national-providential history is the theme of William Haller's *Foxe's Book of Martyrs and the Elect Nation* (Cape, 1963). Foxe's historical vision is the starting-point for William Lamont's study of Protestant eschatology, and its development in a radical direction, *Godly Rule: Politics and Religion 1603–60* (Macmillan, 1969). Needless to say, Protestant historiography was as much concerned with the future as it was with the past, and English historically based religious futurology was by no means concerned only with England. There was indeed a flourishing Scottish sector: see Robert G. Clouse, 'John Napier and apocalyptic thought' (*Sixteenth Century Journal*, vol. 5, 1974), and Sidney Burrell, 'The apocalyptic vision of the early Covenanters' (*Scottish Historical Review*, vol. 43, 1964). The European sources of British eschatology are revealed in Robert Clouse's 'Johann Heinrich Alsted and English millenialism', *Harvard Theological Review*, vol. 68 (1969). Dr Clouse has also written on 'The apocalyptic interpretation of Thomas Brightman and Joseph Mede', *Journal of the Evangelical Theological Society*, vol. 12 (1969). On the most important point in the Christian eschatological programme, the nature and appearance of Antichrist, Christopher Hill has written a succinct study, *Antichrist in Seventeenth-Century England* (Oxford University Press, 1971), tracing the development, extension, radicalisation and finally, internalisation of this figure; for the origins of the figure of Antichrist see Willhelm Bousset, *The Antichrist Legend* (Hutchinson, 1896). A number of recent studies have shown up the all-pervasiveness of millenarianism in early modern England, for example, David Brady's 'The number of the Beast in seventeenth- and eighteenth-century England' (*The Evangelical Quarterly*, vol. 45, 1973). The influence of the vision is traceable through the painstaking study which John F. Wilson has made of sermons, *Pulpit and Parliament: Puritanism during the English Civil Wars, 1640–1648* (Princeton: Princeton University Press, 1969). In *A Great Expectation: Eschatological Thought in English Protestantism to 1660* (Leiden: Brill, 1975), Bryan W. Ball examines the theology of English eschatological thought. The role of apocalypticism in the politics of the early 1640s is studied by Paul Christianson in 'From expectation to militance: reformers and Babylon in the first two years of the Long Parliament' (*Journal of Ecclesiastical History*, vol. 24, 1973), while Tai Liu considers millenialism as a spur to puritan clerical action in *Discord in Zion: the Puritan Divines and the*

Puritan Revolution (The Hague: Nijhof, 1973). Tai Liu has also written about the Barebones Parliament, the very flashpoint of the politicalisation of Congregationalist millenarianism and zeal: 'The calling of Barebone's Parliament' (*English Historical Review*, vol. 80, (1965) gave a full account of the division of purpose in the Nominated Assembly between pragmatists and prophets, traditionalists and visionaries. As for the radicals in the Assembly, James E. Farnell, in 'The usurpation of honest London householders: Barebones Parliament' (*English Historical Review*, vol. 82, 1967), claims that their policies were 'largely those of the London Baptist householders and artisans'. The radical politics of the Baptists, in association with programmatic millenarianism, were examined as long ago as 1912 by Louise Fargo Brown in *The Political Activities of the Baptists and Fifth Monarchy Men in England during the Interregnum* (Oxford University Press, 1912, reissued New York, Franklin, 1965), a work somewhat superseded by B. S. Capp's *The Fifth Monarchy Men: A Study in Seventeenth-Century English Millenarianism* (Faber, 1972). The appearance of Capp's social and intellectual study of the Fifth Monarchists were accompanied by a debate between himself and the author of *Godly Rule*, William Lamont, over terms and over the extent and role of seventeenth-century English millenarianism: see B. S. Capp, '*Godly Rule* and the millennium' (*Past and Present*, vol. 52, 1971); W. Lamont, 'Richard Baxter, the Apocalypse and the Mad Major' (ibid., vol. 55, 1972); and B. S. Capp, 'The millennium and eschatology in England' (ibid., vol. 57, 1972). Another group who took the millennium seriously, though they are themselves seldom taken seriously, were the Muggletonians, subject of a condensed study by Barry Reay in *Journal of Religious History*, vol. 9 (1976). The whole millenarian ethos is examined in Peter Toon's collection, *Puritans, the Millennium and the Future of Israel: Puritan Eschatology* (Cambridge: Cambridge University Press, 1970); the role of Jews in the Protestant eschatological schema is included in Robert M. Healey's article 'The Jew in seventeenth-century thought' (*Church History*, vol. 46, 1977), while the role of the Jews in Jewish expectations is the subject of Gershom Scholem's massive and much acclaimed masterpiece, *Sabbatai Sevi, 1626–1676* (Princeton: Princeton University Press, 1977). Suffused, like Sevi, with futuristic hopes, Gerrard Winstanley has been much discussed in recent literature. George Juretic agrees that Winstanley started out with – in Juretic's view – somewhat naïve millenarian ideas, but he argues that Winstanley went on to become a proper, modern, secular, socialist thinker: 'Digger no millenarian: the revolutionising of Gerrard Winstanley', *Journal of the History of Ideas*, vol.36 (1975). John K. Graham, Lotte Mulligan and Judith Richards prefer not to view Winstanley as a modern man, and in 'Winstanley: a case for the man as he said he was' (*Journal of Ecclesiastical History*, vol. 28, 1977), they set the Digger in a seventeenth-century religious and apocalyptic context. Similarly, in 'Economic and social throught of Gerrard Winstanley' (*Journal of Modern History*, 1946), Winthrop Hudson re-emphasised eschatology and divinity, rather than secular progressivism, in Winstanley's thought. J. C. Davis, in 'Gerrard Winstanley and the restoration of true magistracy' (*Past and Present*, vol. 70, 1976), studies the reliance which the older Winstanley placed upon the state to transform men through discipline. Readers who wish to study Winstanley as he said he was can have ready access to Christopher Hill's Penguin edition of *Winstanley: The Law of Freedom and other writings* (Harmondsworth, 1977), and G. E. Aylmer's edition of *England's Spirit Unfoulded* in *Past and Present*, vol. 39 (1968), which carries a severe warning against the immorality of the Ranters. See also O. Lutand, *Winstanley: socialisme et christianisme sous Cromwell* (Paris: Didier, 1976).

The World of the Ranters: Religious Radicalism in the English Revolution (Lawrence & Wishart, 1970) is the title of A. L. Morton's absorbing collection of papers, which includes an essay on John Saltmarsh. Saltmarsh is the subject of Leo F. Solt's article 'John Saltmarsh: New Model Army Chaplain' (*Journal of Ecclesiastical History*, vol. 2, 1951), which examines the chaplain's development, on the basis of justification by faith, of the ideas of universal social equality and religious toleration; see the same author's *Saints in Arms: Puritanism and Democracy in Cromwell's Army* (Stanford, Calif.: Stanford University Press, 1959). All the variants of mid-seventeenth-century English radicalism are examined in Christopher Hill's *The World Turned Upside Down: Radical Ideas during the English Revolution* (Temple Smith, 1972). All these radical ideas had their roots in social crisis, of which one ingredient was the discontent of the disinherited; for this sense of deprivation see Joan Thirsk's 'Younger sons in the seventeenth century', *History*, vol. 54 (1969). The sociology of Dissent – in the 1670s – is examined by Margaret Spufford in 'The social status of some seventeenth-century rural Dissenters' (*Studies in Church History*, vol. 8, ed. G. J. Cuming and Derek Baker, Cambridge: Cambridge University Press, 1972). These Nonconformists, says Dr Spufford, were recruited from across the spectrum of rural society. Social variety, with a smattering of discontented younger sons, was also present amongst the early Quakers, but as R. T. Vance shows, in *The Social Development of English Quakerism, 1655–1755* (Cambridge, Mass.: Harvard University Press, 1969), a narrowing of the social base took place, whereby Quakerism became in the eighteenth century a middle class, urban movement– an observation also made by Professor Vann in 'Quakerism and the social structure in the Interregnum', *Past and Present*, vol. 43 (1969). Judith Hurwich adds to R. T. Vann's findings (and he replies) in 'The social origin of the early Quakers', *Past and Present*, vol. 48 (1970); see also Arnold Lloyd's *Quaker Social History* (Longman, 1950), and Alan Cole's 'The social origins of the early Friends' (*Journal of the Friends' Historical Society*, vol. 48, 1957). In 'The Quakers and the English Revolution' (*Past and Present*, vol. 10, 1956), Alan Cole revealed the close involvement of the Quakers with militant puritan politics. Their social introversion (if it ever came about) was a feature of the 'bourgeois-quietist' Georgian phase, for, as G. F. Nuttall insists in 'Overcoming the world: the early Quaker programme' (*Studies in Church History*, vol. 10, ed. Derek Baker, Oxford: Blackwell, 1973), early Quakerism, a world-seeking, world-overcoming movement, was characterised by social reformism, militancy, mission and millenialism. The Interregnum Quakers were certainly politically aware people, fond of pestering Parliament – see, for example, Barry Reay's 'The Quakers and 1659: two newly discovered broadsides by Edward Burrough' (*Journal of the Friends' Historical Society*, vol. 54, 1977). Perhaps all this political activism had to do with the presence in the ranks of the first

Friends of men of gentry backgrounds, men conditioned to expect the political involvement to which their caste was entitled. Such a one was William Penn, the subject of a combined biography and political study by Mary M. Dunn, *William Penn: Politics and Conscience* (Princeton, NJ: Princeton University Press, 1966). Melvin B. Endy's *William Penn and Early Quakerism* (Princeton University Press, 1973) examines Penn's religious thought and its influence in his politics; for the most controversial side of Penn's politicking – the involvement of Quakerism with Catholicism in an attempt to use state power to enforce toleration – see Vincent Buranelli, *The King and the Quakers. A Study of William Penn and James II* (Philadelphia: Pennsylvania University Press, 1962). Penn's politics stemmed from his Quakerism; from what did his Quakerism stem? Hugh Barbour's examination of *The Quakers in Puritan England* (New Haven, Conn.: Yale University Press, 1964) revealed the social origins of Quakerism – and its derivation from puritanism, though Barbour is, of course, quick to show the difference between Quakerism and orthodox puritanism. George Fox's own roots were in puritan piety; his *Journal*, of which J. L. Nickalls's 1952 Cambridge University Press edition is the best, has, in part, the character of a puritan autobiography; it forms the basis for Henry van Etten's popular *George Fox and the Quakers* (Longman, 1959). Fox's life seen as a journey was the archetype of seventeenth-century pilgrims' progresses; such pilgrimages ended in rest – but not in inertia. The pages of W. C. Braithwaite's *The Beginnings of Quakerism* (first published in 1912, 2nd edn, with revision by H. J. Cadbury, Cambridge: Cambridge University Press, 1955) exude dynamism, movement and struggle – a baroque air of tension combined with repose which induced contemporaries to liken the Quakers to the Catholics. On the 'sub-apostolic' epoch in Quaker history still the standard work is Braithwaite's *The Second Period of Quakerism*, prepared by H. J. Cadbury for the 1961 reissue by Cambridge University Press. To cap off the famous Rowntree Series, of which the Braithwaite works laid the foundation, Rufus Jones added *The Later Period of Quakerism* (1921, reissued 1970 by Greenwood of Westport, Connecticut), a work whose very title conveys impressions of loss and decay which are part of the fibre of the Protestant attitude to the history of the church.

For the history of Quakerism in its north-western Galilee, the archives of the Lancashire Friends have been a quarry for a number of researchers. In 1976 a calendar was drawn up of this archive and that calendar has been summarised in *The Journal of the Friends' Historical Society*, vol. 54 (1976) and in *Gutenberg-Jahrbuch 1978* (Mainz: Gutenberg-Gesellschaft). Some of the results of study by a group of researchers into the Lancaster Quaker archive have been published in Michael Mullet (ed.), *Early Lancaster Friends* (Lancaster: Centre for North-West Regional Studies, 1978). Also using Lancaster sources, Alan Anderson has written a 'Study of the sociology of religious persecution. The first Quakers' (*Journal of Religious History*, vol. 9, 1977).

A Quaker regional archive similar to that at Lancaster has been systematically catalogued by Russell Mortimer of Leeds University Library. For the West Country, Mr Mortimer has edited the *Minute Book of the Men's Meeting of the Society of Friends in Bristol* 1667–86 (Bristol: Bristol Record Society, 1971). For Welsh Quakerism, note G. H. Jenkins's 'Quaker and anti-Quaker literature in Welsh from the Restoration to Methodism', *Welsh Historical Review*, vol. 7 (1975). For the Midlands, H. C. Johnson has edited the Quaker Sessions Records, 1682–90 for *Warwick County Records*, Vol. VIII (Warwick: Warwickshire County Council, 1953), which volume also includes J. H. Hodson's entries on Warwickshire Nonconformist and Quaker Meeting Houses; then, for Leicestershire, R. H. Evans has produced a study of *The Quakers of Leicestershire 1660–1714* (Leicester: Leicestershire Archaeological Society, 1953). The national Quaker archive is at Friends' House Library, London; its printed collection includes about 60,000 printed books and 60,000 pamphlets; the manuscript collection has all the central records of the Society of Friends, along with such resources as the 1,400 letters and papers of the Swarthmore Meeting.

As it moved into the eighteenth century, Quakerism lost *some* of the harshness of its singularity and was added as a later stratum to the geology of the 'Old Dissent', there to join the established Nonconformists in a protracted campaign against the Anglican stranglehold on the national life. Charting the activities of the Quakers and the three main Nonconformist denominations as prototype pressure groups, N. C. Hunt compares *Two Early Political Associations: The Quakers and the Dissenting Deputies in the Age of Sir Robert Walpole* (Oxford: Clarendon, 1961). B. L. Manning examined the Nonconformists' representatives in *The Protestant Dissenting Deputies* (ed. O. Greenwood, Cambridge: Cambridge University Press, 1952), a work which follows the struggle, lasting nearly a century, of the Nonconformists to find a place in English public life. In Georgian England, in so far as the traditional position of the church was eroded, the erosion benefited secular politicians rather than the Dissenters; in 'Sir Robert Walpole, the old Whigs and the bishops, 1733–1736: a study in eighteenth-century parliamentary politics' (*Historical Journal*, vol. 11, 1968), T. F. J. Kendrick shows how the First Minister reverted, such was his great respect for the power of the episcopal political phalanx, to solid churchmanship after winning tactical victories over the bishops, victories whose chief effect was to consolidate erastianism. Eighteenth-century Dissenters lived, in fact, in conditions of suspended persecution, rather than of toleration, and the carefully circumscribed nature of indulgence contracted the scope of Nonconformity for the planes of nation and world to those of congregation and denomination; this is the view of Russell E. Richey in 'The effect of toleration on eighteenth-century Dissent', *Journal of Religious History*, vol. 8 (1974–5). As has been argued, the limited scope of official toleration was partly a reflection of popular bigotry, a fear of religious deviation whose causes are examined in John Walsh's article 'Methodism and the mob in the eighteenth century' (*Studies in Church History*, vol. 8, ed. G. J. Cuming and Derek Baker, Cambridge: Cambridge University Press, 1972). Popular intolerance, directed against the Catholics, lingered into the nineteenth century but by then the state had acquired the authority to overcome it; 'anti-catholic prejudice', says G. I. I. Machin in 'The No-Popery movement in Britain in 1828–9' (*Historical Journal*, vol. 6, 1963), 'was still profound and widespread', but it could not 'effectively prevent the Government carrying emancipation . . .' A study of the arguments for and against toleration in the late Georgian period, including the regressive but widely adopted views of Burke, has been made by Ursula Henriques in *Religious Toleration in England, 1787–1833* (Routledge & Kegan Paul, 1961).

Some of the wider issues of toleration and Christianity have been explored by Wilhelm Pauck in 'The Christian faith and religious tolerance', *Church History*, 1946. In *The Travail of Religious Liberty* (Hamden, Conn.: Shoestring Press, reprint, 1971), R. H. Bainton surveys Catholic and Protestant intolerance and highlights outstanding individuals – Castellio, for example, and Servetus, Ochino, Milton, Roger Williams and Locke. R. H. Murray examined the views on religious diversity of *Erasmus and Luther: Attitude to Toleration* (SPCK, 1920, reprinted by Burt Franklin, New York). A general survey of toleration in the early modern period is Henry Kamen's *The Rise of Toleration* (Weidenfeld & Nicolson, 1967). For the early Reformation the surprising sympathy of Landgrave Philip of Hesse with Anabaptism is considered by F. H. Littell in *Landgraf Philipp und die Toleranz: ein christlicher Fürst, der linke Flügel der Reformation und der christlicher Primitivismus* (Bad Nauheim: Christian-Verlag, 1957). Landgrave Philip's toleration, though, was influenced by sympathy – not at all the classic liberal toleration of the obnoxious. The wider issues of toleration are explored in Joseph Lecler's *Histoire de la tolérance au siècle de la Réforme* (Paris: Aubier, 1955). The necessity for toleration in France, especially in the circumstances of the religious wars, occupied Sebastian Castellio whose *Advice to a Desolate France*, edited by Marius F. Valkhoff, has been published by Patmos Press of Sheperdstown, West Virginia (1975). Castellio was Stefan Zweig's hero in his highly coloured account of the war of light against darkness, *The Right to Heresy: Castellio against Calvin* (Cassell, 1936). Castellio was perfectly capable of arguing on the basis of the *convenience* of toleration, an argument finding some support in pragmatic England, where *The Development of Religious Toleration* is the subject of a four-volume classic by W. K. Jordan (Allen & Unwin, 1932–40). The case *against* religious diversity is considered by Conrad Russell in 'Arguments for religious unity in England, 1530–1650', *Journal of Ecclesiastical History*, vol. 18 (1967). Tolerationist theory in early Stuart England was the subject of Thomas Lyon's *The Theory of Religious Liberty in England 1603–1639* (New York: Octagon Book reprint, 1972). The problem of toleration was aired with exceptional vigour in mid-seventeenth-century England, as Carolyin Polizzotto shows in 'Liberty of conscience and the Whitehall Debates of 1648–9', *Journal of Ecclesiastical History*, vol. 26 (1975). The tolerationist in a position of power features in George A. Drake's article 'Oliver Cromwell and the quest for religious toleration', in J. C. Brauer (ed.), *The Impact of the Church upon its Culture* (*Essays in Divinity*, Vol. II, Chicago: Chicago University Press, 1968). Toleration after the Restoration is examined in Alexander Seaton's 1911 study *The Theory of Toleration under the Late Stuarts* (reprinted New York: Octagon Press, 1972), and in Charles F. Mullett's 'Toleration and persecution in England, 1660–89', *Church History*, vol. 16 (1949). The impact of revived and intensified persecution on the Nonconformists after the Restoration is traced in Gerald R. Cragg's *Puritanism in the Period of the Great Persecution 1660–1688* (Cambridge: Cambridge University Press, 1957). For the political role of post-Restoration Dissent, see Douglas R. Lacey, *Dissent and Parliamentary Politics in England 1660–1689* (New

Brunswick: Rutgers University Press, 1969).

The reaction of the Dissenters to a brief hiatus in persecution is highlighted by Frank Bate in *The Declaration of Indulgence, 1672: A Study in the Rise of Organised Dissent* (Constable, 1908), and by Richard L. Greaves in 'The organizational response of Nonconformity to repression and indulgence: the case of Bedfordshire', *Church History*, vol. 44 (1975). An account of regional Nonconformity under persecution in a county where relative radicalism was strongly entrenched is G. F. Nuttall's 'Dissenting churches in Kent before 1700' (*Journal of Ecclesiastical History*, vol. 14, 1963); for Dissent in the west after the Toleration, see Allan Brockett (ed.), *The Exeter Assembly: The Minutes of the Assemblies of the United Brethren of Devon and Cornwall, 1691–1717* ... (Exeter: Devon and Cornwall Record Society, 1963). Allan Brockett has also produced a longe-range history of Dissent in a city in which Unitarianism developed markedly: *Nonconformity in Exeter, 1650–1875* (Manchester: Manchester University Press, 1962). Materials for further study of the regional history of Dissent are provided by R. F. Skinner in *Nonconformity in Shropshire, 1662–1816: A Study in the Rise and Progress of Baptist Congregational, Presbyterian, Quaker and Methodist Societies* (Shrewsbury: Wilding, 1964). In the south-west again, the records of an archetypal Baptist church have been published in a new edition by Roger Hayden, *The Records of a Church of Christ in Bristol, 1640–1687* (Bristol: Bristol Record Society, 1974). The vitality of Dissent in the West Country into the eighteenth century is brought home by G. F. Nuttall in 'George Whitefield's "Curate": Gloucestershire Dissent and the Revival', *Journal of Ecclesiastical History*, vol. 27 (1976).

In considering the issue of toleration for Protestant Dissenters in the early modern period, we need to be aware of the subversive reputation which political Calvinism had. For Calvin himself, whose political instincts were authoritarian, there are one or two handy editions of parts of his works, such as Joseph Haroutunian, editor and translator, *Calvin: Commentaries* (SCM Press, 1958), and J. T. McNeil, *John Calvin: On the Christian Faith: Selections from the Institutes, Commentaries and Tracts* (New York: Liberal Arts Press, 1958). Recommended biographies of Calvin are: François Wendel, *Calvin* (Collins, 1963); T. H. L. Parker, *John Calvin: A Biography* (Dent, 1975); and Basil Hall, *John Calvin* (Historical Association, 1967). Calvin's anthropology is explored in Thomas F. Torrance, *Calvin's Doctrine of Man* (Lutterworth Press, 1949), and the results of the Reformer's practical and political work are examined by E. William Monter in *Calvin's Geneva* (Wiley, 1967). In *The History and Character of Calvinism* (Oxford University Press, 1954), John T. McNeil examines, first, the origins of Calvinism in Switzerland and Geneva, then its expansion in Europe and America and, finally, the position of Calvinism in the ecumenical age.

A major study of the impact of Calvinism on early modern politics is Michael Walzer, *The Revolution of the Saints: A Study in the Origins of Radical Politics* (Weidenfeld & Nicolson, 1966). In *Theology Today*, 1948, W. Richter's article 'The Calvinist conception of the state: its tradition and secularisation' traced the derivation of modified democracy from Calvinism, and in 'Democratic freedom and religious faith in the Reformed tradition' (*Church History*, vol. 13, 1946) Winthrop Hudson examined the complex contribution of Calvinism to modern democratic politics. Two case studies of Calvinism in politics are Phyllis Mack Smith's study of applied extremism, *Calvinist Preachers and Iconoclasm in the Netherlands* (Cambridge: Cambridge University Press, 1978), and Richard Schlatter's *Richard Baxter and Puritan Politics* (New Brunswick: Rutgers University Press, 1957), a book in which Baxter's political traditionalism comes across strongly.

Whereas the sixteenth-century Netherlands instance shows Calvinism to have provided fuel for revolutionary vandalism, the seventeenth-century orthodox English Calvinist would seem, or so the case of Baxter would suggest, to have inclined to conservative politics. The same sort of complexities arise over the economic affiliations of the Calvinists: as in politics, so in economics, one asks were the Reformed forward-looking or backward-looking? The best place to begin when discussing Calvinist thought is with John Calvin. Calvin's economic thought is illuminated in two studies: W. Fred Graham, *The Constructive Revolutionary: John Calvin and his Socio-Economic Impact* (Richmond, Va: John Knox Press, 1971), and André Biéler, *La Pensée économique de Calvin* (Geneva: Droz, 1961). The first systematic investigation of the relationship between the religious and economic revolutions of early modern Europe was made by Max Weber in a work translated by Talcott Parsons as *The Protestant Ethic and the Spirit of Capitalism* (Allen & Unwin, 1930). Weber's views were considerably modified by R. H. Tawney in *Religion and the Rise of Capitalism*, originally published by Murray in 1926 and subsequently appearing in Penguin editions (1938 *et seq.*). For a review of the debate see M. J. Kitch, *Capitalism and the Reformation* (Longman, 1969) and the article by E. Fischoff, 'The Protestant ethic and the spirit of capitalism: the history of a controversy', *Social Research*, vol. 11 (1944). Arguing against the identification of Calvinism capitalism, Winthrop Hudson in 'Puritanism and the spirit of capitalism' (*Church History*, vol. 16, 1949) claims that the new economic ethos which came to preponderate from the late seventeenth century onwards was profoundly non-puritan. Several myths about the question of capitalism and Calvinism are exploded by Hugh Trevor-Roper in the title essay of his *Religion, the Reformation and Social Change* (Macmillan 1967). The idea that the early modern entrepreneur was predominantly a God-fearing cautious, industrious Weberian type is demolished by Theodore K. Rabb in 'The expansion of Europe and the spirit of capitalism' (*Historical Journal*, vol. 17, 1974); in this Rabb maintains that early modern 'capitalist' colonial expansion was engineered chiefly by rather piratical characters of a reckless, feckless, workshy and distinctly non-puritan mould. The Quaker role in industrial expansion is examined by Balwant Nevaskar in his interesting comparative study *Capitalists without Capitalism, the Jains of India and the Quakers of the West* (Westport, Conn.: Greenwood Publishing, 1971); and by Arthur Raistrick in *Quakers in Science and Industry* (Newton Abbot: David & Charles, 1968).

If there is a religious link between ideology and capitalism it may originate in the bourgeois culture which grew up in the late mediaeval cities of Europe and which, as Peter Burke shows in 'Patrician culture: Venice and Amsterdam in the seventeenth century' (*Transactions of the Royal Historical Society*, 5th series, vol. 23, 1973), survived strongly into the early modern period. For Amsterdam, and the Netherlands in general, see the two-part study by Pieter Geyl, *The Netherlands Divided 1609–1648* (Williams & Norgate, 1936), and *The Netherlands in the Seventeenth Century, 1648–1715* (Benn, 1964); see also K. H. D. Haley, *The Dutch in the Seventeenth Century* (Thames & Hudson, 1972). The relationship between church and city governments, the magistracy's maintenance of toleration, the rise of commercial capitalism in an officially Calvinist city – these are themes of R. B. Evenhuis's three-part study, *Ook Dat Was Amsterdam: de Kerk de Hervorming in de Gouden Eeuw* (Vols I, II) . . . *in de Tweede Helft van de Zeventiende Eeuw* (Vol. III) (Amsterdam: W. ten Have, 1965, 1967, 1971).

The seventeenth century saw the first stirrings of the rise of the omnicompetent state; the century witnessed the beginnings of commercial capitalism; and it produced a campaign to have religious toleration established on a proper footing. All these interconnected developments seriously affected the position of the churches. The background to these changes can be studied in Trevor Aston (ed.), *Crisis in Europe 1560–1660* (Routledge & Kegan Paul, 1965); in J. P. Cooper (ed.), *The New Cambridge Modern History*, Vol. IV: *The Decline of Spain and the Thirty Years War* (Cambridge: Cambridge University Press, 1970); in Maurice Ashley's *The Golden Century. Europe 1598–1715* (Weidenfeld & Nicolson, 1969); in Henry Kamen, *The Iron Century: Social Change in Europe 1550–1660* (Weidenfeld & Nicolson, 1971); and in D. H. Pennington, *Seventeenth Century Europe* (Longman, 1970).

The modernisation of the state is the subject of Theodore Rabb's *The Struggle for Stability in Early Modern Europe* (Oxford University Press, 1977); of J. H. Shennan's *The Origins of the Modern European State, 1450–1725* (Hutchinson, 1974); and the Marc Raeff's article 'The well-ordered police state and the development of modernity in seventeenth- and eighteenth-century Eruope', *American Historical Review*, vol. 80 (1975). The way in which culture, especially courtly culture, underpinned the ascent of the state is brought home in A. G. Dickens's *The Courts of Europe* (Thames & Hudson, 1977). Going back to the pre-modern period, D. A. Bullough, in 'Games people played: drama and ritual as propaganda in medieval Europe' (*Transactions of the Royal Historical Society*, 5th series, vol. 24, 1974), brilliantly illuminates the ways in which drama and pageantry conveyed religious and political propaganda, and confirmed religious and political assumptions. Courtly political symbolism is examined by Roy Strong in *Splendour at Court* (Weidenfeld & Nicolson, 1973) and the iconography of political propaganda is the subject of two studies by Frances Yates, *The Valois Tapestries* (2nd edn, Routledge & Kegan Paul, 1975), and *Astrea: The Imperial Theme in the Sixteenth Century* (Routledge & Kegan Paul, 1973). A stimulating article on cultural history and its relationship to religion, patronage and political change is H. G. Koenigsberger's 'Decadence or shift? Changes in the civilisation of Italy and Europe in the sixteenth and seventeenth-centuries', *Transactions of the Royal Historical Society*, 5th series, vol. 10 (1960).

The Counter-Reformation was heavily involved with artistic patronage and development. One of the best of many surveys of that episode in the history of Catholicism is A. G. Dickens's *The Counter-Reformation* (Thames & Hudson,

1969). Jean Delumeau's study is now available in English: *Catholicism between Luther and Voltaire* (Burns & Oates, 1977); see also the decidedly Roman Catholic work by Pierre Janelle, *The Catholic Reformation* (Milwaukee: Bruce, 1963); Marvin R. O'Connell has produced a judicious survey, *The Counter-Reformation* (Harper Torch, 1974). In *The Spirit of the Counter Reformation* (ed. John Bossy, Cambridge: Cambridge University Press, 1968), H. O. Evenett viewed the Counter-Reformation primarily as a religious revival. How successful it was on that level, and as a drive to win back hearts and minds, can be assessed by looking at Michael Cloet's figures for Easter communicants in seventeenth-century Belgium – 99+ per cent in Flanders parishes by 1700: see Cloet, *het Kerkelijk leven in een landelijke dekenij van Vlaanderen tijdens de XVIIe eeuw* (Leuven: Éditions Nauwelaerts, 1968). Though a spectacular popular success, the Counter-Reformation may have been so only in the short term – as Professor Bossy argues in 'The Counter-Reformation and the peoples of Catholic Europe', *Past and Present*, vol. 47 (1970). The ways in which post-Reformation Catholicism catered for the needs of philanthropy and association is exhaustively examined by Brian Pullan in *Rich and Poor in Renaissance Venice: The Social Institutions of a Catholic State, to 1620* (Oxford: Blackwell, 1971).

Whether or not women could join religious associations was a crucial issue in the Reformation period and is one of the questions dealt with in Natalie Zemon Davis's *Culture and Society in Early Modern Europe* (Duckworth, 1975), a collection of articles which makes an exceptional contribution to the new study of women's role in religious change. For the mediaeval period, Brenda Bolton has made a study of the tidal wave of female piety in the thirteenth century: 'Mulieres sanctae', *Studies in Church History*, vol. 10, ed. Derek Baker (Oxford: Blackwell, 1973). Heretical women are investigated by Claire Cross in her article ' "Great Reasoners in Scripture": the activities of women Lollards 1380–1530', which appears in Subsidia 1 of *Studies in Church History*, edited by Derek Baker (Oxford:Blackwell, 1978). Moving into the Reformation period, R. H. Bainton has made a number of studies of women's role: his article on Reformation women in the collection edited by L. P. Buck and J. W. Zophy, *The Social History of the Reformation* (Columbus: Ohio State University Press, 1972); his essay on the Protestantism of four well-placed Tudor women which appears in P. Brooks (ed.), *Christian Spirituality Essays in honour of Gordon Rupp* (SCM Press, 1973); and finally Professor Bainton's book, *Women in the Reformation: From Spain to Scandinavia* (Minneapolis: Augsburg, 1977). 'The role of women in the English Reformation' is the title of Patrick Collinson's article in *Studies in Church History*, vol. 2, ed. G. J. Cuming (Nelson, 1965). For the religious emancipation of women in mid-seventeenth-century England, there are two recent studies: Claire Cross, ' "He-goats before the Flocks": a note on the part played by women in the founding of some Civil War churches' (*Studies in Church History*, vol. 8, ed. G. J. Cuming and Derek Baker, Cambridge: Cambridge University Press, 1972), and Keith Thomas, 'Women and the Civil War sects' (*Past and Present*, vol. 13, 1958). In 'Anna Maria van Schurman: from feminism to pietism' (*Church History*, vol. 46, 1977), Joyce Irwin focuses on feminism, learning and religion.

Index